MESSIANIC ZIONISM IN THE DIGITAL AGE

MESSIANIC ZIONISM IN THE DIGITAL AGE

Jews, Noahides, and the Third Temple Imaginary

RACHEL Z. FELDMAN

RUTGERS UNIVERSITY PRESS
New Brunswick, Camden, and Newark, New Jersey
London and Oxford

Rutgers University Press is a department of Rutgers, The State University of New Jersey, one of the leading public research universities in the nation. By publishing worldwide, it furthers the University's mission of dedication to excellence in teaching, scholarship, research, and clinical care.

Library of Congress Cataloging-in-Publication Data

Names: Feldman, Rachel Z., author.
Title: Messianic Zionism in the digital age : Jews, Noahides, and the Third Temple imaginary / Rachel Z. Feldman.
Description: New Brunswick : Rutgers University Press, [2024] | Revision of author's Ph.D. dissertation. | Includes bibliographical references and index.
Identifiers: LCCN 2023032107 | ISBN 9781978828186 (hardcover) | ISBN 9781978828179 (paperback) | ISBN 9781978828193 (epub) | ISBN 9781978828209 (pdf)
Subjects: LCSH: Jewish messianic movements. | Technology—Religious aspects—Judaism. | BISAC: RELIGION / Messianic Judaism | SOCIAL SCIENCE / Sociology of Religion
Classification: LCC BM615 .F45 2024 | DDC 296.3/36—dc23/eng/20231024
LC record available at https://lccn.loc.gov/2023032107

A British Cataloging-in-Publication record for this book is available from the British Library.

References to internet websites (URLs) were accurate at the time of writing. Neither the author nor Rutgers University Press is responsible for URLs that may have expired or changed since the manuscript was prepared.

♾ The paper used in this publication meets the requirements of the American National Standard for Information Sciences—Permanence of Paper for Printed Library Materials, ANSI Z39.48-1992.

rutgersuniversitypress.org

For Yitzhak, my Jerusalem

CONTENTS

PREFACE
Methods and Fieldwork Reflections

"I will tell you why you chose this project," Shoshanna[1] informed me as we sat kneading dough together in her kitchen one afternoon in 2015 in a religious Jewish settlement in the West Bank. I spent time with Shoshanna during my research on the Third Temple movement in Israel: a theocratic movement that strives to rebuild a Temple on the Temple Mount in Jerusalem and revive ancient Israelite ritual practices—actions that, it is believed, will help to fulfill biblical prophecies and catalyze the start of a messianic era. Shoshanna's particular contribution to the movement involved experimenting with and perfecting recipes for the various wheat, barley, and bread offerings that ancient Israelites brought to the Temple to be burned on the altar by priests (*kohanim*). I first met Shoshanna a month earlier, in a workshop that she organized for religious women, training them in the preparation of the *minha* offering, an unleavened dough made from finely ground semolina flour, so they will be knowledgeable and ready to prepare it when the Third Temple is rebuilt. Taking a break for coffee, we sat down at Shoshanna's kitchen table, and I turned on my audio recorder. With a satisfied sigh, Shoshanna wiped the flour off her hands onto her apron and took stock of the mess around us—the metal pans, the measuring cups, and a barley roaster made of recycled machine parts. *Objects from the future*, she had noted earlier with pride. "Are you recording?" she asked. "Okay good you should record this. I wanted to say that, if you chose this project, it is because you also want the Temple, because there is also something messianic in *you*."

We had circled back to this topic a few times in our conversation. Shoshanna was aware that I, an anthropologist from the United States, did not share her desire for Israel to become a Jewish theocracy and did not agree with some of her fundamental theological and political beliefs, which included calls for exclusive Jewish sovereignty over the biblical land of Israel and the forced removal of Palestinians from their ancestral lands. But I was also a Jewish woman, and an observant one at that, with a deep love of Jewish ritual and textual traditions. Shoshanna did not quite know what to do with me and our divergent interpretations of scripture, especially when I candidly responded to her attempts to discern my personal politics.

As we sipped our coffee, I explained that I personally gravitated toward more metaphorical interpretations of the Third Temple in religious Jewish sources. "Perhaps building a 'House for God' on earth could mean striving for a global future of radical equality, justice, and environmental stability," I suggested.

"Look, I also believe there will be a global *tikkun* [rectification] and all of humanity will change when we build the Temple," she responded. "All the *goyim* [non-Jews] will become Bnei Noah [the Children of Noah], and we will be united by worshipping one God in the Temple in Jerusalem. Then there won't be any more wars! All our efforts, the rebirth of our [Jewish] nation is for the sake of humanity. You are a religious Jew so you know that you can't have the spiritual without the material; that is why we have the *mitzvot* [commandments]. Divinity needs a container," she said, holding up and shaking one of her metal bread pans. "That is why we need a Temple and physical sacrifices . . . to heal this broken world."

If we define messianism simply as the desire for social rupture and cultural transformation, for a rebirth of self and society,[2] then I suppose Shoshanna was correct: I was also a messianic activist. We just had different ideas of how to get there practically. " The very fact that you, a Jewish woman from America, are sitting here with me in our ancient homeland with your hands in the dough is a sign that the *geulah* [redemption] is coming! After so many centuries of persecution and suffering we are back in our homeland and witnessing miracles," Shoshanna remarked with a knowing smile. My interest in the topic of the Third Temple was often interpreted by my interlocuters as a sign that the messianic era was approaching, and regardless of my personal beliefs, they tended to feel that my writing about it could be somehow beneficial to raising consciousness of the Third Temple worldwide. I believe that Shoshanna, and indeed most of my interlocuters, saw me as a kind of strategic documentarian and storyteller, one who could, at the very least, disrupt the simplistic portrayals of Third Temple activists as messianic crazies who appeared in secular news reports at the time of my fieldwork in Israel.

Indeed, this was more or less how I saw myself and my own ethnographic mission as I curated and examined stories from my field sites. I wanted to understand why messianic theologies had shaped my informants' daily lives and identities in intimate ways. I wanted to understand how particular messianic imaginations emerged and proliferated, co-constituted by networks of religious and political actors with the help of digital tools. I wanted to comprehend why the Temple, so beautifully abstracted and metaphorized in Jewish thought and mysticism for centuries, had reemerged as an object of desire and as the imagined conclusion of Zionism. Finally, I wanted to understand how messianic visions of global peace and unity became tethered to concrete acts of violence in the present. The latter question in particular weighed on me every day that I set out to conduct fieldwork and every evening as I sat down to type up fieldnotes. I found myself caught in a constant state of cognitive dissonance as interviewees vividly described their Third Temple dreams and the utopian future they longed to manifest, conversations that felt at times utterly disconnected from the tragic political reality playing out on the ground in Israel/Palestine.

The research that I first began in 2012 on the Third Temple movement in Israel evolved over the course of seven years into a global ethnography of messianic Zionism and transnational yearning for the Third Temple. Toward this end, this book includes an account of Third Temple activism in Israel and examines the coeval emergence of the Children of Noah (Bnei Noah) movement, a novel Judaic faith and spiritual identity for non-Jews (primarily individuals exiting Christianity) that developed in tandem and in conversation with the expansion of Third Temple activism in Israel.

It was my intention to productively de-exceptionalize the region, by viewing specific manifestations of messianic Zionism from vantage points *outside* of the geographic center of Israel/Palestine, and contribute to a nascent body of scholarship focused on global Israel/Palestine Studies: the study of transnational ideologies, economies, and political theologies sustaining the Israel/Palestine conflict.[3] Moreover, the expansion of my ethnography beyond Israel's physical geographic boundaries is connected to a second methodological intervention that influenced my research: a choice to continue questioning and disrupting normative boundaries that have come to shape the anthropology of Jews and Judaism.[4] Thus, I extended my research on messianic Zionism in Israel to transnational communities of ex-Christian Noahides, with the intention of revealing new boundary subjectivities emerging on the margins of Judaism among people who see themselves as stakeholders in Israel's messianic future and partners in a project to rebuild the Temple. Much has been written on the impact of Christian Zionism on geopolitics, U.S.-Israel relations, and Western imperialism in the Middle East.[5] The following account considers the relationship of Christians with religious Zionism from a distinctively different angle, specifically by examining how Orthodox Jewish messianic and nationalist ideologies, born in Israel, have reshaped Jewish-Christian relations and transformed Christian identities.

The transnational and multisited ethnographic methodology employed in this research helped me to examine messianic Zionism in motion across multiple geographic domains through offline and online digital forums. It should be noted, however, that attending to multiple transnational field sites has its own inherent limitations: namely, the sacrifice of some of the penetrating depth that can be achieved when focusing on a singular and more restrictively defined locale. In general, I approached my fieldwork with an awareness that the very notion of a field site is an act of social construction carried out by the ethnographer, who arbitrarily sets boundaries for their data collection, thus artificially inscribing and reifying a particular "culture" within a bounded territorial unit.[6]

It is impossible to say definitively where the phenomena that I track in this account (messianic Zionism, the Third Temple, Noahidism) begin and end. The transnational spiritual landscape presented in this book has been shaped by my interlocutors themselves through the particular points of access that they offered to me. Moreover, the question of where to draw boundaries around transnational spiritual communities is made all the more difficult in the twenty-first century when "the field" spans offline and virtual spaces. In addition to a multisited approach, my fieldwork frequently shifted back and forth between in-person and online forums. I examined the way that digital technologies reshaped Jewish and Noahide identities, subjectivities, and theological-political visions while still attending to the ways in which messianic "cyberscapes" remain entangled in the particularities of local contexts.[7] By traveling between Jewish activists and rabbinic leaders in Jerusalem and non-Jewish Noahide communities abroad, I was able to bear witness to the unexpected and often paradoxical engagements of Jewish messianism as it was mobilized for both neocolonial and liberatory ends. The following ethnography captures these two moves as messianic activism furthers settler-colonial dynamics on the ground in Israel/Palestine *and* becomes an empowering spiritual resource for postcolonial communities thousands of miles away.

While my preliminary research on the Third Temple / Children of Noah movements technically began in 2012, the continuous Israel-based portion of my fieldwork was carried out primarily between 2014 and 2016 in Jerusalem and religious West Bank settlements. I conducted follow-up research in Jerusalem with Temple activists and rabbis guiding the Third Temple and Children of Noah movements again in 2017 and 2019. This aforementioned research (presented in chapter 2) draws from more than fifty formal and informal interviews conducted with Third Temple activists, including male rabbis, women, and youth activists. I conducted these interviews primarily in Hebrew and later translated and transcribed them into English. From 2014 to 2019 I observed public events related to the Third Temple movement in Israel that included protests, activist conferences and lectures, and sacrificial reenactments. I also participated in pilgrimage tours to the Temple Mount / Haram ash-Sharif with trained *madrikhim* (guides), one of the central activities of the movement. During these visits I was able to observe the experiences of Jews on the Temple Mount and the work of the pilgrimage guides who narrated the visit for them. My fieldwork in Israel was supplemented with the collection and analysis of print and digital materials such as newspaper articles covering the Temple Mount / Haram ash-Sharif, editorials written by Temple activists, Facebook posts, and interviews with members of the Murabitoun (Palestinian Muslims dedicated to defending Al-Aqsa from Temple activists and Israeli annexation).

My fieldwork in Israel overlapped with a period of intensified political violence that began the summer I arrived in 2014 and continued through 2016. On June 12, 2014, Israeli teens Naftali Frenkel, Gilad Shaer, and Eyal Yifrah were kidnapped and later murdered by two Palestinian men, initiating a two-year cycle of reciprocal violence. On July 2, two Israeli teenagers kidnapped Mohammed Abu Khdeir, a sixteen-year-old Palestinian boy, and burned him alive in the Jerusalem forest. Retaliatory acts continued from both sides as Israel conducted Operation

Brother's Keeper, attempting to arrest Hamas leaders in the West Bank and Gaza. Hamas responded with renewed rounds of rocket fire, prompting Israeli air-strikes and a ground bombardment in Gaza referred to in Israel as Operation Protective Edge. In the end, the 2014 Gaza War left seventy Israelis and two thousand Gazans dead, giving way to a period of continued instability and vio-lence characterized by lone-wolf knife attacks, resulting in the death of thirty-four Israelis and two hundred Palestinians (most killed while attempting attacks).[8] This period lasted through 2016 and became known as the Third Inti-fada or Intifada of the Knives. The political backdrop is important to highlight as it gave me insight into the ways in which political theologies develop in response to daily events and affective experiences. Third Temple activism, I believe, became for many of my interlocuters a channel through which to respond to a bleak political reality in which diplomatic solutions seemed to have been exhausted. A number of my Israeli interlocuters, leaders within religious Zionist activist cir-cles, had personally lost family members to the conflict. As Shoshanna said to me, "I have more faith in the prophets than the diplomats to end this [the conflict]." Moreover, in addition to their disillusionment with diplomacy and peace talks, many of my interviewees articulated a rejection of the secular state itself, viewing democratic ideals and international law as "Western" impositions on the "native" Israelite culture they were trying to revive in Israel.

From 2017 to 2020, I continued the research that I had begun in Israel by extending it to transnational Children of Noah communities, a spiritual move-ment that is testament to the globalization of Israeli-born messianic Zionism and Third Temple activism. Chapters 3 and 4 are based primarily on interviews and participatory observations conducted with Noahides in the United States and the Philippines. This fieldwork was supplemented by additional research (in per-son and conducted by email, WhatsApp, and Skype) with Noahides based in France, Mexico, and Canada, interviews with prominent rabbinic leaders of the Noahide movement in Israel, and three years of regularly monitoring and archiving materials from Anglophone, Francophone, and Hispanophone Noa-hide social media platforms.

Chapter 4 is based on two separate visits (between 2017 and 2019) to the Phil-ippines, home to one of the world's largest Noahide communities, during which I spent a total of five weeks with Noahide communities on different islands. I was introduced to Noahide community leaders in the Philippines through one of my rabbinic contacts in Jerusalem, a rabbi connected to the Third Temple move-ment who was offering advice and mentorship remotely and had noted that the Philippines was a "model community" of Noahides. Not only is the community impressive in size, but it is also one of the earliest examples of a country where local Noahide groups had constructed physical synagogues and adopted prayers and rituals designed for them by rabbis based in Israel. On my end, I was curious to spend time with a vibrant Noahide community outside of the United States.

I had previously visited an American Noahide community in Texas in 2012 (detailed in chapter 3) when I was conducting preliminary research, but as I discovered during my fieldwork in Israel, the largest and most rapidly growing communities of Noahides were actually located in the Global South (specifically, in Latin America, Africa, and parts of Asia), in places where philosemitic and Christian Zionist currents had been on the rise for decades but opportunities for Jewish conversion were limited. I was curious to connect with Noahides in the Philippines to understand better why Noahidism was growing and how it fit into a broader postcolonial context of religious diversification. I was interested in physically crossing the virtual gap that separates most Noahides from their religious authorities based in Israel, rabbis who typically do not visit the majority of the Global South Noahide communities that they mentor regularly online.

After chatting with leaders from the Philippines community on Facebook, I was invited to visit and include the community in my study of the Children of Noah movement. During my trips I documented Noahide ritual life, joining Noahides for Torah study and Shabbat observances, and recorded thirty interviews with English-speaking men and women. The majority of my interlocutors in the Philippines were fluent in English, and in the instances when they preferred to speak in their native Tagalog or Bisayan dialect, I relied on generous translation assistance provided by community members. My inability to interview Filipino Noahides in their native language represents a limitation in the fieldwork presented in chapter 4. Thus, it is important to emphasize that this research should be read not as a definitive account of Judaizing communities in the Philippines but rather as *an* account that is shaped by my own positionality as well as linguistic limitations. It is, like all forms of knowledge, a partial and incomplete account,[9] and perhaps someday an anthropologist fluent in Tagalog or Bisaya will conduct their own study or correct my findings. I openly acknowledge the inevitable "thinness" of my own account and, following the insights of John Jackson, push back on the assumption that Geertzian-style "thick description" can ever produce "full social knowing."[10]

In general, my positionality as a ritually observant middle-class Ashkenazi American Jewish woman with a normative gender presentation facilitated access to my informants in my field sites. Occasionally I was denied interviews with rabbinic leaders in Israel who had grown weary of secular journalists and liberal academics portraying them as religious fanatics. Rabbi Chaim Richman (the former international director of the Temple Institute in Jerusalem who works with Children of Noah communities), for example, refused to meet with me or grant me access to the Temple Institute, an important site of Third Temple / Noahide activism, when he discovered that one of my advisors had previously worked with the New Israel Fund (a social-justice-focused Israeli NGO). However, with grassroots activists, especially women and youth, this sort of gatekeeping was largely not an issue. When I first began the Israel-based portion of my research, I was an unmarried Jewish woman in my mid-twenties and was welcomed by Temple activists who probably perceived me as a young Jewish woman in need of spiritual instruction. That being said, it is possible that upon reading this, interviewees will feel discomfort to see our intimate theological conversations about their most sacred beliefs brought under a critical academic and anthropological lens. It is my hope that regardless of where our opinions diverge in the analysis, my interlocutors will feel that they were humanized in a way that disrupts what are often simplistic and stereotypical presentations of them as fundamentalists or messianic extremists.

It was my goal throughout the research and writing of this account to emphasize the subjective experiences of diverse messianic actors while still carefully situating those same actors within broader power dynamics, gendered and racialized ideologies, and material inequalities. Toward this end, I am deeply indebted to the theoretical and methodological insights of feminist, Mizrahi, and Palestinian scholars who have for decades demanded that we attend to intersections of race, class, and gender in Israel/Palestine.[11] While intersectional, postcolonial, and critical race frameworks are frequently deployed in ethnographies of social justice struggles, they are often underutilized in the study of conservative or right-wing groups.

For years I walked a delicate methodological tightrope as an anthropologist with an insider-outsider status that afforded both intimate access and critical distance. I visually passed as a member of the group I was studying in Israel and yet was very much standing outside of its theological and political orientations. This account is not an anthropology "at home" in the sense that I did not grow up in Israel or in an Orthodox religious-Zionist home. Yet Jewish informants certainly inscribed me in the future messianic Jewish home they were building. And for Noahide interlocuters I was frequently regarded as an honored member of the Children of Israel, a remnant of the biblical world they longed to revive, creating at times an uncomfortable and uneven power dynamic as Noahides emphasized my role as a member of God's "Chosen Nation." Nevertheless, I was able to sympathize and relate to my interlocutors, Jews and Noahides alike, due to our shared love of Jewish observance, Jewish mysticism, and scriptural study.

A NOTE ON PSEUDONYMS, ANONYMIZATION PRACTICES, AND TRANSLITERATION

Almost all of the individuals quoted in the text have been given pseudonyms. I used individuals' real names only when discussing high-profile public figures or quoting previously published materials, such as newspaper articles and YouTube videos, in which their real names appear and the content can be accessed publicly.

I have also taken care to avoid including geographic markers that might reveal the identities of anonymized participants. In a couple of instances, I used pseudonyms for the names of buildings or omitted the name of specific cities or towns in which interviews took place. I understand that these anonymization practices might be frustrating or confusing for certain readers, particularly those with more familiarity with the topic and/or field sites herein. However, I wish to underscore that the primary goal of this work is not to expose individuals to public scrutiny but to render visible new transnational networks, new spiritual and political phenomena, using intrapersonal ethnographic methods.

I chose to be cautious in concealing participants' identities first and foremost out of respect for those who requested confidentiality and, moreover, due to the sensitive political and religious material contained in this account and the various ways in which that material might be perceived or taken out of context by broader public audiences. For example, the growth of the Noahide movement and its appeal to Christians gravitating toward Judaism has led to its condemnation by certain Christian leaders who view it as a theological threat and who have reinvigorated older antisemitic tropes (e.g., Jews as seeking world domination) to describe the Noahide movement, the leaders involved, and Orthodox Judaism at large. Such antisemitic accusations are utterly baseless and dangerous, and I do not wish to expose my interlocuters to harassment.

In my transliteration of Hebrew and Arabic words I adhered, in most cases, to the system adopted by the *International Journal of Middle East Studies* (IJMES). For the names of individuals, organizations, or previously transliterated quotations I left the original transliteration in place even if it did not conform to the IJMES system.

MESSIANIC ZIONISM IN THE DIGITAL AGE

1 · INTRODUCTION

Third Temple Visions and Political Theologies in Motion

The Bethlehem Guest House is an evangelical-owned and biblical-themed hotel in the Philippines. Its walls display a collection of Judaica, golden menorahs, and maps of the biblical Land of Israel. A drawing of the ancient Israelite Temple, portrayed as a heavenly object levitating above the hills of Jerusalem, hangs next to another image: a contemporary photograph of the Temple Mount / Haram ash-Sharif in Jerusalem, with a depiction of the Temple superimposed over the Dome of the Rock and Al-Aqsa Mosque (see Figure 1). I had seen this photoshopped image before in the homes of religious Jews in Israel, on websites, and on Facebook pages, and here it was before me in the Philippines in a Catholic-majority country on the other side of the world—the messianic Temple of Jewish prophecy that is yet to be built and is for my interlocutors a symbol of the eagerly anticipated finale of Zionism.

According to Jewish teachings, the Temple Mount is the site from which the entire world sprang forth during Creation, the place where Noah offered a sacrifice after the flood, and the spot where Abraham came to sacrifice his son Yitzhak. According to the Islamic tradition, Haram-ash-Sharif is the third holiest site in Islam, the place from which it is believed that the prophet Muhammad ascended to heaven. In antiquity (957 BCE–70 CE), the First and Second Temples functioned as the juridical and spiritual centers of Israelite life. The Temple housed the Sanhedrin, a supreme court of rabbis ruling according to Torah Law, and was the domain of the kohanim, Temple priests in charge of daily sacrificial animal offerings. Referred to in Hebrew as the Beit HaMikdash, the holy house, the Temple was believed to be the literal House of God on Earth where the divine presence, the Shekhinah, came to reside—a presence that religious Jews believe was later retracted from the world and sent into exile along with the Jewish people following the Roman conquest of Jerusalem and destruction of the Second Temple in 70 CE. According to certain rabbinic interpretations of biblical

FIGURE 1. An example of circulating Third Temple media similar to what may be seen in the Philippines. The Third Temple of Jewish prophecy has been photoshopped on top of Haram ash-Sharif / Temple Mount in Jerusalem, and in the background we see a construction crane lifting the final pieces of the Temple into place. This particular rendering of the Third Temple was taken from a screenshot of a YouTube video created for the Temple Institute. In the video, which has received nearly 400,000 views, the Temple Institute presents a vision of imminent Temple rebuilding, stating, "This is the generation. The children are ready." (Screenshot by the author.)

prophecies,[1] the Temple Mount will be the location of a Third and Final Temple in the messianic era following the restoration of Jewish sovereignty in the Land of Israel.

Today, there is a growing movement based in Israel that strives to physically build the Third Temple in Jerusalem, to renew a Jewish priesthood and animal sacrifices, and to transform Israel into a biblical-style theocracy, with the ultimate goal of initiating messianic times for all of humanity.[2] The photoshopped image that I stumbled upon in the Bethlehem Guest House continues to circulate transnationally, among religious Jews and non-Jews, and is symbolic of a shared desire for Israeli annexation of the Temple Mount, Temple rebuilding, and the subsequent arrival of a messianic era.

I came to the hotel in the midst of a 2018 research trip in the Philippines to meet with Cecilia and Luis, a Filipino couple in their sixties, who agreed to be interviewed and share their story of leaving evangelical Christianity and becoming Children of Noah: a new transnational Judaic faith whose textual origins, and more recent evolution as a living faith identity, is documented and examined in this account. Many Noahides, as they call themselves, believe it is their destiny as "righteous Gentiles" to play a supportive role to Jews, the Children of Israel (Bnei Yisrael),[3] in initiating messianic times and rebuilding the Temple, the House of God, in Jerusalem.

Cecilia and Luis arrived in the lobby dressed in matching blue T-shirts that they had screen-printed with a Star of David emblazoned on the front. They excitedly recounted their journey out of the Catholic religion that they were raised in. Like tens of thousands of other Noahides worldwide, Cecilia and Luis passed through born-again Christianity and Baptist, Pentecostal, and Seventh-day Adventist churches, together searching for the truth and slowly gravitating toward the Hebrew origins of their faith as a married couple. Most of their children and grandchildren have followed them and embraced a Noahide identity. We ordered a round of mango smoothies, and Luis began to recite the scriptural passages that helped him, in his words, "say goodbye to Jesus" and become a Noahide. He quoted Zechariah 8:22–23 from memory: "The many peoples and the multitudes of nations will seek the Lord of Hosts in Jerusalem. Ten men from the nations of every tongue will take hold: they will take hold of every Jew by the corner of his cloak and say, 'Let us go with you, for we have heard that God is with you.'"

Luis understood these verses as predicting the spread of Noahidism in the messianic era, when, following the return of Jews to Israel, the nations of the world (Gentiles) will figuratively "grab onto" the Jews, God's "chosen people," as spiritual guides who will bring them under the yoke of Torah and a more perfect monotheism. Reviving a particular branch of rabbinic textual interpretation (examined in detail in chapter 3), Noahides consider themselves to be the descendants of the biblical sons of Noah who are destined to assist the Jews, the descendants of Israelites, in fulfilling God's plan: the conquest of Greater Israel and the building of the Third Temple in Jerusalem. While historically there have been a number of philosemitic and Judaizing Christian movements,[4] Noahidism of the twenty-first century is unique in that it involves Christians revoking their faith and belief in the divinity of Jesus and allowing rabbinic authorities to guide their studies and dictate the content of their rituals through a relationship that is largely virtual.

The rabbis guiding the global Children of Noah movement are predominantly members of Israel's religious nationalist demographic, along with certain leaders from the Chabad Hasidic movement who believe that the messianic era begins with the revival of a biblical kingdom in Israel supported by communities of "righteous Gentiles" (Noahides). Much of this rabbinic leadership is ideologically and politically aligned with, if not directly involved in, the Third Temple movement in Israel: a network of activist groups dedicated to physically building the Third Temple on the Temple Mount / Haram ash-Sharif in Jerusalem—in other words, materializing the photoshopped projection of the Third Temple that hung on the wall during our meeting.

As we chatted, Cecilia scrolled through her Facebook feed and paused to show me images from last year's Passover sacrifice event in Jerusalem when Temple activists slaughtered a live lamb at the base of the Temple Mount. "It is amazing to see prophecy coming true. The Jewish people returned [to their land]. We have to return to our identity too, to our place in the Torah," she commented.

Relationships between Third Temple activists based in Israel and Noahides abroad were, I discovered, both direct and indirect. Some organizations, such as the Temple Institute, had made outreach to Noahides a core part of their mission. But even Temple activists who were not at the forefront of Noahide recruitment, I found, were very much aware of emerging Noahide communities. Cecilia proceeded to show me how photographs of her own Noahide community in the Philippines had been shared on the Facebook page of a Temple activist in Israel who was involved in bringing religious Jews to pray on the Temple Mount. The Israeli activist, a young religious man, had posted the photos of Cecilia's Noahide community alongside the following message in Hebrew: "Righteous gentiles in the Philippines helping to fulfill the prophecy of Isaiah who said, 'My House will be called a house of prayer for all nations.'"[5]

OVERVIEW

This book follows an ethnographic object that does not exist:[6] the Third Temple that is now part of a transnational messianic imagination that came of age at the end of the twentieth century through a spiritual and political convergence of religious nationalists in Israel and Christians coming out of evangelical and Hebrew-Roots churches around the world.[7] It tracks the specter of the Third Temple from the streets of Jerusalem where messianic activists prepare for the revival of a biblical kingdom to communities of former Christians who, inspired by visions of a Third Temple future, have adopted a new spiritual identity as the Children of Noah (Bnei Noah).

Drawing on seven years of multisited fieldwork (2012–2019), what follows is an ethnography of messianic Zionism in the digital age, one that documents shifting formations of spirituality and new transnational territories of religious life. In the research and writing of this account, my primary goal was to reveal some of the global entanglements of messianic Zionism as it is mobilized for both neocolonial and liberatory ends. Messianic Zionism, I argue, furthers settler-colonial dynamics on the ground in Israel/Palestine, aiding in state-sponsored territorial conquest while simultaneously becoming an empowering spiritual resource for communities thousands of miles away.

The structure of the book, which takes the reader on a journey from Israel to locations abroad and back to Israel again, underscores the particular methodological intervention that is at stake: to expand Israel studies beyond the territorial boundaries of the Israeli state and to more fully grasp the ways that Israel-based forms of messianic activism and religious nationalism have globalized in the first decades of the twenty-first century, influencing the transformation of religious subjectivities abroad. Toward this end, the book begins in Israel with an account of the Third Temple movement, a growing theocratic movement that, I argue, functions as a supportive appendage of the Israeli state through a symbiotic relationship that has enabled its recent move into the religious nationalist mainstream and access to state resources (chapter 2). The ethnography then departs from Israel and travels to the American Southwest, where Third Temple activists from Israel first began building alliances with Christian Zionists in the 1990s, a spiritual and political convergence of two faith communities that, I argue, played a critical role in the birth of Noahidism as a new Judaic faith (chapter 3).

As this account will demonstrate, the emergence of Children of Noah communities served a strategic role for rabbinic leaders from the Third Temple movement who were eager for transnational allies as they attempted to universalize religious Zionism and promote Temple building as a messianic mission for all of humanity. At the same time, during the first two decades of the twenty-first century, Noahide communities became important new spiritual homes that welcomed growing numbers of skeptical Christians who had gone in search of the Hebrew roots of their faith and found themselves at the doorstep of Judaism. Aided by the internet, rabbinic authorities from Israel's religious right wing became the spiritual guides for former Christians who had adopted the Noahide faith and were searching for Orthodox Jewish mentorship and increased access to Torah studies.

Internet technologies and the rise of social media, I argue, enabled a new form of Orthodox Jewish missionizing to non-Jews and facilitated the emergence of a transnational messianic imagination with the Third Temple at its center. As the following chapters demonstrate, this messianic imagination mobilizes biblical-racial theories of humanity and notions of spiritual-racial difference between Jews and non-Jews to promote a salvific national mission in Israel and a utopian future for humanity. Throughout this account, I use the phrases "biblical-racial" and "spiritual-racial" to demarcate the mythic imagination of messianic Zionism and my interlocuters' attempts to renew biblical categories of subjectivity (Israelite and Noahide) for use in the present toward both spiritual and political goals. Moreover, I invoke the terms spiritual-racial and biblical-racial to reference the co-constitutive nature of race and religion as this relationship played out across the spiritual landscapes included in my ethnography. In other words, I use these phrases to underscore the complex ways in which spiritual identities are *racialized* while at the same time notions of racial difference become *spiritualized*, or imbued with sacred meanings.

After documenting the globalization of Third Temple movement and the coeval birth of the Children of Noah, the ethnography travels to the Philippines, home to one of the world's largest Noahide communities where new forms of Noahide ritual life are thriving (chapter 4). Noahide communities, as I discovered during the course of my research, have grown most profoundly in locations across the Global South, specifically in countries where philosemitic, Judaizing, and Zionist currents have been on the rise for decades but opportunities for

Orthodox Jewish conversion on the ground are extremely limited. The Noahide faith, I contend, has become a viable alternative when economic barriers and forms of racial discrimination foreclose avenues to Orthodox Jewish conversion, providing Judaizing Christians with a Torah-based identity, access to Orthodox rabbinic mentorship, and a role to play in actualizing Jewish prophecy in Israel.

Orthodox Jewish missionizing in the form of the Noahide movement functions, in certain contexts, as a form of spiritual neocolonialism, one that is influenced by Western narratives of modernity and civilization, but it also evades a traditional colonial framework. It is not the Israeli state that is officially spreading the Noahide religion as a means of territorial conquest (although Noahides are certainly regarded by Israeli political leaders as important pro-Israel advocates). The nation here is an imagined *future theocratic state* that does not physically exist but is slowly manifesting in the present through live and virtual arenas. Particular networks of Orthodox rabbis and Noahide preachers work together, collaborating on a messianic vision of biblical revival and Jewish theocracy largely through internet-mediated relationships. The nation (theocratic Third Temple Israel) operates as a kind of speculative design,[8] the blueprint of a possible future, that through the act of design is brought into being in a meaningful way by virtue of eliciting affective states and emotional attachments in the designers.

While the Noahide movement involves certain dynamics of neocolonialism as Judaizing Christians across the Global South engage with rabbinic mentors who function as proxy-state actors on behalf of a future theocratic state, it is a spiritual exchange that is not unidirectional or whose outcome is determined. As a traveling political theology, the Third Temple imagination allows for the interaction and merger of religious systems, enabling modes of spiritual empowerment alongside patterns of neocolonial spiritual influence. Indeed, anthropologists and historians of religious colonization have emphasized the reciprocal nature of colonial interactions that refashion the spiritual and national subjectivities of *both* colonizer and colonized as well as the agentive power of colonized subjects to resist, syncretize, and transform missionized religions as their own.[9] Messianic Zionism, I contend, has become a powerful motor of spiritual reinvention as Christians in Latin America, Africa, and Asia adopt Noahide identities and increasingly demand access to Orthodox Jewish conversion.

By alternating vantage points from Israel to the United States and to the Philippines, this account attempts to render visible some of the global circuitry of messianic Zionism, a political theology in motion that simultaneously bolsters Jewish ethnonationalism in Israel, enables digital missionizing, and serves as a rich ideological substrate nourishing new postcolonial spiritual identities. After following the Third Temple to locations abroad, I return the reader to the geographic space of Israel. This account concludes with a consideration of the contemporary political stakes of a growing theocratic movement in Israel and its alliance with emerging Noahide communities and Christians around the world (chapter 5). While the social phenomena I examine here (the Third Temple / Noahide movements) are quantitatively small (in the order of tens of thousands worldwide), their qualitative impact, I will demonstrate, is not. Furthermore, I remind the reader that not all Jews are religious and/or Zionist and that the messianic ideologies featured in this account represent a minority stream within the broad and complex ideological world that is Orthodox Judaism—albeit a minority stream that has gained traction in recent decades and continues to pose a distinct challenge toward the establishment of a just peace in Israel/Palestine.

TOWARD AN ANTHROPOLOGY OF POLITICAL THEOLOGY

As an ethnographic account of messianic Zionism in the digital age, this work, in its broadest formulation, might be characterized as an *anthropology of political theology*.[10] Political theology typically refers to the study of how theological concepts are secularized, entering into and shaping a wide range of political ideologies, discourses, and practices, influencing national politics and forms of international intervention from colonial conquest to humanitarian aid. More simply, political theology is the nexus of religion and politics in society. In this particular ethnography of messianic Zionism, I am primarily interested in the *social life and subjective experiences* of political theology by individual actors and localized communities (while still mapping broader national and geopolitical implications along the way). My encounters with Third Temple activists and Noahide communities impelled me to ask questions: How do traveling political theologies change us in intimate ways? Why and how do political theologies enable liberating forms of spiritual reinvention alongside patterns of political domination and conquest? I asked these questions in the hope that they would shed light on the intersections of messianism and ethnonationalism in Israel today and on the diverse ways in which messianic Zionism is now taken up worldwide.

Producing an anthropology of political theology demands an acute attention to the textured lifeworlds and intersectional positionalities of religious actors, to their own ways of seeing and being that evade the religious/secular binary, complexities that can get lost when we pigeonhole messianic actors in a "fundamentalist" category. The mainstream Israeli and Anglo media, and Israel studies literature to a large extent, continue to replicate the religion/secularism binary by presenting the conflict over the Temple Mount / Haram ash-Sharif as a "powder keg" ready to ignite a regional "Armageddon" due to the actions of "extremist" Jews and evangelical Christian supporters who wish to demolish Al-Aqsa and rebuild a Jewish temple on the site.[11] The danger of this impending regional "Armageddon" is still largely pinned on religious actors and a "clash of cultures" between Jewish and Muslim nationalisms.[12] In addition to framing the Temple Mount conflict as Jewish fundamentalism, the existing Israel studies literature tends to focus on Ashkenazi male rabbinic authorities and takes their disproportionate representation in the Temple movement leadership for granted, overlooking the deeper role of racialized and gendered power dynamics in enabling forms of Jewish messianic activism as well as the critical roles that religious women have played in mainstreaming the movement (an issue I address in chapter 2).

While I do not wish to downplay the potential of messianic activism in Israel to incite violence, the religious fundamentalism paradigm is problematic because, as Joyce Dalsheim argues, it artificially separates out "radical" religious-nationalist Jews, especially West Bank settlers, from the population of "Israel proper" in order to maintain the legitimacy of more acceptable forms of secular Zionism.[13] Such an approach obscures the junctures where religious piety and liberal secular ideologies actually hybridize to support state violence and land annexation (junctures that I continue to explore in chapter 2).

I note for the reader that in this account of messianic Zionism and its transnational lifeworlds I purposely eschew the term "fundamentalism." In lieu of "fundamentalism," I invite the reader to think deeply with me about the ubiquitous nature of political theologies in the digital age, what Gil Anidjar calls the "theologico-political," which undergirds all aspects of our so-called "secular" and "religious" lives. Explaining his use of this analytic category in his scholarly work, Anidjar underscores that it is impossible to "separate the human from the divine, the sacred from the profane, the holy and the eschatological from the secular . . . all terms that are produced at the same time that they are distinguished."[14] In other words, it is impossible to untangle the theological from the political, to delineate where religion or secularism begins or ends, as the very concepts co-constitute one another. The fundamentalist label continues to replicate an artificial religious/secular binary that, as Talal Asad has argued, is itself a product of European modernity and has been used to justify Western superiority and imperialism.[15] Secularism is not void of religion but has come to stand in for what is rational, ethical, and modern and functions as a mechanism for policing and assimilating the religious (i.e., what is deemed irrational, dogmatic, or non-Western/European), dictating the proper boundaries, content, and meaning of religious activity within and according to the needs of the nation-state.[16]

Susan Harding, reflecting on the fraught nature of representing religious fundamentalists in anthropological research, characterizes this as the "problem of the repugnant cultural other."[17] According to Harding, fundamentalists are mistakenly represented as homogenous groups of people (in terms of beliefs and socioeconomic conditions) whose existence is then used to reify the presumed binary between that which is secular/modern/rational/progressive and that which is religious, antithetical to modernity, and "backward."[18] To be a fundamentalist, Harding reminds us, *is* to be thoroughly modern, to be produced by "modern discursive practices."[19] Even as my informants cited scripture and biblical prophecies, their readings of these texts and application of them to their daily lives was motivated profoundly by contemporary political ideologies and the material power dynamics of their local context.

This account is an ethnographic examination of the ways in which traveling theologico-political imaginaries such as messianic Zionism not only influence national politics and state policies but also interact with all dimensions of material and ideological human life, including but not limited to religious subjectivities, ritual expression, racial and gendered constructs, and class inequalities. Bruce Lincoln's work on religion, empire, and violence underscores the historical fact that religious beliefs and material interests are "dialectically related and mutually sustaining" in political projects of empire.[20] Messianic political theologies effectively sustain and legitimize forms of state violence and discrimination, employing what Richard Hughes calls (referring to the U.S. context) the *myth of the innocent nation*: "the conviction that, while other nations may have blood on their hands, the nobility of the American cause always redeems the nation and renders it innocent."[21] In Israel, messianism is also dialectically related to forms of state violence and land annexation. Inspired by Jewish messianic traditions that emphasize Jewish national restoration as part of a redemptive process, religious Zionism relies on a mythology of divine election in order to justify territorial conquest: the notion that God chose Israel for a special mission in the world, including control over the biblical Land of Israel. Messianism provides the theological and eschatological underpinnings for more secularized expressions of Jewish ethnonationalism, bolstering biopolitical strategies aimed at ensuring a Jewish demographic, territorial, and political dominance over Palestinians.[22]

The combined nationalist *and* settler-colonial origins of the State of Israel are at this point well established in the academic literature.[23] While a complete review of this literature is beyond the scope of this book, I wish to address it here briefly in order to situate the Third Temple / Noahide movements in relationship to political dynamics on the ground in Israel before moving on to examine global expressions of messianic Zionism.

The European Jewish leaders who initiated the Zionist movement at the end of the nineteenth century were deeply influenced by pervasive ethnonational, colonial, and Orientalist ideologies of the era. Early Zionist leaders were, on the one hand, seeking a practical solution for centuries of Jewish persecution and the failure of modern European nation-states to secure equal rights and protections for their Jewish-minority populations. On the other hand, though, founding political Zionists like Theodor Herzl came to view the creation of a Jewish-majority nation-state in Palestine as not only a project of Jewish self-determination in the ancestral Jewish homeland but also a colonizing and civilizing venture to be carried out by Europeans in the Middle East, and they articulated the Zionist project in these terms in their writings.[24] Faced with European ethnonationalist movements and rising antisemitic trends at the turn of the century, many European Jews felt that they had to choose between assimilating, which meant trading Jewish religious and cultural particularity for socioeconomic mobility and acceptance, and building an exclusive ethnonational movement of their own. As Zionist settlers arrived in Palestine with the aim of fleeing persecution in Europe, they brought with them dominant notions of European superiority and viewed the Palestinian population that they encountered according to prominent Orientalist frameworks of the time.[25] Palestinian locals and Mizrahi (Jews from North Africa and the Middle East) immigrants to the State of Israel were regarded as primitive natives in need of "civilizing," and Zionist leaders were convinced they would be grateful for the modernization that technologically and culturally "superior" European Jews would bring.[26]

While early waves of European Jewish immigrants became members of the preexisting political community in Palestine, by the Second Aliyah (1900–1923) Revisionist Zionist leaders like Vladimir Jabotinsky had developed explicit plans to displace and dominate the native Palestinian population until Jews were firmly secured as the national majority in the land under the protection of a Jewish state.[27] The violence resulting from Zionist settlement in the twentieth century was witnessed most profoundly during and after the 1948 War of Independence, a period that Palestinians refer to as the Nakba (catastrophe), when approximately four hundred Palestinian villages were destroyed by Jewish paramilitary groups and 80 percent of the Palestinian population fled (either out of fear or due to forced and coordinated acts of expulsion) and were later prevented from returning to their lands and homes by the Israeli state.[28] As a result of the displacement, approximately 700,000 Palestinians became refugees, a number that has grown into 4.3 million Palestinian refugees and their descendants currently living in United Nations–sponsored refugee camps in Lebanon, Jordan, and Syria.[29] By the end of the war, the State of Israel's new leadership had implemented strategies of ethnic cleansing, including population transfer, surveillance, and control over the Arab population, ultimately aimed at securing a Jewish national majority.[30] The dispossession of those who fled or were expelled or internally displaced in 1948 was further legalized through the 1950 Absentee Property Law, which enabled the Israeli government to confiscate Palestinian properties and transfer ownership to Jews.[31]

As Shira Robinson has argued, Israel is best characterized as a *liberal-settler state*.[32] Beholden to the human rights norms of international law, Israel formally extends the category of citizenship to Palestinians within the Green Line while maintaining the ethnocratic nature of the state, with access to political power, economic resources, and immigration rights dependent on Jewish nationality.[33] Expansionist territorial policies, Jewish ethnonationalism, and forms of racial segregation continue to drive Israeli policies across the political spectrum.[34] In the West Bank, for example, Palestinians live under de facto Israeli sovereignty but are not granted citizenship rights or the protections of civil law. They are subject to martial law, trials in military court, land expropriation, home demolitions, economic hardship due to the loss of agricultural lands, and severe restrictions of movement due to Israeli-controlled checkpoints and segregated road systems.[35] Since 1967, Jewish settlement expansion into Israeli-controlled Area C of the West Bank has concentrated Palestinian populations into fragmented cantons, creating a landscape that now seems to architecturally foreclose the possibility of a contiguous Palestinian state and a two-state solution.[36] In short, Palestinians live under the authority of a Western-identified state that flaunts its liberal inclusivity yet continues to restrict Palestinian access to civil rights, a regime that is bolstered by messianic political theologies of Jewish redemption and national restoration.

POLITICAL THEOLOGY IN MOTION AND NEW RELIGIOUS SUBJECTIVITIES: GLOBALIZING ISRAEL AND ZIONISM STUDIES

The following ethnography places Israel within larger global currents of messianic desire and postcolonial power relations, exploring how political and theological developments in Israel shape lifestyle choices and religious identities and influence forms of affective belonging in *other* geographic regions. By journeying between ancient scriptural sources and contemporary websites, between the messianic epicenter of Jerusalem and sites of postcolonial spiritual reinvention (such as emerging Noahide communities in the Philippines), this book attempts to grasp the shape and scope of messianic Zionism in the digital age. I approach messianic Zionism, and more specifically Third Temple Israel, as one "imagined world"—that is, as Arjun Appadurai explains, collectively constituted, brought into being by the perspectival and locally situated imaginations of persons around the world.[37] While Appadurai did not write specifically about religion, anthropologists of religion have more recently extended his theoretical work on globalization to the examination of transnational spiritual geographies that emerge through global flows of migration and mobile forms of print and digital media.[38]

Since the early 2000s, the internet has enabled Jewish teachings to travel far beyond the boundaries of established Jewish communities. New channels for Torah study online have connected rabbis in Israel to non-Jews around the world who are searching for rabbinic mentorship. Non-Jews coming primarily from different streams of evangelical and Hebrew-Roots churches have converged with Orthodox rabbinic authorities through online platforms where they negotiate theological questions and their own place within a messianic Zionist vision, slowly adopting a Jewish interpretation of the Hebrew Bible and the Noahide faith. While previous research on digital religion has provided rich analyses of the discursive dynamics, ideological practices, and online leadership roles through which digital authority is constructed and conveyed,[39] my own contribution to the literature on digital religion focuses on the *offline* context of those on the receiving end of digital missionizing efforts. More specifically, I am interested in how localized conditions and inequalities impact the authoritative potentialities of digital religion. The offline power dynamics that impede access to Orthodox Judaism in the Global South, I will demonstrate, have actually helped to deflect spiritual seekers to Noahide resources online, channeling them into an arena of religious Zionist rabbinic authority that welcomes them with open arms when local synagogues shut the door.

The internet has opened powerful channels for transnational missionizing that are successful especially when they work in conjunction with the socioeconomic differentials of Judaizing communities in the Global South relative to rabbinic mentors coming primarily from Israel and North America. As Marla Brettschneider previously argued in her research on Judaizing communities in sub-Saharan Africa, Global North Jews, despite historically being subject to persecution as a religious minority, often unconsciously replicate "aspects of historical Christian European modes of imperialism" and inadvertently exert a neocolonial influence on Judaizing communities in the Global South when they serve as educators, rabbinic mentors, and communal gatekeepers.[40]

Through the Noahide movement, Judaizing Christians come under the influence of virtual rabbinic mentors who function as proxy-state actors on behalf of a speculative future theocratic state. However, it is a spiritual exchange that is not passive or unidirectional. I am interested in how this Israel-centered project is taken up, negotiated, and eventually altered from the perspective of Noahides on the ground coming from Hebrew-Roots Christianity. Thus, this ethnography offers a grounded analysis of globalization that takes into account homegrown power structures and institutions and the subjective experiences of local actors.[41] Each of my field sites provided a situated vantage point from which to observe the transnational construction of a messianic imagination that converges around the desired Third Temple in Jerusalem. Moreover, by viewing transnational religion as a multidirectional process, this work contributes to efforts to nuance unidirectional portrayals of global religion as straightforward cases of cultural imperialism, where religious influences are assumed to travel from one geographic center of power to a passive periphery.[42] Thomas Csordas proposes that we envision the world as a "neural-network" in which new spiritual impulses emerge and spread out from any nodal location."[43] With this image in mind, the chapters in this book might be read as interconnected yet heterogeneous nodes that reveal the mobile nature of political theologies in our digitally mediated world while simultaneously grounding messianic Zionism in the histories of specific locales where it gives rise to new religious subjectivities.

Careful attention to local nodes reveals the particular power dynamics that invigorate the globalization of spiritual and political ideologies. Anna Tsing, in her own anthropological work on globalization, urgers ethnographers to consider the "messier" features of global interactions and to attempt to document the "awkward, unequal, unstable, and creative qualities of interconnection across difference that lead to new arrangements of culture and power."[44] By traveling between Third Temple activists, rabbinic leaders in Jerusalem, and non-Jewish Noahide communities abroad, I was able to bear witness to unexpected and paradoxical engagements of messianism Zionism as it was mobilized to support forms of state violence, Judaization, and land annexation on the ground in Israel/Palestine while simultaneously becoming an empowering spiritual resource for Judaizing communities on the other side of the world.

This work considers how traveling political theologies like the Third Temple imaginary function as energizing motors of religious transition. Like Cecilia and Luis, the dozens of Noahides whom I met with had been born into Catholic families and traveled through multiple Protestant and Hebrew-Roots denominations in adulthood before gradually adopting a Noahide identity. They described to me a process of "purifying" their Christian faith and reexamining scripture from a "Hebrew mindset" in order to discern what was truly divine and not corrupted by "pagan" Roman beliefs. As they traveled through different denominations and continued to study the Hebrew Bible, tuning into YouTube lectures by Orthodox rabbis online, Cecilia and Luis slowly arrived at a complete rejection of Christian replacement theology, the trinity, and the divinity of Jesus—a sequential theological journey that was simultaneously motivated by an underlying messianic Zionist ideology that identifies the Land of Israel and the Jewish people as vehicles of salvation.

Previous anthropological research has revealed the tremendous potential for religious practice and conversion to remake political and spiritual geographies in the postcolonial era.[45] On the one hand, scholarship on transnational religion in the postcolonial era has emphasized the transformative potential of religion to refashion identities and extend forms of belonging beyond the territorial bounds of the nation-state.[46] On the other hand, this research has challenged the idea that global forces necessarily exert explosive or disruptive force on local worlds, attuning instead to preexisting conditions of religious fluidity that enable new transnational spiritual engagements.[47] Thus, it is imperative to underscore that even as forms of digital proselytizing have shaped the Noahide movement, my interlocutors in the Philippines exercised agency in their spiritual transitions, and these transitions were progressive, from Catholicism to Protestantism, from Protestantism to Messianic churches or Seventh-day Adventism and finally to Noahidism.[48] This sequential journey toward the Hebrew roots of their faith reflects broader trends experienced by Noahide communities across the Global South, with similar theological journeys and evolving Jewish ritual expressions enabled by the increasing availability of internet resources in places where living Jewish communities are inaccessible or absent.[49] Even as my informants slowly relinquished Christian theological precepts and embraced the Noahide faith, a core messianic Zionist political theology remained constant as informants changed churches, swapping New Testaments for Hebrew Bibles and Jewish prayer books, crosses for Stars of David and modest Orthodox-style clothing.

While the idea of tens of thousands of Christians abandoning their faith for a new identity (Noahide) subsumed under Orthodox Judaism and derived from Jewish legal debates may seem dramatic, the spiritual journeys documented in this account challenge characterizations of religious conversion as total ideological rupture. In early twentieth-century anthropological and sociological literature, conversion was often characterized as an act of rupture catalyzed by experiences of personal crisis.[50] Max Weber's work on charisma, for example, set a precedent for thinking about religious conversion as a manipulative psychological process involving the influence of a charismatic leader over a mentally susceptible convert who experiences a religious epiphany. Theories of religious conversion were subsequently dominated by a "crisis model" that emphasized predisposing conditions, such as tension, alienation, and frustration, as the catalysts for individual religious conversions.[51] Moving away from the individualistic psychological models that dominated early research on this topic, later research reconceptualized converts as active, rational, and agentive subjects who utilize available resources and social networks in their search for religious meaning.[52] Instead of being seen as a process of acquiring new members through control and manipulation, conversion was reframed as a socialization process, a progressive spiritual journey guided by interpersonal attachments.[53]

More recent scholarship on transnational and postcolonial religious movements has replaced conversion with concepts like "religious transit" that better index the fluid passages between multiple religions that an individual may undergo throughout a lifetime.[54] Writing from a postcolonial Brazilian context, Patricia Birman, for example, rejects the very notion of conversion, which she claims overemphasizes interior belief and underplays the social context where different religious systems merge, particularly in the Spanish postcolonies where the Catholic hegemony is weakening and a vibrant spiritual marketplace of alternative options is growing.[55] Likewise, scholarship on Pentecostalism in Latin America and Africa has questioned the notion of religious conversion and its applicability inside of spiritually fluid and syncretic cultural contexts.[56] In my own work, I am interested in how globalizing political theologies and reinvigorated spiritual-racial ideologies motivate processes of religious transit. Noahides like Cecilia and Luis seek to recover a "lost" or "original" biblical identity, one that is rooted in a notion of genealogical descent from Noah and viewed as belonging to a precolonial time and space. "We were colonized by Spain and now we are waking up from this idol worship. We have to go back to our original identity from Noah and the covenant God made with us," Luis explained to me at the end of our interview. "But Noahide is not really a religion," he quickly interjected. "It is just an identity for people who follow a universal moral code."

Noahidism is not a religion. This is a refrain that I heard repeatedly from self-declared Noahides and their rabbinic mentors throughout years of fieldwork in multiple countries. Despite that fact that I was witnessing and documenting a rapid proliferation of Noahide ritual life and communal infrastructure (elaborated in chapter 4), my interlocuters often made a point of reminding me that Noahidism was *not* an organized religion but simply an umbrella term for non-Jews who follow a universal moral code (Seven Laws of Noah) dictated by the Torah. Noahide, they explained, was the true or original identity intended by God for Gentiles. I paid careful attention to these comments and found that my interlocuters' desire to situate Noahidism outside the category of religion was intricately connected to a broader set of theological, racial, and political power dynamics that I unpack in the following chapters. Writing as an anthropologist, however, I refer to Noahidism as an emerging "Judaic faith" or new "religious identity" and examine it as a form of organized religious and ritual life in order to capture the complex ways in which contemporary Noahidism now extends far beyond a theoretical or philosophical attachment to a moral code.

In the anthropology of religion, it is now widely recognized that there is no single objective definition of religion, and current scholarship tends to operate with maximally expansive and inclusive definitions that capture a broad range of spiritual experiences. The very process of granting specific communities the status of religion is inherently political and biased: rather than having an objective foundation, the category of religion is arbitrarily conferred to delineate which groups and practices are acceptable according to a society's normative moral and social standards in a given historical moment.[57] By framing Noahidism as a new "religion" or "Judaic faith," it is my intention to simply render Noahidism visible as a meaningful spiritual practice and new religious subjectivity in the twenty-first century. I categorize it as "Judaic" in the sense that Noahides locate religious authority exclusively in Jewish textual sources and in Orthodox rabbis coming primarily from religious Zionist theological orientations.

As an anthropology of a globalizing messianic imagination, this work aims to capture the complex interplay between mobile, deterritorialized political theologies and localized forms of religious transformation. It is necessary at this point, however, to pause and contextualize the particular political theology that connects the Jewish and Noahide actors throughout this account by providing some of the theological, historical, and political background surrounding the rise of messianic Zionist activism in Israel.

JEWISH MESSIANISM AND MESSIANIC ZIONISM: THE THEOLOGICAL AND HISTORICAL BACKGROUND

At the heart of the Jewish messianic narrative is a vision of national restoration and return based on scriptural and rabbinic sources that view the destruction of the Second Temple in 70 CE as part of a divine plan for the redemption of humanity. Jewish prophetic texts predict the return of Jewish exiles to the Land of Israel, the rebuilding of a central Temple, and resurrection of a sovereign Jewish kingdom (actions facilitated by the leadership of a yet-to-be-revealed messiah) as part of a messianic process.[58] While Orthodox rabbinic interpretations concerning the messianic era vary, the aforementioned events are typically included in Jewish messianic timelines and were famously elaborated by Maimonides (1138–1204), generally considered to be one of the most authoritative rabbinic commentators. According to Maimonides, the messianic process will not involve any supernatural wonders or miracles but will be carried out through practical earthly actions under the political and spiritual leadership of a human messiah, a righteous Jewish scholar and descendant of the ancient King David who will facilitate the process of national revival in the Land of Israel.[59]

Jewish messianic thought contains both particularistic and universalistic theological elements. It is particularistic in the sense that it does not seek the conversion of non-Jews to Judaism and is focused on the national and spiritual redemption of Israel. Yet the very restoration of a Jewish polity in the Land of Israel is believed to have universal significance. According to Maimonides, Jewish national revival will usher in a utopian era of peace and global monotheism as Gentiles, who are not required to convert, recognize the one true God of Israel and adopt the Seven Laws of Noah (a basic moral code and the foundation upon which the contemporary Children of Noah movement is based).[60]

Following the destruction of the Second Temple, Jewish messianic aspirations found expression through symbolic ritual action and prayer. Pleas for the rebuilding of the Temple and restoration of Israel became embedded in the liturgies that Jews pray three times a day. In the absence of a physical temple space, rabbinic Judaism focused on the cultivation of what Abraham Joshua Heschel referred to as "holiness in time":[61] sacred ritual events that could be performed in a state of dislocation from the Israel and axis mundi of the Temple Mount. It is noteworthy, however, that abstract and symbolic notions of the Temple actually *predate* the destruction of the Second Temple and the advent of rabbinic Judaism. Aspirations for a future, more perfect messianic House of God were articulated in antiquity to critique corruption within Second Temple institutions.[62]

Rabbinic Judaism developed a ritual and textual tradition that responded to the geographic dispersal of the Jewish people from their holy land and the loss of a central Temple. Jews could connect with divinity from anywhere in the world through Torah study, the performance of *mitzvot*, the commandments required by Jewish Law, and daily prayers, considered to be equivalent substitutions for the animal sacrifices that once took place on the Temple Mount.[63] The very absence of a physical Temple inspired a rich canon of Jewish thought that elaborated the symbolic and metaphysical importance of the House of God.[64] The Jewish body, for example, was imagined at times as a microscopic temple, a material container for holiness that must be cultivated through righteous actions.[65] Specific ritual actions, previously enacted by Temple priests, were relocated onto the individual Jewish body and into the private Jewish home. For example, the ritual handwashing that Jews perform upon waking in the morning represents the actions of the high priest who would purify his hands before offering an animal sacrifice on the Temple Mount.[66] Likewise, the dinner table inside the Jewish home came to be viewed as a symbolic temple "altar" for the blessing and elevation of food (to be consumed and transformed into spiritual sustenance by one's digestive "fire").[67]

Mystical and macroscopic notions of the Temple also proliferated, beginning with postbiblical rabbinic literature, in which the entire world was conceived as a potential temple and vessel for divinity to reside within.[68] While abstracted notions of the temple played an important role in shaping Jewish practice, connection to and longing for the physical temple persisted in liturgy and ritual; for example, on Tisha B'Av (the ninth day of the month of Av) religious Jews collectively fast and mourn the destruction of the Second Temple while praying for its eventual rebuilding.

Rabbinic sources, including the Talmud and kabbalistic works, expanded metaphysical interpretations of the House of God, broadening it beyond its national/historical role on the Temple Mount. In the early kabbalistic work *Sefer Yetzirah*, the Temple appears as part of the sacred architecture of the universe, the container through which divine creative power flows and gives rise to the material world.[69] In addition to abstracting the Temple, rabbinic commentators downplayed apocalyptic visions of the end of times, developing passive and individualized approaches to redemption and the messianic era. The end of times was not something to be hastened through radical actions; instead, the initiation of the messianic era was considered a matter of divine decree,[70] or, alternatively, as contingent upon personal spiritual cultivation and gradual collective *tikkun* (rectification or world fixing) through pious actions.[71] Medieval kabbalists like Isaac Luria emphasized the ability of human actions to influence the divine realm; through the performance of daily mitzvot and prayer Jews could collectively and slowly "raise up the divine sparks" and help draw the Shekhinah, the divine presence, back out of exile.[72] From this perspective, the arrival of the messianic era would occur at an unrevealed time when Jewish repentance and righteousness would be sufficient to merit national restoration in the Land of Israel.

In tension with more passive theological orientations toward the messianic era are the acute moments of messianic fervor that punctuate Jewish medieval and modern history, including the emergence of self-proclaimed messiahs and attempts to return to the Land of Israel.

During the seventeenth century, Jewish rabbi and kabbalist Shabbatai Tzvi claimed to be the long-awaited Messiah who would lead Jews back to the Land of Israel.[73] A century later, the Gaon of Vilna, one of the most influential rabbinic figures of his time, predicted the imminent arrival of the Messiah in 1781. The Gaon rejected the messianic passivity of his rabbinic contemporaries and defied admonitions against prematurely hastening the arrival of messianic times. Decades before the birth of the Zionist movement, he encouraged his disciples to immigrate to the Land of Israel and begin physically rebuilding a Jewish theocracy.[74]

The birth of the Zionist movement at the end of the nineteenth century intensified theological debates regarding passive and active messianic attitudes as the immigration of European Jews to Palestine brought to the fore questions surrounding the role of practical human action in initiating messianic times. Despite the secularity of the founding Zionist philosophers and general lack of religious observance among European Jewish settlers arriving in the second and third waves of Zionist immigration, Zionist discourses in the prestate years were saturated with nationalist messianic tropes inspired by the Jewish prophetic tradition. Immigration to Israel to work the land through collective farming was viewed as part of an effort to redeem not only the nation but also the Jewish body and soul. Diasporic Jews would be transformed into "native" Hebrews firmly bonded to their ancestral homeland, and the biblical past became an important resource for socializing Jewish natives in Israel.[75] The imagined degenerate and bookish Jew of Exile would be refashioned into a muscular, proud (European-like) man through agricultural work and military power, resurrected in the imagined image of his biblical Israelite ancestors.[76]

As the Zionist movement gained political momentum in Europe at the turn of the century, the majority of the Orthodox Jewish leadership in Europe remained opposed, rejecting the idea that the long-awaited return to the Land of Israel would be carried out by secular socialists who did not respect Torah Law. Political Zionism was viewed as a heretical attempt to artificially rush messianic times that would actually delay the coming of a Jewish messiah.[77] Rabbinic leaders from across the diaspora generally held to the theological principle that one must wait patiently for divine intervention to initiate the process of national restoration. There were, however, notable exceptions among rabbinic leaders in the early twentieth century who articulated an active messianic theology compatible with the nationalist goals of the secular Zionism movement.

Rabbi Avraham Isaac Kook (1865–1935), generally considered the founding father of modern religious Zionism, took the stance that practical earthly labor was required to initiate redemption in the Land of Israel and that the establishment of the State of Israel by secular Zionists was a necessary part of the messianic process.[78] Drawing on kabbalistic theory, which identifies holiness hidden inside of secular profanity, Kook, like the Gaon of Vilna before him, taught his disciples that mundane actions in the earthly realm were necessary to awaken and inspire reciprocal action from the divine realm above—that redemption began with individual actions and extended outward to all of humanity and the universe. From this perspective, even the secular Zionist pioneers who desecrated the Shabbat could be regarded as holy vehicles for the initiation of biblical prophecies, responsible for building a nation-state that would eventually enable the return of Jewish exiles to the Land of Israel and the rebuilding of the Third Temple. By sanctifying the national project, Rabbi Kook's theological innovations set the stage for a religious Zionist partnership with a secular state apparatus as evidenced by the eventual establishment of a Chief Rabbinate in 1921, the integration of religious Zionists within subsequent socialist governments, and the participation of religious nationalists in the army.[79]

By the 1950s, the religious Zionist movement fractured between those who remained within Israel's 1967 borders and practiced a moderate version of Orthodoxy and those who drifted even further to the political right while adopting increasingly Ultra-Orthodox norms of observance.[80] Rabbi Kook's son, Tzvi Yehuda, mobilized his father's poetic and esoteric writings toward more ambitious and messianically driven territorial goals, developing a political theology that would eventually transform religious Zionism into the influential political bloc that it is today. Israel's seemingly miraculous victory in the 1967 war energized the messianic yearnings of religious Zionists, who came to view themselves as a vanguard paving the way for the arrival of the messianic era. In 1974, Tzvi Yehuda's disciples from the Merkaz ha-Rav yeshiva went on to found Gush Emunim (Bloc of the Faithful), a religious-nationalist movement dedicated to Jewish settlement in all of "Greater Israel" (the West Bank, Gaza, and the Golan Heights).[81] Gush Emunim considered the expansion of Jewish settlements as an urgent and divinely mandated project that would hasten the arrival of the messianic era and eventual reestablishment of a Jewish theocracy in the Land of Israel.[82] As the political dominance of secular-socialist Labor Zionism declined following the Yom Kippur War (1973), religious Zionism began to play an increasingly prominent role in the public sphere, in part due to an increasing religionization of Israeli society, but more profoundly due to religious Zionism's ability to offer an alternative and attractive interpretation of the changing political reality following the war—namely, one that championed an expansionist territorial vision while also supporting the hard-line security stance and neoliberal economic policies of the newly governing secular right-wing Likud party.[83]

While religious-nationalist ideologies were a driving force in Israel's settlement project in the West Bank, far more mundane motivations (e.g., affordable housing, education, and social services) now account for the expansion of Israel's large settlement blocs and the growth of a settler population numbering around six hundred thousand (out of Israel's total population of eight million), with the majority located just over the Green Line in the middle-class suburbs that constitute a de facto annexation of East Jerusalem by Israel.[84] West Bank settlements must be viewed not as existing inside of a messianic bubble that is the antithesis of "Israel proper" but rather as a contiguous part of the administrative, economic, and residential landscape of Israel.[85] The rapid expansion of Jewish settlement over the Green Line exposes the intricate interplay of underlying messianic political theologies with changing social and economic conditions that enable territorial expansion.

According to different estimates, approximately one-fifth to one-fourth of Israel's population actively identifies as "religious nationalist," but a much broader cross section of the right wing votes in alignment with core religious-nationalist ideologies: a shared resistance to territorial withdrawals, skepticism toward peace negotiations following the failure of the Oslo Peace Accords and the Second Intifada, and the belief that Jews have an undisputable biblical right to all of "Greater Israel." The strength of Israel's religious right wing was enhanced in the 1980s and 1990s due to the widespread support of Mizrahi voters (Jews from North Africa and the Middle East). Mizrahim defected to the right in protest of the discrimination they faced under Ashkenazi-led Socialist Zionism during the first decades of statehood and the continued inability of left-wing parties to address intra-Jewish racial injustice, in conjunction with a broader pattern of religionization of Mizrahi communities and their increasing presence in religious Zionist institutions.[86]

In summary, the original messianic fervor of Gush Emunim has given way to a more far-reaching right-wing nationalism, one that joins together a broad spectrum of secular and religious Israelis through dovetailing political interests.[87] As the following chapter will continue to elaborate, it is within this context of right-wing nationalism and Jewish territorial domination over the West Bank that the Third Temple movement has been reinvigorated in the twenty-first century. Once an ostracized movement on the margins of religious Zionism,[88] the Third Temple movement has gained access to state resources and successfully slid into the religious and political mainstream. In the wake of the "success" of West Bank settlement projects, religious Zionists (along with secular nationalist allies) have refocused their sights on the Temple Mount as the last unconquered frontier of Zionism—a territorial conquest that is not only viewed as critical for securing Jewish sovereignty over the Land of Israel but also considered to have profound spiritual and global implications. In effect, the Temple Mount has, according to Tomer Persico, become the "centerpiece and point of convergence for national feelings and desires" in Israel today, a contested sacred site that sits at the center of ongoing cycles of political violence.[89]

As mentioned previously, Jewish messianism contains both particularistic and universalistic dimensions. While the Third Temple movement aims to complete a process of Jewish ethnonational revival, the Children of Noah movement purports to *extend this redemptive process to all of humanity*, effectively unifying the two poles of Jewish messianic thought. Throughout the course of my fieldwork, rabbinic informants repeatedly referred to the Noahide movement as the "final stage" of Zionism, in which Israel "turns outward" and actualizes its prophesized role to be a "light unto the nations."[90]

A NOTE ON RACE AND RELIGION

Noahidism effectively universalizes Israel-based religious Zionism, transforming an ethnocentric and territorial project into a deterritorialized one concerned with the spiritual welfare of humanity. Even though religious ideologies and identities may appear as universalizing and transcendent, they are, as Su'ad Abdul Khabeer reminds us, always produced through "intersubjective relationships charged by the complexities of race."[91] As I followed the Third Temple from Israel to Noahide communities around the world, the question of race became inescapable as informants drew upon biblically inspired categories of difference to narrate their spiritual journeys and messianic visions. Informants described Jews and Noahides as two separate spiritual and genealogical lineages branching off from the sons of Noah—two divinely ordained categories of humanity with different roles to play and spiritual potentials to actualize. For Third Temple activists this meant completing a process of ethnonational and spiritual revival, one that had begun with the birth of Zionism and would end only with the rebuilding of the Third Temple on the Temple Mount. As Jews became Israelites, interlocuters explained, non-Jews would return to their own biblical identity as the Children of Noah, bound to the God of Israel through their own unique Noahide covenant inside the Torah.

I note for the reader that the idea of reviving an imagined Israelite past has historically been a core part of Zionist ethnonational ideology since Israel's pre-state years. Throughout the twentieth century, religious and secular Zionist groups alike have relied on a romanticized visions of the biblical past; in addition to biblical texts, they have utilized scientific disciplines like archaeology and genetic science as resources for reconstructing Jewish indigeneity and authenticating the Jewish national project.[92] State-funded archaeological projects, for example, helped to present a narrative that seamlessly linked an Israelite antiquity to a Jewish national present, erasing Palestinian history in the process and contributing to the Judaization of Palestinian lands and holy sites.[93] As Nadia Abu El-Haj explains, archaeological excavations were critical in the early years of state building because they provided the empirical "scientific evidence" of Israelites as a category of people, affirming "the Israelite nation as a material-historical fact."[94] Through the development of archaeological science in Israel, the past became a means for generating the national legitimacy needed to carry out large-scale Jewish settlement alongside the domination and displacement of Palestinians.

I employ the notion of race, and more specifically what I refer to as the "biblical-racial" or "spiritual-racial," to identify sacralized ideologies of bloodline, biblical genealogies, and notions of spiritual hierarchy that circulated in my field sites. In general, biological discourses, which attempt to ground racial constructs in genetic evidence, were less pronounced in my particular field sites, as informants primarily invoked biblical and prophetic narratives to organize and classify humanity for spiritual and nationalist purposes. Religious texts have historically served as flexible resources for constructing categories of difference and classifying humanity in hierarchical ways. While the biblical story of Noah and his three sons has been used for centuries by the Abrahamic religions to support notions of universality and equality, common descent, and God's covenant with all of humanity, it has also been used at particular historical moments to construct seemingly primordial and divinely sanctioned racial categories into which humanity could be classified for political aims.[95] A common passage used in this way is Genesis 9:18–27, which I have summarized below:

> When the Flood ended, Noah walked out onto dry land accompanied his three sons: Shem, Ham, and Japheth, whose descendants would become the "70 nations of the world."[96] Noah, being a farmer, immediately began to till the earth. He planted a vineyard and fermented his first harvest of grapes to produce a wine that he drank to intoxication. He was later discovered lying naked in his tent by his son Ham. Rather than assisting his father, Ham gazed upon Noah's nudity before notifying his brothers. Modestly averting their eyes, Shem and Japheth promptly covered their father's naked body. When Noah awoke and learned of Ham's indecency, he proclaimed a curse upon Ham's son Canaan: "Cursed be Canaan; the lowest of slaves shall he be to his brothers."

Through postbiblical Jewish and Christian exegesis, Noah's son Shem was identified as the ancestor of all Semitic peoples, Japheth became the progenitor of northern white Europeans, and Ham became the "cursed" ancestor of Black-skinned peoples inhabiting the southern hemisphere (despite the fact that the actual biblical verses do not describe Ham as Black and, moreover, identify only Canaan—the son of Ham—as being punished for his father's actions). As David M. Goldenberg demonstrates in his recent historical investigation of the "Curse of Ham," centuries of Jewish, Christian, and Islamic exegesis have used this biblical story to conceptually join Blackness and slavery, to argue that Blacks are the descendants of Ham and also subject to the curse of eternal slavery, which is interpreted as extending beyond Canaan to all of Ham's (Black) progeny.[97] Goldenberg argues that interpretations of the biblical story of Noah effectively established the idea that "color means something," providing a convenient theological rationalization for Black inferiority in the medieval Christian world.[98] The "Curse of Ham," in turn, became one of the most widespread religious justifications for Black slavery, persisting into the modern era as a moral defense for the transatlantic slave trade and later for the continuation of racial segregation in the United States following the Civil War.[99]

During the colonial period, European Christian missionaries continued to draw upon biblical-racial theories to develop what became known as the "Hamitic Hypothesis," dividing Africa into "Hamitic" and "Negroid" lineages, in order to determine which groups were racially closest to Semites and Europeans.[100] In effect, biblical-racial imaginaries became, according to Edith Bruder, a "highly flexible tool for demarcating either racial superiority or inferiority" and justifying colonial domination well into the modern era.[101] To be clear, in writing about the use and derivation of "biblical-racial categories," I am not implying that the Bible itself or entire religious traditions are inherently racist. Racial constructs are not in fact "biblical" at all but rather represent the *imposition* of more modern racial ideologies read back into the Bible through subsequent exegesis— the grounding of contemporary racial ideologies in divine providence for the sake of specific political or economic goals at particular historical moments. Biblical-racial theories are interpretations of the Bible that, when examined from a critical anthropological gaze, can inform our understanding of dominant ethnonational and political ideologies in a given era.[102] In the following ethnography, I continue to examine particular constructions of spiritual-racial identity at stake in the biblical revival projects of Jewish Third Temple activists and non-Jewish Noahide allies who draw on scriptural resources to support projects of spiritual self-fashioning as well as political/territorial goals.

I note for the reader that just as religious source texts served as malleable tools for *sacralizing race* by anchoring notions of physiological or blood-based difference in divine providence, the biological sciences were subsequently invoked in the modern era to *racialize religion*. At the end of the nineteenth century, European notions of racial hierarchy and white supremacy, previously justified through scriptural exegesis, were reinforced through new scientific technologies. The field of genetic science, for example, led to the development of eugenic social policies and a racialization of Judaism that reinvigorated antisemitism in Europe and was ultimately used by the Nazi regime to justify genocide. In the first decades of the twentieth century, Jewish religious and cultural difference became increasingly fused with notions of *biological difference* as Nazi propaganda portrayed Jews as Semitic foreigners and racial degenerates who threatened to "contaminate" superior European races.

With the development of racial science at the turn of the century, European Jews in turn internalized notions of themselves as a kind of race group and began adopting the blood metaphors commonly found in European nationalist discourse of the era as a *response* to antisemitism, specifically as a means for articulating Jewish nationalism and advocating for the creation of a sovereign Jewish nation-state.[103] As Nadia Abu El-Haj's research has documented, a renewed post-Holocaust interest in Jewish genetics has continued to drive diverse projects of "Jewish self-fashioning," including the use of genetic studies to bolster Zionist territorial claims (staked on notions of Jewish racial homogeneity and indigeneity in the Land of Israel) and to validate (or invalidate) the identities of Jews of color vying for recognition and/or immigration to Israel.[104]

In the wake of twentieth-century scientific racism and the Holocaust, religious communities continue to be racialized through their interactions with genetic scientists,[105] and religion has continued to play a role in the process of racialization, used to demarcate and render meaningful various categories of difference in order to bestow privilege and/or marginalize a group accordingly. In the United States, for example, Muslims are racialized and marginalized through Islamophobic attitudes,[106] and in Israel, new immigrant groups, initially marked by ethnic or cultural difference, may gain acceptance and inclusion as Jewish citizens through the performance of proper Orthodox religiosity.[107] In summary, religious resources have been used to construct racial categories, and religious communities have been racialized through the interplay of ethnonational ideologies and scientific epistemologies. In this account, I am particularly interested in the transnational circulation of biblical-racial constructs like "Israelite" and "Noahide," as a move away from biological/genetic racializations of Jews and Judaism and back toward asserting the primacy of scriptural evidence.

I emphasize for the reader that the religious and racialized ideologies documented in the following chapters, including notions of Jewish spiritual-racial supremacy articulated by some of my Noahide and rabbinic informants, are not representative of any Jewish cultural or theological consensus. Not all Jews identify as religious and/or Zionist, and Jewish religiosity comes in a broad and diverse spectrum of ideological stances and ritual practices. Moreover, the Jewish textual tradition, including the Hebrew Bible and postbiblical rabbinic literature, is replete with countertraditions attesting to the equality of Jews and non-Jews created in the image of God and depictions of non-Jews as righteous individuals, as well as more modern theological challenges to Jewish ethnonationalism. Maimonides, one of Judaism's most authoritative rabbinic commentators, famously rejected a minority opinion that Jews are ontologically different from or superior to non-Jews. He argued that Jews could and should acquire wisdom and truth from non-Jewish philosophers and held that all human beings had equal capacity to achieve knowledge of God.[108]

Finally, I note for the reader that, in addition to documenting manifestations of biblical-racial or spiritual-racial ideology, this research also considers "race" in the sociological sense, as an analytic category that helps identify structural inequalities and power dynamics operating within my field sites. Producing an anthropology of political theology requires the careful excavation of messianic political theologies to reveal the localized power dynamics that make their global proliferation possible. Thus it became imperative to ask the following: How are messianic Jewish activists positioned within Israeli society in relationship to intra-Jewish power dynamics? And how are emerging Noahide communities positioned vis-à-vis rabbinic mentors in Israel and their own surrounding national and religious contexts? The following chapters attempt to render visible some of the intersecting gender, race, and class positions of Jewish messianic activists and Noahide actors.

The Third Temple movement in Israel is, for example, predominantly led by educated middle-class Ashkenazi Jews (descendants of European Jewish communities) who occupy a privileged status within Israel's racial hierarchy relative to Palestinians and Mizrahim (the descendants of Jewish communities from North Africa and the Middle East).[109] The relative racial and socioeconomic privilege of their leadership has enabled the Third Temple movement to access financial resources and police protection for their activities. While Mizrahi Jews are certainly present in the contemporary Temple Movement, I found that they were better represented in youth groups and tended to participate as lower-ranking activists rather than as members of the rabbinic elite.

Instead of referring to "ethnic" divisions between Jews and Palestinians, as well as between Ashkenazi and Mizrahi Jews in Israel, as is more commonly done in Israel studies scholarship, I use the word "race" because it better reflects the psychosocial reality on the ground in Israel/Palestine. As more recent interventions by Israeli anthropologists and feminist theorists have demonstrated, race better enables us to understand the mechanics of power in this particular context. Scholars have illustrated how the Israeli state categorizes residents and citizens and distributes privileges and resources through racial frameworks, attaching Jewishness, and even more specifically Ashkenazi whiteness, to many symbolic and material forms of capital.[110] Ashkenazi Jews benefit from a form of white privilege within Israeli society relative to Mizrahi Jews and Palestinians and continue to disproportionately dominate Israel's upper class as well as elite professional and political positions of leadership in the country. Mizrahi Jews, who technically make up the majority of Israel's Jewish population, have been subject to forms of racial discrimination by the ruling Ashkenazi minority and continue to experience a lack of socioeconomic mobility that dates back to the early years of statehood when Mizrahi immigrants were channeled into working-class labor and resettled in periphery zones.[111] As Smadar Lavie argues, racial divides within contemporary Israeli society are obscured by a pervasive Zionist ideology that continues to coalesce all Jews into one purified racial category that is continually positioned in opposition to the enemy "Arab Other."[112] Moreover, Lavie writes, the sacred Zionist formula of "chosen people–chosen land" is utterly dependent upon upholding a smokescreen of Jewish unity, one that must be forcefully reinvoked whenever racial and gendered differences threaten to be revealed in everyday life.[113]

The replication of the Jewish/Arab and Jewish/Muslim binaries is critical, as it maintains the founding logic of the Israeli state itself, confirming the miraculous ingathering of Jewish Exiles, stripped of their differences and revitalized as "natives," to the land granted only to them by God. Contemporary Jewish messianism in Israel relies on this same logic but takes it to its prophetic conclusion, promising a utopian messianic future where all Jews are united and ethnic differences erased through a return to a common "Israelite" or "Hebrew" identity inside of a restored theocratic kingdom.

Concurrently, as I discovered during the course of my research, non-Jewish Noahides see themselves as living out a parallel and supportive messianic trajectory. As Jews become Israelites, non-Jews imagine themselves as returning to their own original "biblical" identity, and "Noahide" becomes its own spiritual-racial category dictating the spiritual potentialities and destinies of Judaizing Christians. Biblical-racial imaginaries intersect with localized postcolonial power dynamics as Noahides, in the process of exiting Christianity, come in contact with rabbinic mentors in Israel through new digital channels. This book takes up considerations of new forms of digital proselytizing, transnational religious authority, and spiritual neocolonialism to capture the power dynamics that link my separate field sites together and sustain a messianic Zionist imagination, one that, while enabling empowering forms of postcolonial religious shifting, remains tethered to expansionist and exclusive ethnonational practices on the ground in Israel/Palestine.

2 · BIBLICAL REVIVAL IN CONTEMPORARY ISRAEL

Temple Builders as Proxy-State Actors

When Denis Rohan, an Australian tourist visiting Israel in 1969, set fire to an eight-hundred-year-old pulpit in the Al-Aqsa Mosque, he believed that he was carrying out a sacred mission: one that would enable Israel to begin building the Third Temple on the Temple Mount. As an evangelical Christian, Rohan was convinced that the rebuilding of the Temple was a necessary precondition for the Second Coming of Jesus. A decade later, American-born Israelis Baruch Ben Yosef and far-right rabbi and political leader Meir Kahane were arrested in Israel for plotting to use a rocket launcher to destroy the Dome of the Rock. In the words of Ben Yosef, their intention was to "attack Arabs and incite them, until the government would have no choice but to carry out a massive exile of Arabs."[1] After he was released from prison, Rabbi Meir Kahane continued to promote a militant messianic agenda throughout the 1980s in Israel and abroad, participating in transnational outreach to leaders from the emerging Children of Noah movement in the United States just months before he was assassinated in 1990 (a history I return to in the following chapter).[2]

In 1984, a few years after the attempt by Ben Yosef and Kahane, the Jewish Underground, a militant group of West Bank Jewish settlers staunchly opposed to the territorial concessions proposed by the Camp David Accords (1978), were caught planting bombs on Palestinian buses in East Jerusalem. During their interrogations, it was discovered that the Underground had amassed a cache of weapons and was preparing to blow up the Al-Aqsa Mosque, again with the aim of igniting a regional war that would pave the way for the removal of Palestinians from the land and the rebuilding of the Temple. In Israel, these actors were characterized as religious fundamentalists and psychologically unstable individuals (during his trial in Israel Denis Rohan was labeled mentally disturbed and hospitalized before he was returned to Australia). The subsequent signing of the Oslo Accords (1993–1995) seemed to signal, at least briefly, Israel's triumph over religious radicals who opposed territorial concessions and a two-state solution. Meanwhile, their messianic vision of temple building and theocratic biblical revival was already traveling far beyond the bounds of Israel's religious margins.

Since the 1984 arrests of the Jewish Underground, desire for the Third Temple has not dissipated. The first two decades of the twenty-first century saw the reemergence of new and allegedly "nonviolent" channels for Temple Mount activism. This included the appearance of a coalition of Third Temple activist groups and organizations dedicated to preparing architectural plans and sacred objects for the future Temple, instilling a desire for the Temple within the public consciousness, and bringing increasing numbers of Jews to the Temple Mount for daily pilgrimage tours. This chapter tells story of a Third Temple imaginary that was born in Israel. It begins by providing necessary historical background to contextualize a public grassroots campaign for the Temple that materialized in the wake of the attempted Al-Aqsa bombings of the 1980s. Since 2012, the Third Temple movement has grown significantly, migrating from Israel's religious margins to a position where it has gained broad-based support from Israel's religious-nationalist sector, secular nationalists, and a diverse coalition of ministers in Parliament.

Third Temple activism, I will argue, has been able to thrive, gaining unprecedented access to state resources and police protection on the Temple Mount, precisely because it is aligned with liberal Zionism rather than separate from it and functions as a supportive appendage of the Israeli state. Messianic Zionism is an ubiquitous political theology that functions collaboratively and symbiotically with Israeli state institutions, even as actors within the Temple movement work toward the transformation of Israel into a theocratic Torah state. This chapter renders visible the complex ways in which messianic activists, including rabbinic authorities, women, and youth, function as proxy-state actors who hybridize messianic political theologies and religious piety with liberal Zionist ideologies to accomplish spiritual and territorial goals on the ground in Israel/Palestine.

THE THIRD TEMPLE MOVEMENT: FROM MARGINS TO MAINSTREAM

The Third Temple movement's origins can be traced back to the early years of Israeli statehood with groups such as Brit Hachashmonaim, a militant religious-Zionist youth movement, that saw national renewal as dependent on reestablishing a Jewish theocracy and rebuilding a temple on the Temple Mount in Jerusalem. However, support for rebuilding the Third Temple coalesced into an organized movement only after Israel's victory in the 1967 war, which religious Zionists (both Jews in Israel and Christians abroad) interpreted as a sign that Jewish prophecies were materializing and messianic times were approaching. According to historian Motti Inbari, when the Israeli government returned the

Temple Mount to the Jordanian Waqf, religious Zionists experienced a sense of disillusionment, no longer viewing the secular Israeli state as a means for bringing redemption.[3]

In the years following the 1967 war, Inbari demonstrates, there was a proliferation of messianic activist groups in Israel committed to taking matters into their own hands.[4] Temple activists in particular began to more brazenly challenge a long-standing rabbinic ban against entering the Temple Mount.[5] Temple activists dedicated themselves to practical preparations for the rebuilding of the Temple, including the rigorous study of biblical and Talmudic sources that describe the *halachic* (Jewish Law) minutiae of sacrificial practices and architectural dimensions of the ancient Temple.[6] The Temple Mount Faithful, one of the first Third Temple organizations led by Israel Defense Forces (IDF) veteran Gershom Salomon, organized a broad coalition of religious Jews and secular right-wingers in Israel while forging close connections with American evangelicals coming from premillennialist churches during the 1980s and 1990s.[7] By emphasizing the role of Christians as allies and active participants in a universal Temple-building project, the Temple Mount Faithful began laying the groundwork for the transnational Christian allyship that would finance Temple-building activities in Israel and eventually give rise to the contemporary Noahide movement (a history that I detail in chapter 3).

By the end of the twentieth century, newly formed coalitions of Temple builders sought to connect the theoretical and textual study of Temple *halakha* (Jewish Law) with practical grassroots actions. In 1990, the Temple Mount Faithful famously attempted to lay a "foundation stone" for the future Temple. Israeli police prevented their entrance to the Temple Mount, but the provocative nature of the act sparked demonstrations by Palestinian Muslims who threw rocks at Jewish worshippers at the Western Wall below, resulting in a day of deadly clashes with Israeli police. The event foreshadowed the incendiary nature of Third Temple activism on the Haram ash-Sharif compound.

For Palestinians, Haram ash-Sharif is a sacred Islamic site, home to the Al-Aqsa Mosque, from where it is believed that the prophet Muhammad ascended to heaven, and it is an aspirational symbol of Palestinian national sovereignty. On a practical and communal level, as the largest Islamic site in Jerusalem, Haram ash-Sharif provides a daily respite from the violence and pressure of life under Israeli military occupation and is home to a number of Islamic charities and schools. For Palestinians and indeed many Muslims worldwide, the growing Third Temple movement represents a direct threat to the Islamic nature of this holy site and an obstacle to peace in the region.[8] The increasing presence of visibly religious Jews entering the Haram ash-Sharif compound accompanied by armed Israeli police signals to Palestinians, especially those already living within a context of ongoing Judaization, land annexation, and housing evictions in East Jerusalem, that Temple activists have state support to annex the compound in the near future.[9]

In response to the Temple Mount Faithful's foundation stone attempt, an organized Palestinian campaign for the protection of Al-Aqsa emerged in 1990 under the leadership of Sheikh Raed Salah. The campaign intensified after 1996 when Israel opened the Western Wall tunnels, an action that Salah claimed was definitive proof that the State of Israel had systemic plans for destroying Al-Aqsa.[10] Sheikh Salah subsequently established the Al-Aqsa Foundation (Moasasat Al-Aqsa), an organization dedicated to protecting Al-Aqsa and raising awareness of Israeli incursions on Islamic holy sites across the country. Salah's campaign to protect Al-Aqsa from annexation gained international support following Ariel Sharon's infamous visit to the Temple Mount in 2000, which helped ignite the Second Intifada. According to the Al-Aqsa Foundation,[11] between 2010 and 2016 (years when the Temple movement grew significantly in numbers and political support), distinct changes took place in daily life at Haram ash-Sharif as Israeli police facilitated the entry of Third Temple activists and Palestinian worshippers were subject to increasing restrictions in the name of security interests.

The increasing numbers of visibly religious Jews—including prominent rabbis, members of the rabbinate, heads of religious seminaries, and Knesset members—visiting the Haram ash-Sharif / Temple Mount on guided tours with Third Temple activists have played a role in inflaming ongoing cycles of violence in Israel/Palestine. This occurred, for example, in the wake of the 2014 Gaza War during a period of intensified violence that became known as the Third Intifada or Intifada of the Knives, which was characterized by lone-wolf knife attacks targeting Jewish Israelis. The stabbings were largely spontaneous and imitative, carried out by teenage Palestinian males experiencing humiliation and desperation from life under military occupation coupled with the lack of any diplomatic solutions or future prospects. Family members of the assailants linked their motivations to Israeli incursions at the site of the Al-Aqsa Mosque, where during the same period activists from the Third Temple movement had been increasingly visible due to their public campaign for Jewish prayer and pilgrimage to the Temple Mount.[12] While the growth of the Temple movement and Jewish messianic activism was certainly not the sole provocation that ignited the so-called Third Intifada, the images of religious Jews ascending to the Temple Mount, prostrating themselves on its sacred ground, and singing songs about rebuilding the Temple (daily actions that were recorded by Muslim worshippers at Al-Aqsa and circulated widely on social media) spurred rumors that Israel was planning an imminent annexation of the Temple Mount / Haram ash-Sharif compound.

By 2010, an alternative paradigm of grassroots Third Temple activism, characterized by a broad-based coalition, had clearly been established, spearheaded in part by the first generation of Temple builders who had initially sought explosive means to catalyze the messianic era. After he was released from jail, Yehuda Etzion, a leading organizer of 1984 Jewish Underground plot to blow up Al-Aqsa, dedicated himself to refounding a nonviolent Temple movement in Israel focused on changing public opinion. In 2013, Etzion publicly unveiled plans for his Jerusalem Rebuilt project, a professional city plan that he designed in collaboration with a secular-nationalist architect detailing the incorporation of the Third Temple into the future landscape of Jerusalem: an updated version of a plan first proposed forty-three years prior by Etzion's mentor Shabtai Ben Dov, a former member of Lehi (a militant Zionist group that operated during the British Mandate).[13]

The plan that Etzion presented to the Jerusalem municipality includes blueprints for the transformation of Jerusalem into a global capital the size of London through an eastward expansion that would annex Ramallah, Bethlehem, and the Gush Etzion settlements. The proposal includes the installation of an underground high-speed bullet train to carry thousands of international pilgrims daily into the center of Jerusalem at three hundred kilometers per hour. According to the plan, the Temple Mount will be the official location of the Third Temple, the House of the King, and the Court of the Sanhedrin, a council of seventy-one rabbis who will constitute a new legislative body of Israel, ruling over the country according to Torah Law.

I had an opportunity to speak with Etzion at his home in May 2016. He reflected on his change in strategy in the first decades of the twenty-first century and his decision to move away from violence and focus instead on nonviolent grassroots organizing in collaboration with state officials and secular political allies. The goal, he explained, was to slowly cultivate a wide base of public support for rebuilding the Temple. When I asked him about Jerusalem Rebuilt, he emphasized the importance of professional design as a means to liberate the imagination and begin taking practice steps toward a new future, even if that imagination feels utterly detached from the present reality. Just the very act of designing, producing schematics, was a way to begin materializing the future and initiate a paradigm shift.

Etzion, it seemed, was deeply aware of the power of *speculative design*, the envisioning and planning of possible futures to change moral and political perceptions in the present. Speculative design, also commonly referred to as "critical design" or "futurescaping," is a design methodology aimed at creating "alternative ways of being" and is typically used to develop design solutions for large-scale economic, political, and social justice issues such as climate change or alternatives to capitalism.[14] Design collectives, often working in collaboration with social scientists or ethicists, use this form of conceptual design that is free from industrial production to design *ideas* that can "act as a catalyst for collectively redefining our relationship to reality."[15] Jerusalem Rebuilt is an attempt to use technology to create a new kind of future modeled after a biblical past, where humanity will allegedly be united through a perfected monotheism, recognition of the Torah, and restoration of Israelite nationhood.

Intentionally or not, Etzion's remarks on Jerusalem Rebuilt, both in our conversation and in other published public interviews on the project, echo the basic tenets of speculative design theory. He believes that his plans will unshackle the imagination of his Jewish viewers, allowing them to suspend their connection to the present and consider a new kind of post-Zionist reality. While discussions and practices of speculative design typically occur in liberal academic circles in response to social justice issues, speculative design work may also be employed for ethnonationalist projects aimed at redefining the relationship of a nation to an imagined past and desired future. Etzion's design, which includes the mass removal of Palestinians through financial incentives to emigrate, also emphasizes the universal significance of the Third Temple as a future "house of prayer for all nations."[16] The Jerusalem Rebuilt plan includes a House of Nations, a kind of welcome center for "righteous Gentiles" (Noahides) who will also travel to the Third Temple as religious pilgrims.

In summary, the Third Temple movement, now consisting of at least two dozen affiliated activist groups and organizations (according to my last count in 2018), has successfully rebranded itself as a nonviolent initiative in Israel focused on teaching the public about their biblical heritage through lectures, public reenactments of Temple rituals, and the re-creation of sacred Temple vessels including the iconic golden menorah on display in the Old City of Jerusalem overlooking the Temple Mount.

For most Israelis and tourists passing by, the menorah, a common national symbol, does not resonate as inherently controversial. But for Temple activists, this particular menorah is an item on loan from the future. It is, in fact, a reconstruction of the menorah that once stood in the Second Temple that has been carefully replicated by the Temple Institute according to specific measurements recorded in the rabbinic literature, and it stands in a glass case across from the Temple Mount, waiting for the day that it will be put into ritual use in the Third Temple (see Figure 2). The sign below it explains that the menorah "was recreated for the first time since the destruction of the Second Temple according to the research conducted by the Temple Institute."[17]

The Temple Institute, founded in 1984 by Rabbi Yisrael Ariel, is one of the leading organizations of the Third Temple movement and exemplar of the "nonviolent" approach developed in the 1990s and early 2000s by Temple activists. The Temple Institute has played a key role in supporting emerging Noahide communities abroad, viewing them as critical non-Jewish allies for achieving Temple-building goals (the relationship between the Temple Institute and Noahides abroad is detailed in chapter 3). Rabbi Ariel previously served as a paratrooper in the Israeli brigade that took control over the Temple Mount during the 1967 war, an experience that inspired him to devote his life to building the Third Temple.[18] Ariel, who graduated from the Mercaz HaRav Yeshiva (one of the most influential religious Zionist seminaries), is also a former member of Rabbi Meir Kahane's

FIGURE 2. Menorah created by the Temple Institute on display in the Old City of Jerusalem. (Photo by Rabbi Drew Kaplan.)

ultranationalist KACH party that was outlawed in Israel and banned from Parliament in 1986. Like Kahane, Ariel has used religion to justify violent conquest and has advocated for the transformation of Israel into a Jewish theocracy. Yet, through the establishment of the Temple Institute, he has found an avenue to advance his goals in a manner that seems nonthreatening and appeals to a much broader audience beyond Israel's religious far right.

In its mission statement, the Temple Institute describes itself, first and foremost, as an *educational* organization dedicated to teaching the Israeli public about the importance of the Temple through "research, seminars, publications, and conferences, as well as the production of educational materials" and promises to "do all in our limited power to bring about the building of the Holy Temple in our time."[19] To support its daily activities, the institute receives national service volunteers (noncombat army duty) from the Israeli state and substantial annual funding from the Ministry of Culture, Science and Sports, the Ministry of Education, and the Ministry of Defense to support its projects as well as donations from Jews, Christians, and Noahides abroad.[20] Located across from the Western Wall in the Old City of Jerusalem, the Temple Institute has become a popular tourist destination for Israelis and internationals who visit its gallery of reconstructed Temple objects including priestly garments, instruments for Temple musicians (Levites), and altars for animal sacrifices. Visitors can even purchase from the gift shop "Temple incense" to take home with them.

In addition to preparing sacred objects, the Temple Institute supports an ongoing project to train Jewish men who descend from a priestly lineage so that they will be ready to take up priestly service in the future Third Temple. Part of this training takes place through the public staging of *tirgulim* (exercises), live animal sacrifices that reenact rituals that once took place in the Second Temple but were converted into verbal prayer following its destruction by the Romans. During these events, such as the Passover sacrifice conducted annually by the movement since 2000, Israelite indigeneity is choreographed and staged by the kohanim, Third Temple priests in training, who perform the ritual onstage for hundreds of spectators while dressed in the biblical white robes that they refer to as *beged ivri* (Hebrew clothes).[21] In August 2016, Baruch Kahane, the son of the late Meir Kahane, was nominated by Temple activists to serve as the Kohen Gadol, the high priest, should the political situation change and allow for the construction of the Third Temple.[22]

This revival and reembodiment of Israelite religion represented by Temple priests in training is further enhanced by the authority of scientific knowledge and DNA symbolism as the Temple Institute emphasizes the genetic authenticity of the kohanim in its publications. The following example was taken from the Temple Institute's online campaign to raise money for Nezer Hakodesh, its Jerusalem-based institute for training kohanim.

> The first kohen, the founder of the priestly clan of Israel, was Aaron, brother of Moses, of the tribe of Levi. Levi was the patriarch Jacob's third son, and Aaron was a fourth generation descendant of Levi. Aaron and his four sons were designated as the first priests; Aaron served as the first High Priest. As the verses indicate, all of his male descendants were chosen by G-d to be priests forever; it is an eternal covenant. Thus, even today, a kohen among the Jewish people is genealogically a direct descendant of Aaron. In our time, new advances in science and medicine have established the identity of the descendants of Aaron beyond any doubt, through DNA.[23]

More than simply romanticizing the biblical past, which has long been an important theme in secular-Zionist ideology, the practice sacrifices are part of an ongoing project to continue transforming Jews into "natives" of the land through embodied practices and participatory experiences (at the end of the Passover event, participants are invited to consume the flesh of the sacrificial lamb). Through public sacrificial reenactments, Third Temple activists construct a sensorium of Israelite indigeneity as a spiritual and political resource, transmitting their vision of biblical revival to increasingly diverse audiences.[24] During my fieldwork, I documented the attendance of modern Orthodox religious nationalists, Ultra-Orthodox nationalists, Hasidic Jews identifying with Chabad and Breslov streams, and even secular nationalists, who all view the renewal of animal sacrifices as an important demonstration of Jewish sovereignty. In 2016, the religious newspaper *Arutz Sheva* found that out of 681 readers surveyed, about 68 percent believed that reinitiating the Passover sacrifice was a "worthy and good" endeavor. The survey exposed the growing acceptance of the tirgulim within the religious-nationalist community in Israel and indicated that questions regarding the legitimacy of animal sacrifices had become a topic of interest among this demographic. For example, in 2016 a digital flyer for the Passover Sacrifice event was distributed widely on social media. The flyer utilized the growing level of public support from religious-nationalist rabbis to advertise the event as one legitimized by mainstream rabbinic authority. The flyer listed the names of eleven prominent rabbis who had endorsed the event, including Rabbi Aryeh Stern, the Ashkenazi Chief Rabbi of Jerusalem, and Rabbi Shmuel Eliyahu, the Chief Rabbi of Safed.

The motivations behind the staged practice sacrifices are multiple. On one level, sacrificial reenactments cohere with the Third Temple movement's nonviolent rebranding, appearing as nonthreatening and educational and, according to some of my informants, focused primarily on instilling a "temple consciousness" in a younger generation. By reorienting children and teens toward the Temple Mount, sacrificial reenactments promote the idea that the Temple Mount is the last unconquered frontier of the Zionist project. At the same time, the sacrificial spectacles have a deeply subversive mission, functioning as an arena for proposing a future theocratic order centered around the Temple. Sarina Chen's research on the sacrificial reenactments examined the symbolic significance of sacrifices in proposing a new source of religious and political authority, namely the reconstitution of the Sanhedrin, a rabbinic high court, intended to one day replace the Israeli Supreme Court and rule on all matters according to halakha.[25] In 2004, Temple activists announced the revival of this rabbinic Parliament, referred to now as the "nascent Sanhedrin," a project that was backed by prominent rabbinic leaders including Rabbis Moshe Halberstam and Adin Steinsaltz. The nascent Sanhedrin, which does not have any official legal authority in Israel, continues to serve as an intellectual forum generating halakhic opinions related to Third Temple revival activities including Temple Mount pilgrimage, animal sacrifices, and emerging Noahide communities.

Establishing a Sanhedrin is a central element of the future ethnotheocracy that Temple activists hope to establish in Israel, one fully subsumed under Torah Law that distributes rights according to biblical definitions of citizenship. According to Temple Institute founder Rabbi Yisrael Ariel, all non-Jews who wish to remain in the Land of Israel following the rebuilding of the Third Temple must profess adherence to the Seven Noahide Laws and recognize the supremacy of the Torah. This applies to Palestinians, who will be allowed to remain in Israel only if they declare themselves to be Noahides, accept their secondary status as *ger toshav* (a biblical category typically translated as "resident alien"), and submit to the yoke of Torah Law. In a speech from 2015, delivered during a public conference for Temple Mount activists, Rabbi Ariel described this impending era of Jewish theocracy and conquest of Greater Israel when the Sanhedrin will be reestablished and Jews will go from city to city imposing Torah Law.[26] Rabbi Ariel's messianic dream of an imperialist halachic state illustrates his disregard for international laws or borders, his focus on military conquest, and his goal of replacing manmade political systems with a divinely sanctioned biblical hierarchy: the kohanim, Israel, and the rest of the world as Noahides.

During the 2016 Passover sacrifice event in Jerusalem, I had the opportunity to speak with members of the self-elected Sanhedrin who spoke openly about using the sacrifices to prepare the public consciousness for a refounding of the state as a Jewish theocracy. As one affiliated rabbi explained: "We hope that that practice and everything around it, the ethics, and so on will have a big echo. This is actually the most important thing about it. This [building the Temple and sacrificing animals] will build more peace and more liberation than all the peace conferences that the politicians are doing to bring peace in the world," he explained. True liberation for the Jewish people required embracing and revaluing ethnocentrism: "Today the highest value is equality. But the whole exodus from Egypt is based on discrimination. God discriminated between Israel and Egypt. And every slave in world chooses the exodus from Egypt as a symbol of liberation." According to the rabbi, rather than embracing secular values such as equality and democracy, redemption required the reincarnation of sacred biblical-racial hierarchies, the "discrimination" of God's chosen nation vis-à-vis the other nations.

Democracy, he continued to explain to me, "is shallow because it leads to equality," erasing the distinct categories and roles that the Torah prescribes: "the cohanim, kings, men, women, the nation of Israel, and other nations." Other Temple activists shared similar sentiments in our discussions. These ancient roles, these biblical categories of citizenship, are what linked Jews to the Land of Israel and thus had to be renewed and sanctified: "That is why we are standing here [at the Passover sacrifice] in a struggle for the revival of holiness and a different reality; for the chosenness of Israel. God chose Israel and brought the Temple as a place for God to reside in and to be a place of prayer for the nations," he concluded with a universalistic twist, portraying Israel's ethnocentric project as necessary for the broader spiritual welfare of humanity.

Historian Motti Inbari labels the ideology articulated by Third Temple movement leaders as "theocratic post Zionism,"[27] a political theology that developed in response to Israel's territorial concessions, including the return of the Temple Mount to the Jordanian Waqf in 1967 and the Gaza Disengagement in 2005. These actions were considered treasonous by certain groups of religious nationalists and led to a strengthening of messianic desire among those who felt they could no longer rely on the state as a vehicle for annexing all of Greater Israel and rebuilding the Temple. According to Inbari, the "fear of losing," of prophecies not coming true, creates a "cognitive dissonance that leads to messianic radicalization."[28] By reviving Temple rituals and the rabbinic platform of the nascent Sanhedrin, Temple activists have taken upon themselves the responsibility of gradually transforming the State of Israel into a premessianic theocracy. Post-Zionist theocrats such as the late Meir Kahane (with whom Rabbi Ariel from the Temple Institute worked closely) view Zionism as a project of "purification" from exile and the degrading influences of Western assimilation on the Jewish people during diaspora. Such negative influences include democracy, which they consider to be a foreign "Gentile" ideology that hinders the return of the Jewish people to their biblical roots.[29] They are "post-Zionist" in the sense that they utterly reject secular Zionist and more moderate religious Zionist visions of Israel as a liberal nation-state situated among the nations of the world and subject to international law. Rather, as Shaul Magid argues in his recent work on Kahanist ideology, theocratic post-Zionism promotes an "ethos of conquest and domination" over the Land of Israel that justifies Jewish violence toward non-Jews and, moreover, is driven by a fundamentally "biblical worldview of separation."[30] The sacred "separation" between God's Chosen Nation (Israel), subject to divine laws and mandates, and the Gentile nations is considered necessary for redemption.

Following the advent of social media platforms in the early 2000s, the Third Temple movement gravitated from the right-wing margins into the religious-nationalist mainstream, gaining endorsement from prominent rabbinic leaders including Ashkenazi Chief Rabbi David Lau.[31] A 2013 survey indicated that one-third of Israeli Jews support building a Temple on Haram ash-Sharif / Temple Mount and 59 percent agree that there should be a change to the status quo, such as extending Israeli control over the site or establishing separate visiting hours for Jews and Muslims, as was previously done at Abraham's tomb in Hebron.[32] Since 2015, increasing numbers of Knesset members have openly supported the Third Temple movement and attended guided pilgrimage tours on the Temple Mount with Third Temple activists.[33] On November 7, 2016, ministers from the Likud and Jewish Home parties announced the establishment of a new Temple Lobby dedicated to advancing the issue of Jewish visitation and prayer on the Temple Mount.[34] In 2021, following an escalation of violence that began on Jerusalem Day when Israeli forces entered Al-Aqsa, prominent rabbinic figures, including the heads of religious nationalist seminaries and members of the Israeli rabbinate, issued statements of support on social media for Jewish pilgrimage to the Temple Mount.

With the failure of the Oslo peace process, ongoing Jewish settlement, and the Gaza Wars of 2014 and 2021, the Temple movement has gained political traction, leading to the unlikely alliance of secular and religious nationalists in the Knesset who support the idea of annexing the Temple Mount and rebuilding a Jewish temple as an act that will once and for all ensure Israel's complete sovereignty over the land.[35] Israel's passing of the "nation-state law" (2018), which declares self-determination in Israel as exclusive to the Jewish people and promotes Jewish settlement as a national value, further reflects these ethnocentric and antidemocratic trends. Political representation for the Temple movement was enhanced by Israel's recent 2021 parliamentary elections when members of the far-right Jewish Power Party (Otzmah Yehudit), a reincarnation of the previously outlawed KACH party, led by the late Rabbi Meir Kahane, managed to gain seats in the Knesset for the first time in thirty-three years. Party leader Itamar Ben-Gvir is a prominent supporter of Third Temple activist groups and regularly participates in pilgrimage tours to the Temple Mount.

I note for the reader that support for Temple Mount activism is hardly limited to Israel's extreme right. In 2021, thirty-one Knesset members from across Israel's secular and religious nationalist spectrum (representing the Likud, Yamina, Jewish Home, Yesh Atid, Otzma Yehudit, United Torah, Religious Zionism, and New Hope parties) had issued statements of support for the Temple movement, advocated for increased Jewish access to the Temple Mount during parliamentary debates, and/or participated in a Temple Mount pilgrimage tour. On November 16, 2021, the Knesset's Education Committee met to consider a proposal by Temple activists to enhance Temple Mount content within the mandatory school curriculum and to include visits to the Temple Mount during mandatory school field trips to Jerusalem.[36] On January 6, 2021, the question of extending Israeli sovereignty over the Temple Mount again took center stage in the political arena as Knesset members debated adding the Temple Mount to Israel's list of protected holy places. While the number of dedicated Third Temple activists participating regularly in the sacrificial rituals and Temple Mount pilgrimages is still arguably small (in the order of tens of thousands compared to Israel's population of nine million), the political trends described above indicate broad-based support for the idea of Temple building and/or Temple Mount annexation, support that has yet to be definitively quantified in survey data.

The decentralized nature of the Temple movement, in conjunction with its social media savviness, has contributed to its growth and its ability to reach increasingly diverse supporters across age, gender, and ethnic categories. While the Temple Institute focuses on training kohanim and preparing Temple objects, the organization Women for the Temple, for example, works to organize Orthodox Jewish women from across the country to participate in Temple Mount pilgrimages and practice Temple "crafts," such as sewing clothes for the kohanim and preparing the bread sacrifices for ritual reenactments. Returning to the Mount caters to teenagers and young adults in their early twenties, while Students for the Temple organizes college students around the country in support of rebuilding the Temple, appealing to religious youth as well as secular nationalists. Beyadenu: Returning to the Temple Mount focuses on political lobbying in the Knesset and securing increased Jewish access to the Temple Mount.

While the Temple movement does not have a rigid hierarchical structure, there are leading rabbis, predominantly Ashkenazi men, whose theological and political interpretations play an important role in guiding the movement and the actions of grassroots activists. In Israel, Ashkenazi Jews occupy a position of racial and economic privilege vis-à-vis Mizrahi Jews and Palestinians, disproportionately occupying positions of power and leadership within state-sponsored religious and political institutions. During my fieldwork in Israel, Mizrahi Jews were notably absent from the leadership ranks of Third Temple organizations but were certainly present as rank-and-file activists (according to my own fieldwork surveys, they made up at least one-third of the activist base regularly participating in demonstrations, workshops, and pilgrimages). Many Mizrahim in Israel continue to follow the religious legal rulings of the late chief Sephardic rabbi Ovadia Yosef, who forbade Jews from entering the Temple Mount, and the Ultra-Orthodox Mizrahi religious leadership generally remains opposed to pilgrimages to the Temple Mount or using political action to rebuild the Temple. When Mizrahim do participate as grassroots activists, they do so in ways that notably conform to Ashkenazi religious Zionist standards of theological interpretation and ritual practice. For example, at the time of my research, out of the approximately one hundred active members of the Returning to the Mount youth movement, at least forty members came from Mizrahi or mixed Mizrahi/Ashkenazi families and most were attending Ashkenazi-led religious-Zionist schools. Similarly, five out of the fifteen women activists with whom I conducted interviews identified as Mizrahi but were notably married to Ashkenazi men and identified with Ashkenazi-run political parties and religious institutions. Such findings are in line with previous research highlighting the role of religion in incorporating Mizrahim into the nationalist project and making them proper Zionist subjects. As Yehouda Shenhav has argued, adopting a religious-Zionist identity, as defined and performed according to Orthodox Ashkenazi standards, enabled Mizrahim to access Israel's public and political sphere while diminishing their Arab identity.[37] Ashkenaziness, then, does not necessarily imply European descent but stands for an Israeli version of whiteness that, Orna Sasson-Levy argues, functions as a kind of "symbolic capital" that can be learned or adopted.[38] According to Nissim Leon, the absorption of Mizrahim into Ashkenazi religious standards illustrates how Ashkenazi Orthodoxy has "become the yardstick for determining normative religiosity" in Israel.[39] Although the Third Temple movement is often labeled as "extremist" or "marginal," it is positioned within a broader culture of normative Ashkenazi religiosity that has enabled the movement to move into the mainstream and access state resources, police protections, and political representation in recent years.

As Jews were discursively condensed into an ethnic unity through the Israeli Zionist account of the "ingathering of exiles," they were also gathered under an Ashkenazi universalist umbrella. While Mizrahim were marked as culturally particular in the early years of state formation, Ashkenaziness was de-ethnicized and has come to stand for the entire Jewish collective.[40] This reality was reflected in the confusion expressed by Temple activists when I attempted to talk to them about the ethnic composition of the movement in Israel. While almost all of my informants agreed with me that the movement, and certainly its leadership, was predominantly Ashkenazi, they could not understand why this would be significant information. "But we are all Jews," they would often insist, and emphasize that rebuilding the Temple was fundamentally about "Jewish unity," about rectifying the Jewish divisions that caused the destruction of the Second Temple. The messianic discourse employed by activists further concealed intra-Jewish racial divisions in the present by promising the imminent arrival of a utopian existence that would make such divisions irrelevant.

While ideologically unified around the goal of rebuilding the Temple, each activist group differs in the extent to which they rely on state resources and cooperate with the Israeli police, mirroring the wide spectrum of pro-state and anti-state sentiments present among Israel's religious-nationalist demographic. Government-supported organizations like the Temple Institute work to maintain cordial relationships with state authorities, right-wing politicians, and government ministries. To maintain the public image of a nonviolent and educational organization, spokespeople for the Temple Institute typically refrain from speaking openly about destroying the mosques on the Haram ash-Sharif compound. Supportive Knesset ministers also tend to present peaceful visons of Temple building, drawing on liberal discourses that frame Jewish access to the Temple Mount as an issue of "religious freedom" that should be a concern for Israel as a "democratic state."

In contrast, youth activists from Returning to the Mount view such approaches as capitulating to a secular state and constraining the movement. Teens and young adults openly confront Israeli police and Muslim worshippers and are frequently arrested for provocative activities such as praying, prostrating, and attempting to sacrifice lambs on Haram ash-Sharif / Temple Mount during the Passover holiday.[41] During my fieldwork, I found young women to be among the most passionate and committed of the approximately one hundred active members of Returning to the Mount. These teenage girls saw it as their job to provoke state responses. On Israeli Independence Day—May 12, 2016—fifteen of these activists were arrested for participating in an illegal protest and attempting to march to the Temple Mount through Palestinian East Jerusalem. The arrested included three young women who were carrying their infants while attempting to cross a police blockade.[42] The majority of these young women activists grew up in West Bank settlements, and for them it was not enough to simply educate and raise awareness of the Temple. They saw themselves as carrying the Zionist settlement project in the West Bank to a new border: the Temple Mount in Jerusalem. Shira was a sixteen -year-old activist in the youth movement from a Mizrahi family who had been arrested three times when I interviewed her in 2016. She explained, "We don't play by rules the way the other groups in the movement do. We aren't afraid to say openly that we want to destroy the mosques. Other groups talk about democracy and religious freedom on the Mount but that is not our message." As Shira explained with pride, her group was the kav 'esh—or fire line—that is willing to "push things forward" for the movement by confronting Israeli police and Palestinians. Mizrahi youth like Shira reported that they did not feel beholden to their parents' tradition of observing the rabbinic ban on Temple Mount pilgrimage and were willing to be arrested for praying on the Temple Mount or carrying out illegal protests.

TEMPLE MOUNT PILGRIMAGE

The most publicly visible and influential form of Temple activism is Jewish pilgrimage to the Temple Mount and the ongoing campaign for Jewish prayer there. Following the Second Intifada (2000–2005) when the Temple Mount / Haram ash-Sharif opened back up to non-Muslim tourists, religious Jews largely continued to avoid the Temple Mount, upholding long-standing rabbinic rulings that forbade Jewish pilgrimage for fear that Jews would desecrate the site by entering in a state of ritual impurity. Gradually, the idea of returning to the Temple Mount grew in the public awareness, and from 2011 to 2016 a distinctive new mode of religious Jewish pilgrimage to the Temple Mount emerged. Religious Jews began entering the Mount on guided pilgrimage tours with trained madrikhim (pilgrimage guides) affiliated with Third Temple organizations, and the number of religious Jews participating annually in the tours has increased steadily, from 5,658 in 2009 to approximately 20,000 in 2021 and as many as 44,000 in 2022.[43] At the time of my fieldwork (2014–2016), religious nationalist men, typically teens and young adults studying in yeshivot (religious seminaries), constituted the majority of daily Temple Mount pilgrims. With the mainstreaming of the Temple Mount movement and its increasing coverage in national media in recent years, there has been a greater diversity of pilgrims beyond the Orthodox religious Zionist demographic, including a growing number of Haredim

(Ultra-Orthodox Jews traditionally staunchly against pilgrimage to the Mount) who, in 2017, had been given permission by certain prominent rabbis to stand and pray in the entrance of one gate.[44] When I returned for follow-up interviews and observations in 2019 and again briefly in 2022, the numbers of religious Jews waiting in line daily to ascend the Temple Mount had very visibly swelled and diversified to include those across the modern Orthodox and Ultra-Orthodox spectrum and spanning an age range from toddlers to the elderly.

A growing contingent of secular nationalists now also participates in the guided tours as pilgrimage to the Temple Mount is not only a spiritual journey but also an important form of nationalist activism: one that is used to send a pointed message to the Israeli government and the international community. According to activists whom I spoke with, the Jewish presence on the Mount reminds the world that Jews have not forgotten their holiest site and will not relinquish their claims to it or to the rest of the Land of Israel. David, a member of Students for the Temple Mount, explained to me in 2016 that "I used to think the Kotel [Western Wall] was the holiest place on earth. But eventually I realized that is a lie. It was like waking up from a dream. Of course it's the Temple Mount [that is the holiest site]! But no one will realize this unless we start going there again."

Ari, David's friend and classmate at university, added, "It is really important for people to go to the Temple Mount as Jewish pilgrims following the purity laws even if they aren't religious because that has a nationalist meaning. This kind of visit is saying that the State of Israel needs to go back and raise the flag and be sovereign over the Mount. Many people in our group are not religious but they feel the Temple Mount is part of our entity as the Jewish people."

By promoting Temple Mount pilgrimage, Temple activists have succeeded in gaining national attention and access to state resources in recent years, building support for Israeli annexation of the Temple Mount. During 2016, while conducting interviews with some members of Women for the Temple, I joined the group to observe a women's *aliyah* (ascent) to the Temple Mount, led by Yehudit, a member of the group and experienced tour guide. The example of Women for the Temple illustrates how grassroots spiritual projects become entangled with nationalist projects of territorial expansion, specifically by hybridizing messianic ideologies with liberal discourses. Moreover, this organization shows how gendered, sexual, and racial dynamics further mediate religious activists' relationships with the state, enabling them to function as proxy-state actors who carry out territorial conquest.

PORTRAIT OF A TEMPLE MOUNT GUIDE: SEPTEMBER 2016

I arrived at entrance to the Temple Mount promptly at seven thirty in the morning according to Yehudit's instructions. The Mughrabi Gate, adjacent to the

Western Wall, is the access point through which non-Muslims (Israelis and international tourists) may enter the Haram ash-Sharif compound during specific visiting hours. I searched for Yehudit, a pilgrimage guide from Women for the Temple who was leading a group of religious Jewish women to the Temple Mount that day. A week prior I had explained to Yehudit on the phone that I was an anthropologist interested in observing a pilgrimage firsthand, and she invited me to attend and document the trip so long as I, being a Jewish woman, agreed to prepare for the visit according to the purity regulations of Jewish Law. I prepared for the *aliyah* (literally ascent, in this case pilgrimage)[45] to the Mount according to Yehudit's detailed instructions, immersing the night before in a *mikveh* (ritual bath) to purify my body before entering the Temple Mount where it is believed that the Shekhinah, the divine presence, still lingers even after the destruction of the Second Temple by the Romans. I wore plastic flip-flops per Yehudit's warning regarding the prohibition against leather shoes, which carry the impurity of death and could desecrate the sacred ground.

Yehudit grabbed me by my elbow and pulled me out of my place in a growing line of international tourists, cutting us straight to the front gate where Israeli police were stationed. "We are not *tourists*," she remarked, regarding me with a skeptical raised brow. The eight other women in her group soon arrived with babies and small children in tow. They varied slightly in observance levels, from Ultra-Orthodox nationalist (hardal) to more modern Orthodox nationalist (dati-leumi), identifiable by slight differences in the stringency of their modest dress and hair coverings. Yehudit gathered our identification cards and handed them over to the border police who screen religious Jews before they enter the Mount, checking to see if any of them are on a blacklist of Third Temple activists known for committing politically inflammatory acts like audible prayer, Israeli flag waving, or prostration. The police briefed the group, explaining that carrying any religious objects or engaging in audible prayer was strictly prohibited while on the Mount. According to Israel's "status quo" arrangements with the Jordanian Waqf, visibly religious Jews may enter the Mount only in small, staggered groups and must be accompanied by Israeli police and representatives of the Waqf at all times. This meant that the wait to ascend could take up to an hour, but Yehudit had come prepared. She used the time to distribute bottles of water and readied the women mentally and physically for the Temple Mount, explaining that they could pray secretly and avoid detection by the Waqf by pretending to talk on their cellphones. As we waited to walk up the ramp to the Temple Mount, Yehudit gave a motivational speech for first timers: "When we enter the Muslim women will begin screaming at us. They call them the Murabitat. They will shout 'Allah Hu Akbar.' That means God is great. Sometimes I yell back, 'Yes I agree with you!' . . . You have to transform their screams in your mind, and focus on your relationship with Hashem [God] when you are up there. Erase the screams and erase the mosques in your mind. Remember that you are returning home!"

Women for the Temple was first founded in 2000 by a group of religious-nationalist Jewish women primarily from Jerusalem and West Bank settlements, and since then the group has brought hundreds of women from across the country to the Temple Mount. Since 2010, women activists have played an increasingly important and public role in Third Temple activism, in the process challenging patriarchal power and rabbinic rulings on matters of Jewish Law through efforts such as their work to provide single women access to ritual baths prior to ascending. Jewish Law requires married women to immerse themselves in a ritual bath after monthly menstruation in order to become pure for sexual relations. Single women are often discouraged from or denied entry to a mikveh because rabbis consider that this enables premarital sex. In response, Women for the Temple carried out a successful campaign to convince mikveh workers not to ask women their marital status or reasons for taking the ritual bath.[46]

According to a mission statement published online in 2014, Women for the Temple is an "apolitical movement" striving to utilize the "feminine force" to "prepare hearts for the establishment of the Third Temple." At the time of my fieldwork, the group was regularly offering Jewish women lectures and courses focused on Third Temple theology; teaching them "temple crafts," such as sewing priestly garments; providing hands-on educational workshops for children and programs for schools; and training women to serve as pilgrimage guides. By recruiting and training female pilgrimage guides fluent in additional languages (English, French, Spanish, and Russian), Women for the Temple has been able to mobilize increasingly diverse Jewish women to ascend the Mount, including new immigrants. During the training courses that I observed in 2014, religious women were schooled in the geography and history of the Temple Mount, religious laws regarding women's purity, and methods for making the pilgrimage a meaningful spiritual journey for women.

Through their activism, members of Women for the Temple cultivate and perform a messianic femininity that emphasizes maternal domestic duties and redemptive women's power in Judaism. The women, most of whom are mothers, define themselves as guardians of domestic space and the House of God (the future Third Temple) and caregivers who protect and redeem the Jewish nation through their spiritual labor. This emphasis on maternal care of the House of God is depicted in the group's logo, which shows a woman lovingly cradling the Temple Mount in her arms like a child.

Yehudit's group was finally escorted up the ramp to the Temple Mount by Israeli police, one Mizrahi and one Ethiopian, dressed in riot gear. As is the case in many of Israel's hotspot military checkpoints in the West Bank, the Haram ash-Sharif is predominantly policed by Mizrahi Jews, Ethiopian Jews, Druze, and Christian Palestinian soldiers, who do the work of protecting a predominantly Ashkenazi religious elite.[47] As the women entered the compound, they were joined by two additional escorts from the Jordanian Waqf and were confronted immediately by Palestinian protestors, who regularly document and film the growing numbers of religious Jews entering on guided pilgrimage tours. The women in Yehudit's group took out their iPhones and filmed them back, capturing footage that would later be posted to Facebook as evidence of Jewish harassment on the Mount by "Islamic extremists" who, in the words of one woman on the tour, "refuse to share the holy site peacefully." According to Yehudit, this footage was also proof of a weak and capitulating Israeli state that had failed to properly secure the sacred compound and its own sovereignty.

Third Temple activists often repeated the refrain, "Whoever controls the Temple Mount, controls Jerusalem, and whoever controls Jerusalem controls the Land of Israel."[48] As my fieldwork overlapped with the 2016 Intifada of the Knives, activists would sometimes describe their pilgrimages as a "response to terror," as critical to ensuring Jewish "safety and sovereignty" in the Land of Israel. On June 30, 2016, Hallel Ariel (the daughter of Rina Ariel, a cofounder of Women for the Temple) was stabbed to death in her home in the settlement of Kiryat Arba by Mohammad Nasser Tra'ayra, a Palestinian teenager from a nearby village. For Rina, the murder of her daughter only reinforced the need for Israeli sovereignty over the Temple Mount and the rebuilding of the Third Temple. According to Rina, the state's "exiling" of Jews from the Mount was effectively "giving a prize to Islam" and motivating Palestinians to continue their attacks.[49]

Yehudit began her guided tour by walking around the perimeter of the compound (thereby making sure not to step on the actual location of the Second Temple). She used a laminated map of the Second Temple to help orient the women and explain where specific Temple rituals were once performed. According to Yehudit, an effective Temple Mount guide must be able to transform the discomfort and tension on the Mount into an inspirational journey, one that leaves participants feeling empowered to return again. To do this, the guide participates in a creative act of place making. Yehudit provided vivid descriptions and narrated the biblical drama of sacrificial offerings that took place in the Second Temple. She asked the group to imagine the smell of Temple incense wafting through the air and to hear the songs of the Levites, Temple musicians who once played harps and sang songs of devotion. She paused, gesturing to the location where the *mizbeah* (the altar where Temple priests sacrificed animals) once stood, and explained that a column of smoke would have reached from the altar all the way up to the heavens.

The imaginative exercise that Yehudit carried out during the tour was coupled with a search for traces of the Second Temple. She pointed to golden remnants on marble columns, neglected piles of rubble, and different stone textures where original walls of the Temple could still be seen. She directed the group's attention to a pair of large dumpsters containing wooden debris and explained that these were beams from the Second Temple that Islamic authorities were systematically trying to destroy, along with all sorts of antiquities from the Second

Temple period that had been discovered under the surface of the Mount. "They don't realize that this place is for all of humanity, not just Jews," she explained. "Someday, when the Temple is rebuilt, the world will wake up. Representatives from all the nations of the world, righteous Gentiles [the Children of Noah], will also come here to pray in the House of God."

A few weeks after my pilgrimage with Yehudit, I was invited by two of the women from the tour group to observe their weekly "outreach" efforts, attempts to spread the vision of a Third Temple future to non-Jews, to the "righteous Gentiles" whom Yehudit had mentioned. I met up with the women at the tomb of King David in the Old City, where they approached visiting Christian tourists, handed out pamphlets, and spoke to them about the Seven Noahide Laws and the role of "righteous Gentiles" in the rebuilding of the Third Temple. The women, followers of Rabbi Yitzhak Ginsburgh who lived in the West Bank settlements, had been encouraged by Ginsburgh himself to undertake this form of messianic outreach and proselytizing as a means of hastening the redemption.[50]

I had to admit that Yehudit was highly articulate and engaging as my guide for the day. She covered an impressive range of topics during the tour, including Jewish Law, biblical history, and archaeology. As a grandmother, she projected an air of maternal care, initiating the women on her tour into a sisterhood for the day, forging a common bond between women who, as she reminded them, had courageously ventured into a "new frontier" together. She did not speak openly about destroying the mosques on the compound. Rather, she interwove a messianic narrative about rebuilding the Temple and reestablishing a future theocracy with liberal demands for human rights and religious freedom from the Israeli state in the present, affirming for her participants that they were the true victims in the story. If Israel were truly a democratic state, she reminded them, then certainly Jews would be allowed to pray in their holiest site whenever they wanted. She explained to the women that they were righteous Jews and "civil rights activists," nonviolently using their bodies and prayers to demand access to their holiest site.

To this end, Yehudit orchestrated a small act of civil disobedience. She took out a small bag of fruits and nuts so that the women could bless the food before eating it as a snack (Orthodox Jews are required by custom to bless foods before consuming them). At the time of my fieldwork, religious Jewish activists were frequently expelled from the Mount for audible prayer, so for Yehudit the action had several aims: it afforded the group a moment of spiritual catharsis as they engaged in prayer at the holiest location in Judaism, and in the event that they would be expelled, it would become a tool for demonstrating the violation of Jewish rights on the Mount. "Today we are lucky," she stated. The escorts from the Waqf realized what Yehudit was doing but allowed the short and relatively unobtrusive blessings to proceed in a quiet corner of the compound.

Yehudit encouraged the group to take a final photo in front of the steps lead-ing to the Dome of the Rock (Qubbat As-Sukhrah), which is, according to the Jewish tradition, the location of the foundation stone (*even hashtiyah*), from which it is said the entire world sprang forth. She positioned the women so that the golden dome became a glowing centerpiece in the background. Despite her earlier instructions to erase a Muslim Haram ash-Sharif and see the Third Temple in its place, Yehudit insisted on staging a final photograph in front of the iconic Islamic shrine and encouraged the women to share the picture on social media so that others would feel inspired to ascend. This iconic photograph, often used as the Facebook profile picture for Third Temple activists, became for the pilgrims a souvenir of their participation in reclaiming the Mount.

While the women posed for pictures, a young Jewish man with a white knit-ted kippah and long blond side curls who was attending a pilgrimage tour organized by his *yeshiva* (seminary), suddenly threw himself on the ground in an act of prostration before God. Another young man from the same tour group began to loudly recite the "Shema" prayer, the Jewish declaration of faith, fla-grantly violating Israel's agreement with the Waqf that forbids Jewish prayer on the site. The Israeli police reacted quickly and escorted the men's group off of the compound. Concerned that the boys' actions would inflame tensions with Pales-tinian worshippers, the police informed Yehudit that her group's visit would also end prematurely. As they were ushered off the Mount into East Jerusalem, one woman attempted to speak with one of the guards from the Waqf. "We just want to be able to pray in our holiest site. If we could work together it doesn't have to be like this," she tried to explain in English.

He responded, "Many times in our history we protected Jews. But we cannot work together when you occupy us and kill our children."

She shook her head in disbelief: "But the Third Temple will be a house of prayer for *all* nations."

Finally off the Mount, the women in Yehudit's group huddled together in the Muslim quarter of the Old City in Jerusalem and sang a tearful round of "Yibaneh Hamikdash" ("Let the Temple Be Restored") as Palestinian protestors, mostly women members of the Murabitat (guardians of Al-Aqsa) who had been banned from the Temple Mount, stood at the exit gate and continued to protest. With the growth of the Third Temple movement, Palestinian women members of the Murabitat have played an important role in the defense of Al-Aqsa, using their bodies, voices, and prayers to protest the entry of Jews. By keeping the presence of Muslims in Haram ash-Sharif high throughout the day, protesting and shout-ing "Allah Hu Akbar" when groups of Jewish pilgrims enter or exit, studying and reading the Quran outside in the different terraces of Haram ash-Sharif, and per-forming *al-i'tikaf* (meditative prayers), they attempt to send a message that Al-Aqsa is a Muslim holy site and will not be annexed or Judaized.[51] In the Israeli media, the Murabitat have been frequently portrayed as intolerant, potentially violent women who refuse to "share" the space with Jews who come to pray there. In contrast, Women for the Temple, escorted by armed Israeli guards, appear as the calm, pious, and respectful victims of the Murabitat, who refuse to allow them the space and silence to pray. With police turned defensively toward the Murabitat during these confrontations, the religious claims on the space of Women for the Temple are tacitly reinforced. From the Israeli media gaze, "Allah Hu Akbar" is registered as a political statement, while the songs and chants of Women for the Temple are depoliticized and registered as pious acts. Israeli media perceptions of the Murabitat have promoted the idea that they are political instruments of male Islamic leaders and that their actions are "aimed at fueling and shaming men into participation" and "mobilizing public support for further violence."[52]

Like Women for the Temple, the Murabitat are pious women, transcending traditional domestic roles in their effort to defend a House of God. One leader, Aisha, a Palestinian woman from East Jerusalem, was working as a Quran teacher in Al-Aqsa when she became a spokesperson for the Murabitat. This role evolved naturally, she explained to me, as more and more religious Jews began entering Al-Aqsa during the times when she was teaching. I spoke with Aisha in 2016 after finishing my fieldwork with Women for the Temple. I was introduced to Aisha through contacts at the Al-Aqsa Foundation, a Palestinian NGO based in East Jerusalem and dedicated to monitoring Third Temple activism and raising global awareness of the situation on the Haram ash-Sharif. Prior to meeting with Aisha, I had visited the NGO and conducted an interview with one of their senior researchers. Representatives from the Al-Aqsa Foundation agreed to meet with me only after I submitted letters of recommendation from academic Palestinian colleagues who reassured the organization that I was not working on behalf of the State of Israel and that I was an independent researcher examining the growth of the Temple movement.

Aisha emphasized the unique role that Palestinian women had come to play in the struggle to defend Al-Aqsa: "Men are more often arrested and held in jail for periods of time. And when this happens the whole family suffers because the man is bringing the main source of income. So we as women decided that we must take responsibility and do something." Aisha acknowledged the particular strategic value of religious women's activism and insisted that the motivation for her activism stemmed from theological principles: "They are using weapons, money, and power, but our only weapon is our faith. We scream 'Allah Hu Akbar' and hold up the Quran. It is a religious duty to fight the occupation and defend Islam. This is about *rubat* [defending Islam] not *sumud* [usually translated as steadfastness]." Aisha's distinction between rubat and sumud is an important one. Sumud is often used by Palestinians to describe a political strategy of resisting occupation by remaining firmly attached to their land despite the consequences they face. Sumud has a political, nationalist connotation, while rubat references a religious struggle, a defense of land and holy places, that is tied to a defense of Islam. According to Aisha, the Murabitat were not a group of organized activists; instead, they were individual women who felt a "spiritual call" to come to Al-Aqsa every day and defend it against the "Temple builders." "We follow them closely on social media and know what they are planning, how they want to destroy Al-Aqsa and build a Temple. We also know this goes against their own religion," Aisha added, referring here to the traditional rabbinic ban on Jewish pilgrimage to the Temple Mount and prohibitions against artificially hastening the messianic era through human action.

A television crew filmed the tense scene at the exit gate as Yehudit's group sang in Hebrew and members of the Murabitat protested next to them. One journalist pulled Yehudit aside for a quick interview. She calmly emphasized the "shame and humiliation" that Jews face as they are denied the freedom to worship in their holiest site. "As you can see," she said, gesturing to the women in her group, "women are leaders in struggle today." The "struggle" that she was referring to is more than a demand for Jewish access and worship on the Temple Mount, although such accomplishments would be celebrated by Temple activists as an intermediary goal. For Yehudit, it was also a struggle for the completion of the Zionist project itself and the start of a messianic era that she believed would reverberate outward from Israel and transform humanity.

During the course of my fieldwork, Women for the Temple activists articulated their desire to rebuild the Temple as a logical move from theory to action for the Jewish people, part of reviving and deepening their spiritual practice. Miriam explained this concept when I interviewed her in 2015: "Why should we continue to abstract the Temple and the animal sacrifices into prayers? We pray three times a day for the rebuilding of the Temple. Now that we have returned to Israel we can act. What is stopping us? It is the mental slavery, the mentality of *galut* (exile)." Miriam was one of Women for the Temple's pilgrimage guides and public educators. She believed that there were signs from God everywhere that the time had come for the Jewish people to build the Temple: "Now there is country of six million Jews, museums, and hospitals. All the signs are here. The redemption is going forward, and whoever doesn't see that is crazy. There is an ingathering from all over the world. Jews are returning to Orthodox observance and the land is being settled. The Temple is part of this process. There is an awakening going on. . . . And even the Gentiles realize this and are coming to the Torah," she explained, referring to the emerging Children of Noah movement abroad.

Similarly, Sarah believed that the moment had come to transform messianic dreams and theories into action. As she shared in one interview, "It is convenient to sit in your synagogue and dream about the Third Temple falling from the sky, like we waited, dreaming for the Messiah. But we know what happened in the end, they [European Jews] waiting so long so God had to push them. This is why we had the Holocaust. So it is our job as women to put the subject of the Temple into the air."

According to other women activists such as Shoshanna, the best way to raise consciousness of the Third Temple, to move from theory to action, is through embodied activities and experiential education with a focus on women and youth: "We have to just start doing and talking about the Beit Hamikdash. . . . We start with younger children because they are more open-minded. Begin in school or summer camp. More people just need to be connected. People say prayers on Tisha b'Av like a mantra but who really believes what they say? People need to *do something*. Stop crying and get up and do." Toward this end, Shoshanna uses her talents and experience as a baker to reconstruct recipes for the bread offerings once used in Temple rituals and teaches women how to prepare these offerings. "The best part of history is the rebuilding of the Third Temple and the coming of messiah," Shoshanna reflected. "I asked myself, what can I do about it as a woman? I don't expect men to start making dough."

In our conversations, Women for the Temple often drew comparisons between their spiritual labor and the trials and tribulations of biblical matriarchs, viewing the matriarchs as archetypes for the modes of messianic femininity they longed to embody. Miriam the prophetess, for example, figured strongly in their accounts as a model of female spiritual power, inspiration, and redemptive potential. Adinah compared members of Women for the Temple to the biblical Miriam, who led Jewish women in song and dance with her tambourine after crossing the Red Sea. In her exegesis of the Exodus story, Adinah shifted the focus away from Moses as savior and emphasized the role of women in leading the Jewish people out of slavery and toward national redemption in the Holy Land. Women for the Temple saw themselves as "modern day Miriams," leading the Jewish people out of the final stages of galut (exile in diaspora) toward the fulfillment of Jewish sovereignty in the Land of Israel and reconnection with God on the Temple Mount. As guardians of the family and the Jewish home, they viewed themselves as uniquely positioned to guard the national home and the House of God.

Women for the Temple activists emphasized their roles as spiritual leaders alongside male rabbis within the Temple movement, and as college-educated religious-Zionist women they had clearly been influenced by feminist currents that permeated the strictly Orthodox world in profound ways at the end of the twentieth century. In Israel and religious settlements, women's seminaries for advanced Torah study flourished, greatly expanding the number of women religious teachers and spiritual leaders in the Orthodox world.[53] Idit Bartov, for example, is a leader from Women for the Temple and one of the first Orthodox women to receive a special ordination from Midreshet Lindenbaum in Jerusalem, allowing her to assist both men and women with Jewish legal questions.[54] In 2016, Idit used her expert knowledge of Jewish Law to assist Women for the

Temple in their campaign to secure mikveh access for single women wishing to ascend to the Temple Mount in a state of ritual purity. In one interview, Idit explained how women's pilgrimage to the Mount is part of a larger effort by Orthodox women to study Jewish Law, update it, and make it more relevant to women's experiences in the twenty-first century. Rather than chasing after male rabbinic authorities for halachic decisions, she encourages women to study and take matters into their own hands: "There is a war on the opening of the Temple Mount to women that begins and ends with the mikveh. . . . We are dealing with laws that have been frozen for two thousand years. . . . In the beginning, there were voices that wanted to go door to door and collect Rabbis who will give their approval and blessings. I am not in this game. I see how they belittle us."[55] Taking control of purity practices based on advanced religious training challenges a rabbinic hierarchy that traditionally excluded women from the interpretation of Jewish Law.

Idit's assertion that women should play an active role in updating Jewish Law, on the one hand, and the deep traditionalism of the Temple movement, on the other, expose a paradox at the heart of Women for the Temple's activism: it is at once a venue for women's spiritual/nationalist leadership and a kind of Orthodox feminism while remaining in service to patriarchal rabbinic authority. Boundary pushers like Idit, who evoke religious and liberal values, were welcome as they help to enhance the public profile of the movement, but, as my informants reminded me, there were limits to women's empowerment, which remained circumscribed by normative gender expectations.

Despite Women for the Temple being a women-initiated and -led movement that often challenges male authorities and patriarchal restrictions on female behavior, only two of the fifteen activists from the organization with whom I spoke were willing to identify as "feminists" (the same word in English and Hebrew), and these two women did so with some reluctance, given the negative connotations within religious circles. Anat explained, "You ask me if I am a feminist. I don't really like the title, but yes. We are in the middle of a big change for women and it is part of God's plan. The feminine light is becoming more revealed in the world and it is a sign of the messianic era. Yes, feminism is coming for the Temple! But it is not about waving a flag and saying that I am feminist. The entire process of feminism is developing in order to bring the Temple." According to Anat, her activism for the Third Temple was not the result of secular feminist values seeping into the religious world but rather a sign of the divine messianic process unfolding in Israel, leading to a prophesized revealing of the hidden "feminine light" in the world at the end of times.[56]

Most women whom I spoke with firmly rejected the term "feminist" and framed their leadership as a form of women's "empowerment" that capitalizes on the traditional domestic roles and inherent spiritual skills of Jewish women to further the Third Temple movement. For example, according to Naomi, "The work we do is very empowering for women. As women we bring certain skills that men do not have. For example, we know how important the family home is so we understand how important the House of God is. But most women in our movement do not consider themselves feminists. Most will agree that the house and the family always come first. And then second is working outside [the home] for the sake of Israel. The house of Israel cannot be built unless the personal house is complete." Women for the Temple saw themselves as uniquely positioned to bring about a change in public consciousness regarding the importance of Temple building precisely because of their "natural" domestic roles and talents. "As women, we understand this [the importance of building the Third Temple] because the relationship of Israel to God mirrors the relationship of husband and wife," Adinah explained. "Like the husband and wife, Israel and God need a house, vessels, and clothes. It's not just a spiritual or mystical union. We need to do something physical so that love can enter into a real container. Women for the Temple are helping to prepare the container, to get the house ready by sewing clothes for the kohanim." Adinah mobilizes an image of heterosexual partnership, comparing the relationship between husband and wife with that of Israel and God in a messianic process. As Women for the Temple members ascend the Temple Mount, they enact Jewish religious language that articulates the Temple as the site for pairing with God.

Similarly, Tamar, a university student at the time of my research, stated, "I go to the Temple Mount in purity . . . like a bride on her wedding night. It is the place I go to join in a union with the divine presence. When the Temple is rebuilt, the entire nation of Israel will have this new marriage with God." Young Jewish women today are also literally ascending the Temple Mount as brides. As part of their campaign to bring more Jews to the Mount, Women for the Temple offer special guided pilgrimages for brides on their wedding day.

THIRD TEMPLE ACTIVISM IN A ZIONIST EXPANSIONIST CONTEXT

The example of Women for the Temple illustrates how grassroots spiritual projects become entangled with nationalist projects of territorial expansion and, moreover, how gendered and sexual dynamics mediate this relationship. Women's gendered bodies play important roles as territorial markers within nationalist movements.[57] Women often serve as metonym of the nation, sacred bodies that must be protected from defilement by enemy "Others" and motherly guardians of family, caretakers of land, and reproducers of national identity and religious traditions.[58] As Women for the Temple members ascend the Mount, they embody the traditional feminine and sexualized language used to refer to the House of God in the Jewish tradition, where the Temple is the bodily receptacle of the divine presence that comes to dwell within it.

Activists reinforced the idea of the Temple Mount as a feminine body that is victimized and humiliated by police who prevent Jews from ascending and Muslims who "occupy" and "defile" the site. Messianic femininity as spiritual theory and embodied practice promises to undo this humiliation, enabling women to care for the Temple Mount—the House of God—just as they care for the private family home. As women ascend the Mount in a state of bodily and spiritual purity, they believe that they are helping redeem the nation by reestablishing a direct link between the Jewish people and God. Women for the Temple have played a role in mainstreaming the Third Temple movement precisely because they cultivate their project as informed by values of piety, motherly caregiving, and feminine empowerment rather than those of violent national conquest. The gender of my informants, their predominantly Ashkenazi and middle-class status, and their integration into a patriarchal rabbinic order have better enabled the Third Temple movement to access resources and operate symbiotically with the state security apparatus that continues to Judaize East Jerusalem. Although they belong to a so-called fundamentalist messianic movement, Women for the Temple activists craft an identity of pious womanhood in the service of state power. In turn, they rely on and expect the Israeli police to protect them and Israeli institutions to amplify their cause.

Feminist scholars have challenged the practice of naturalizing connections of militarism with masculinity and pacifism with femininity because representations of the "moral mother" are often enlisted to support violence or reinforce the subjugation of women.[59] The conservative maternal activist is by definition both empowered and constrained by a patriarchal logic that assumes and expects women to be naturally domestic and caretaking. Accordingly, Women for the Temple informants often reiterated their nonviolent intentions in rebuilding the Third Temple, arguing that their primary aim was to further a *spiritual* connection to the site, yet they were also explicit in their hopes to push the State of Israel to eventually divide and annex the compound away from Palestinian control. Women who worked as pilgrimage guides, in particular, saw themselves as leading a "spiritual revolution" that only women were uniquely positioned to accomplish. It is women, they believe, who will normalize the movement for Jewish control of Haram ash-Sharif / Temple Mount. As Naomi explained during a course for prospective pilgrimage guides, "Why are women leaders in the Temple movement? Because women are naturally more spiritual than men, much closer to divinity and the will of God. Men need the structure to pray three times a day to remember God. Women are naturally more connected to the Temple. Men may be out in front and get into physical confrontations on the Mount, but women are leading the spiritual revolution there. And when women come there to pray, society begins to see it as something normal."

The increased presence of Jewish women on the Mount as pilgrims has contributed to its wider acceptance in the religious nationalist mainstream. In contrast with the way they represent male activists, Israeli newspaper articles and television reports are more likely to portray Women for the Temple activists as pious subjects than as political provocateurs. Israeli media frame the women as victims: innocent religious pilgrims who are discriminated against when the state restricts their ability to pray.[60] In the religious and right-wing media especially, the activists are portrayed as harassed by dangerous Muslims who riot and scream "Allahu Akbar" (God is the greatest) at them when they appear on the Temple Mount / Haram ash-Sharif.[61] These representations depict the activists as pious mothers of the nation rather than instruments of land annexation. As Tamara Neuman has argued in regard to Jewish women activists who establish settlement outposts in the Palestinian territories, such representations facilitate Israeli annexation of the West Bank by relying on stereotypes that cover violence with a façade of maternal care.[62] Scholars have argued that right-wing Zionist activism has been feminized as Jewish women strategically use maternalist discourse to achieve goals such as land annexation.[63] Maternal discourses play on the notion of women belonging to the private realm, facilitating their appearance as apolitical protectors of children and family; thus, they are less likely to be subject to police intervention.[64] Israeli soldiers are less likely to evict a woman settler activist in the West Bank because she is seen as representing feminine ideals of peace and rootedness in the home.[65] Likewise, still images and videos of women with children on the Temple Mount who are prevented from carrying food or breastfeeding during the pilgrimage frame them as victims, which appeals to Jewish publics beyond the religious right wing. The rise of social media and widespread use of smartphones have played a role in spreading such videos and pictures of the victimization. Accompanying verbal or written accounts by Temple Mount activists depict the site as under the control of "foreign occupiers" protected by Israeli police, who enforce an "apartheid" system that robs pious Jews of their religious and civil rights.

By bringing larger numbers of Jews to the Temple Mount every year through the format of pilgrimage, Temple activists hope to cultivate a situation where the state will no longer be able to ignore their demands and ultimately will be forced to divide the space or provide separate visiting hours for Jews and Muslims just as the Ibrahimi Mosque / Abraham's tomb in Hebron was divided into separate Jewish and Muslim prayer spaces (following the massacre of Palestinian worshippers by Israeli American Baruch Goldstein in 1994).

It must be noted that the confluence between touristic pilgrimage and land annexation has a long history in Israel and has played a critical role in the transmission of Zionist ideology. Even before the creation of the State of Israel, during the British Mandate period, Jews in Palestine were working to build a biblical tourism industry in order to promote nationalist goals, inspired by the ethos of *yedi'at ha'aretz* (knowledge of the land).[66] Since the 1920s, practices of yedi'at ha'aretz have been implemented and funded by nonprofit organizations, private donors, and the Israeli school system.[67] These practices included guided walks (*tiyulim*), meant to connect new Jewish immigrants to the territory of Israel and cultivate a cohesive national identity. The walks, which emphasized both natural as well as biblical sites, were led by professional madrikhim (tour guides),[68] who mediated the transmission of historical knowledge and interaction with the landscape.[69] In 1922, the first professional tour guiding course was opened by the Zionist Trade and Industry Department, institutionalizing the tour guide as a spokesperson for the Zionist movement.[70] According to Kobi Cohen-Hattab, the professional tour guide became another "soldier in the national struggle," working to transmit and legitimize Zionist ideology in order to carry out plans for large-scale Jewish settlement.[71] After 1948, the new Israeli state made a concerted effort to develop and market a sacred landscape.[72] Professional Israeli tour guides helped to reinforce this sacred geography for Jewish immigrants and Christian visitors, validating the prophecy of Jewish return from exile to the ancient homeland.[73] It is this narrative of the sacred, strengthened through tourist experiences in the land and the ethos of yedi'at ha'aretz, that has also been used strategically to cover up the destruction and displacement of Palestinian communities during and after the Nakba.

Since 1967, the entanglement of pilgrimage, tourism, and land annexation has dramatically altered the urban landscape of East Jerusalem. The lands surrounding the Temple Mount have been converted into symbolic national monuments, woven together by strategic landscaping projects that help ensure Israeli sovereignty over the areas surrounding the Old City.[74] Within this symbolic national landscape, Hava Schwartz argues, the Temple has been constructed as the "supreme absentee," where the promise of its future existence has seeped into the national consciousness even as state authorities continue to deny any plans to harm Al-Aqsa or annex the Mount.[75] Today, the strategic relationship of religious tourism and land annexation continues to play out in the Palestinian neighborhood of Silwan, located adjacent to the Temple Mount, where the Israeli settlement organization Elad has created an archaeological theme park dedicated to uncovering artifacts from the ancient city of King David, believed to have stood on the site. In the name of uncovering a sacred Jewish past, the Elad organization uses legal schemes to evict Palestinians from their homes surrounding the site.[76] With the help of the Israeli Nature and National Parks Protection Authority, the Elad organization has been given a contract to manage the City of David National Park, a hugely popular touristic destination for Israeli families and visitors from abroad.

The increasingly popular practice of Jewish pilgrimage to the Temple Mount must be viewed within this larger context of land annexation occurring in East Jerusalem under the guise of biblical tourism. Similar to the way an earlier generation of Zionist tour guides implemented practices of yedi'at ha'aretz in order to lay claim to the Land of Israel, today we see Temple Mount guides carrying on this legacy, fashioning Jewish pilgrims/tourists into willing participants in nationalist conquest.

THIRD TEMPLE ACTIVISTS AS PROXY-STATE ACTORS

The Third Temple movement has successfully migrated into Israel's religious and political mainstream, I argue, specifically because activists function as proxy-state actors conjoining messianic ideologies with concrete modes of territorial expansion. In thinking about proxy-state relationships, I draw on a body of anthropological scholarship that has disaggregated the imagined centrality and coherence of the nation-state, illustrating that what we call "the state" is actually composed of local, national, and transnational networks and institutions.[77] James Ferguson and Akhil Gupta, for example, point to a new modes of "transnational governmentality," challenging the classic spatial metaphors of state power as "vertical" bureaucratic control over populations or the state as "encompassing" the local.[78] Furthermore, by questioning the idea of the state as a unified sovereign power, ruling over a bounded national territory, anthropologists have turned their attention to the ways different actors *perform as the state*, with grassroots political organizations or private corporations increasingly taking up state functions.[79] According to Christopher Krupa, these trends have to led to the production of different forms of "fragmented, competitive statecraft," including manifestations of the "state-by-proxy" that often occur in state margins or frontier spaces.[80]

The Third Temple movement is not explicitly backed by the Israeli state through any official policy but receives state resources in the forms of funding, police protection, and endorsement from Parliament members. This kind of tacit support follows in the wake of the settlement movement in the West Bank, which likewise functions as a kind of "state-by-proxy" operating in the frontier spaces of Israel/Palestine (sites yet to be formally annexed under full Israeli sovereignty). Settlement councils take up state functions, providing security, education, and infrastructure, and continue to carry out Zionist goals, annexing land and natural resources as part of maintaining Jewish territorial domination. Settlements represent a dynamic form of state sovereignty where grassroots actors may exist simultaneously as adversaries *and* strategic accomplices to the "official state." Temple Mount activists, for example, function as strategic accomplices to the Israeli state even though, at times, they appear to be policed and antagonized by the state security apparatus, which requires that their tours be conducted under police supervision and evicts Jews from the Temple Mount if they attempt to pray there in too flagrant of a manner.

This relationship of state support combined with public displays of policing reflects, in Shira Robinson's words, the "contradictions of liberal settler sovereignty,"[81] wherein keeping up the liberal appearance of the Israeli state requires that it distance itself from "extremist" Third Temple activists. Yet the state continues to back the Third Temple movement financially and facilitates the organized entrance of Jewish pilgrims onto the Temple Mount. As they lead Jewish pilgrims to the Mount, guides like Yehudit help to produce the evidence of "native" Jewish belonging to the land by reviving biblical modes of worship and completing Zionism's reterritorialization of Judaism through reclamation of the Temple Mount.

Before leading groups, Temple Mount guides undergo training courses, offered by Third Temple activist organizations, where they learn to provide historical, spiritual, and political content as Jewish pilgrims complete their circuit around the perimeter of the compound. On the Mount, they mediate between their tour participants and the police, teaching Jewish pilgrims how to pray discreetly. They offer emotional support and legal advice to participants who wish to engage in acts of "civil disobedience" such as attempting to pray or revealing an Israeli flag during the tour, actions that will result in their immediate expulsion and possible banning from the Mount. Most vitally, the guides provide a metanarrative framing for their group: pilgrims should see themselves entering the Mount as pious protestors reclaiming their holiest site and leave the Mount as victims of religious discrimination. As victims of religious discrimination, pilgrims then can argue for increased access to the Mount under the pretext of strengthening the liberal democratic state.

The madrikhim, often licensed graduates of Israel's national tour guiding schools, carry with them a legitimizing force, an aura of state power operating on the Temple Mount that is evident to pilgrimage participants as well. Talia, a university student and member of Students for the Temple Mount, explained to me in 2016 that pilgrimage guides are not doing anything radical; they are simply taking up the business that the Israeli state left unfinished when it handed back jurisdiction over the Temple Mount to Jordan in 1967: "They are finishing the job. [The guides] realize that we cannot wait for the state to act. They are taking matters into their own hands and showing everyone that the Temple Mount belongs to Israel."

On the Temple Mount, the madrikhim and their Jewish pilgrims subjectively enact Israeli sovereignty through the relational nature of their encounters with Muslim worshippers when they enter escorted by armed Israeli guards, whose bodies are turned defensively toward the Muslim population. The ability of the madrikhim, along with their pilgrimage participants, to perform state sovereignty on the Temple Mount is acutely felt and internalized by Palestinians. A survey conducted in 2015 by the Palestinian Center for Policy and Research revealed that 50 percent of Palestinians "believed that Israel was intent on destroying the Al-Aqsa Mosque and Dome of the Rock to make way for a third Jewish temple."[82] Palestinian members of the Mourabitoun whom I spoke with did not see religious Jews *as pilgrims*, referring to them instead as "settlers" and their visits as an uninvited "entry" or more commonly a "break in" (using the Arabic *iqtahamu*).

Moreover, Jewish pilgrims become accomplices to the state when their performances of Israeli sovereignty provoke violence and, subsequently, the state security apparatus responds by extending Israeli control over Haram ash-Sharif. In other words, when Palestinians carry out attacks in the name of defending Al-Aqsa from Temple builders, the Israeli state can then justify increased military control over the site in the name of security. On July 14, 2017, two Israeli police (both Druze) were patrolling Haram ash-Sharif when they were shot and killed by three Palestinian men in the name of defending Al-Aqsa from Temple activists. In response, Israel took control of the site, blocked access for three days, and installed new metal detectors in front of Muslim entrances. Referring to the shootings, Knesset member Ari Dicter (chairman of the Foreign Affairs and Defense Committee at the time of my research) stated that "Israel is the sovereign on the Temple Mount, period. The fact that the Waqf became a sovereign on the Temple Mount ended last Friday [the day of the shootings]."[83]

In addition to performing state sovereignty on the Temple Mount, Third Temple activists function as proxy-state actors in the way that they filter down a liberal discursive framework to participants, teaching Jewish pilgrims to describe their experiences on the Temple Mount in terms of "human rights" and "religious freedom" violations within a democratic state. Through the format of a piety ritual, Temple Mount guides help provide the appropriate moral justifications for land annexation (i.e., Jewish access as a "human right") by adopting the language of the liberal state.

This kind of discursive posturing was first popularized by Rabbi Yehudah Glick, a Temple Mount activist, rabbi, and former member of the Israeli Knesset who helped to build representation for the Temple movement within the Israeli political establishment as well as garner support from international Christians and Noahides. Glick's move from grassroots Third Temple activist to minister in the Knesset occurred alongside the broader trend of Temple activism moving from the margins toward the religious and political mainstream, gaining support from respected rabbis and politicians and secular nationalists from 2017 to 2020. Glick, who immigrated to Israel from the United States with his family as a child, is the previous director of the Temple Institute. He left his position in 2009 in order to obtain a tour-guiding diploma and to focus on building a public outreach campaign for Jewish prayer on the Temple Mount. Glick first gained national notoriety during his hunger strike in October 2013, which he commenced after he was banned from the Temple Mount by police who feared that his presence would incite violence with Muslim worshippers. In the same year, he founded the Organization for Jewish Freedom on the Temple Mount. According to Glick, in his many public appearances, the fact that Jews cannot pray on the Temple Mount is an issue of the "civil rights" and "freedom of worship" that all citizens are entitled to in a democratic Jewish state. Glick builds his argument on top of the popular perception of Zionism as a fundamentally "humanitarian enterprise" that "produces human rights" amid a sea of backward and oppressive Arab nations.[84] In 2014, Yehudah Glick became a household name in Israel when he amazingly survived an assassination attempt by Mutaz Hijaz, a Palestinian man from East Jerusalem, and in 2016 he entered the Israeli Parliament as a member of the majority Likud party.

Glick's unique blend of liberalism and messianic Zionism reflects contradictions inherent in the larger religious Zionist demographic in Israel, which views itself as part of the liberal Western world and also feels beholden to ethnocentric principles embedded in Jewish Law.[85] Moreover, the Temple movement's use of human rights discourse can be situated within a larger phenomenon exhibited by right-wing prosettlement organizations in Israel, which have learned how to mobilize human rights discourses to their advantage in recent years.[86] Human rights discourses are powerful tools in political projects of domination and conquest precisely because human rights appear as neutral, transcendent, and apolitical values.[87] Yet their mobilization at the local level is always political because, as Nicola Perugini and Neve Gordon argue, human rights effectively "demarcate the borders of human," establishing a hierarchy of civilians who fall under their purview.[88] Participating in Temple Mount pilgrimage allows activists like Glick to strategically utilize the human rights language of the secular left wing. During my fieldwork, some activists described even themselves as victims of "apartheid" on the Temple Mount.[89] They explained that the Temple Mount was currently being "occupied" by Palestinian Muslims with the help of the Israeli government, which restricts non-Muslim access to a few hours a day and limits the ability of religious Jews to pray and perform rituals on the site. Temple Mount pilgrimage, as a carefully crafted piety practice, illustrates the political mobilization of human rights through the format of a public ritual meant to invert the relationship of settler and native.

By promoting Temple Mount pilgrimage and hybridizing their messianic vision with democratic language, Third Temple activists have been better able to access the national conversation and national resources in recent years. Temple Mount pilgrimage guides who coordinate with state institutions and appear in the image of state power on the Temple Mount prompt us to question religious fundamentalism narratives and the distinction between the secular and the religious. What we refer to as "secular" and "religious" spheres are not opposites but co-constitute one another in intricate ways as secularism dictates the proper boundaries, content, and meaning of religious activity.[90] We can observe the policing function of the secular in the way that the Third Temple movement has learned to adopt liberal discourses and formed symbiotic relationships with the police, politicians, and state institutions in order to advance its goals. The Third Temple movement, born in the wake of the violent actions of the Jewish Underground in the 1980s, has gained traction and acceptance in Israel by transforming activism on the Temple Mount into a popular "civil rights struggle." Secularism operates not as a realm void of religion but rather as a means for *assimilating religion*, making it an aid to state power and expansionist territorial aims.

Yehudah Glick cannot step out on the Knesset floor and speak about animal sacrifices or reestablishing a theocratic kingdom, but he can make demands for Jewish prayer on the Temple Mount using human rights discourses. At the same time, his nonviolent and humanistic discourse that casts access to the Temple Mount as an issue of religious freedom has helped garner international support for building the Third Temple movement (largely from Evangelical Christians and Noahides) specifically because he *universalizes* Jewish ethnonationalism. Glick commonly portrays open access and prayer on the Temple Mount, along with eventual Temple rebuilding, as an endeavor for the benefit of all three Abrahamic faiths: an interfaith project that will finally bring peace to the region.

In a 2020 interview, Glick reflected on the success of Temple Mount pilgrimage in securing Jewish access to the holy site, explaining that a sea change took place after 2015 as religious Jews began ascending in greater numbers, learning how to work collaboratively and effectively with police to suppress the activism of the Mourabitoun (Palestinian men and women dedicated to guarding Al-Aqsa from Israeli annexation).[91] Glick goes on to compare the aspirations of the Temple movement with those of Theodor Herzl, the founding father of Zionism, who was once considered radical and is now an icon of mainstream Zionist ideology: "When Herzl talked about Zionism, he was far from consensus. They thought he was putting the Jewish people at risk. When we started to visit the Mount, we were seen as a radical, belligerent curiosity. I saw it as a place of human rights and respect for every person." From his perspective, the Temple movement will eventually become a central and accepted component of the Zionist metanarrative of return and revival, authenticating national identity and extending Israeli sovereignty across its final frontier. Yet even as the Third Temple movement works to extend Israeli state sovereignty over the Temple Mount, much of its rabbinic leadership arguably works to *undo* the state, advancing a vision of Jewish theocracy that will one day replace Israel's parliamentary democracy. It is this vision of biblical revival that has proliferated globally in recent years, aided by the advent of social media, capturing the imagination of Christian Zionists in particular. In addition to building pro-Israel ideological and financial allyship abroad, as the following chapters will demonstrate, the mobile Third Temple imaginary is refashioning the very boundary lines between Judaism and Christianity and catalyzing the emergence of new religious subjectivities.

3 · "BORN AGAIN, AGAIN"

The Emergence of Noahidism as a Transnational Judaic Faith

As the Temple movement was reenergized at the beginning of the twenty-first century in Israel, coalescing into a coordinated grassroots struggle of activist groups and NGOs, a parallel movement was emerging abroad. Noahide communities, made up of individuals exiting Christianity, began forming online spiritual networks and physical congregations under the guidance of Orthodox rabbis affiliated with the Temple movement in Israel. This chapter examines the theological origins of the Bnei Noah (Children of Noah) concept in ancient and medieval rabbinic source texts and its more recent transformation into a living faith identity. It chronicles the journeys of the first American Noahide converts who were "born again, again"[1] after leaving conservative Protestant churches in the 1990s and the subsequent expansion of the Noahide movement in the twenty-first century, most notably in the Global South. The transformation of Noahidism from a legal/philosophical construct to a contemporary religious movement was enabled, I argue, by two primary factors: the political ascent of religious Zionism in Israel and the connective power of the internet.

This chapter reveals a spiritual and political convergence that occurred in the 1990s between rabbis from Israel's religious right wing with transnational communities of Christians dually invested in a messianic Third Temple future. Furthermore, it demonstrates how the internet has afforded unprecedented pathways for religious missionizing, facilitating the extension of Orthodox rabbinic authority to new locales where questioning Christians have been gravitating toward the Hebrew origins of their faith for decades. In turn, a new class of digitally savvy Noahide preachers (typically ex-Christian ministers) has emerged as important non-Jewish "subcontractors" of rabbinic authority, bridging the gap between virtual rabbinic mentors based in Israel and Noahide congregations abroad. In effect, in addition to documenting the birth of a new transnational Judaic faith, this chapter tells a story about the authoritative potentials of religion in the digital age, about the simultaneous modes of spiritual exploration and forms of neocolonial control the internet affords.

By examining the recent transformation of the Children of Noah (Bnei Noah) from an abstract concept in Jewish texts to an embodied practice and living religious identity, this chapter reveals the far-reaching influence of messianic Zionism and the Third Temple imaginary, a political theology in motion that is catalyzing the formation of new spiritual subjectivities, while remaining tethered to a program of territorial conquest playing out on the ground in Israel/Palestine.

FINDING THE THIRD TEMPLE IN TEXAS

The twenty-fifth anniversary celebration of the Temple Institute (Machon Hamikdash), a Jerusalem-based NGO dedicated to building the Third Temple on the Temple Mount in Jerusalem, took place in Dallas, Texas, on November 15, 2012, the same day that Israel launched Operation Pillar of Cloud, an eight-day airstrike on Gaza. When I saw the event advertised online I quickly registered and flew to Texas two weeks later, expecting to find a crowd of evangelical Christian Zionists bankrolling the Temple Institute in order to actualize their own messianic goals. Since the 1970s, evangelical Christians in America have been crucial supporters of the State of Israel and religiously motivated settlement in the West Bank, providing considerable financial backing for settlements and organizations connected to Israel's religious right wing.[2] For some evangelical sponsors of the Temple movement, rebuilding the Temple is a Christian obligation; it is a prerequisite for the Second Coming of Christ and eventual mass Jewish conversion to Christianity.[3]

I wandered around the hotel lobby examining the Third Temple–themed Judaica for sale and mingling with guests who had flown in from across the American Southwest. The banquet's centerpiece, a painting of the future Third Temple, would be auctioned off later in the evening. The painting depicted Yehuda Etzion's architectural masterplan for Jerusalem Rebuilt (described in chapter 2). A massive, reconstructed Temple stands where the Haram ash-Sharif and Al-Aqsa Mosque used to be. In the foreground, a Jewish father and son gaze at the Third Temple, and below them a mass of non-Jewish pilgrims from around the world wait in a parking lot for the arrival of a high-speed train that will take them to the Temple Mount.

I scanned the room, taking in the cowboy boots, yarmulkes, tzitzit fringes, and women in Orthodox-style headscarves; feeling unnerved by my inability to classify the attendees, I noted in my journal that Magen David (Star of David) necklaces far outnumbered the crosses. Were they Texan Jews? Or messianics? I wondered.[4] After about an hour, I discovered that the majority of attendees did not identify as Christians but referred to themselves as the Children of Noah (Bnei Noah) or simply "Noahides": a new Judaic faith that gained momentum in the United States in the 1990s through a convergence of Christians with rabbis from Israel's religious right wing.

Several attendees explained to me that they had recently left Christianity, which they now considered to be a form of idolatry, to follow the "truth and revelation of Torah" but were not considering conversion to Judaism. "Why I don't convert?" explained Bill, a middle-aged engineer from Texas. "Because God did not create me as Jew. As the Torah explains, there are roles for Jews and Gentiles to play in bringing the Third Temple. As a Gentile, as a Noahide, I have a unique role. And it is thanks to rabbis from the Temple Institute that I have been able to realize my role in serving Hashem [God]." Other participants echoed this sentiment with statements such as "I do not have a Jewish soul" or "I am not one of the Chosen People," explaining that Jews and Noahides are separate and divinely instated statuses in the Torah, with collaborative roles to play in bringing about messianic times.

Since the early 1990s, rabbis from the Temple Institute have been cultivating relationships with emerging Noahide communities in the American Southwest. Rabbi Chaim Richman, former director of the International Department of the Temple Institute, is an important spiritual leader for American Noahides, who provide some of the financial backing for the Temple movement in Israel. Through annual lecture tours, weekly webinars, and YouTube videos that have received hundreds of thousands of views, Richman offered spiritual guidance to Noahides around the world using internet technologies. Under the tutelage of rabbis like Richman, Noahides have been able to fill the void in their spiritual life that was created when they left their former Christian communities. And for most, this gap could not be filled by Torah study alone but required the cultivation of a distinctly Noahide lifestyle. American Noahides have adopted Orthodox Jewish styles of modest dress; they may eat kosher foods, celebrate Jewish holidays, and choose Hebrew names for themselves; and some marry (or remarry) their spouses through a Noahide wedding ritual officiated by an Orthodox rabbi.

Dinner was about to begin in the hotel ballroom. I spotted an empty chair at one of the banquet tables and introduced myself to the couples already seated. After I outed myself as a Jewish woman and an anthropologist interested in the Third Temple movement in Israel, my dinner companions were eager to share their stories of leaving Christianity. "I wish more of the Jewish world knew about us, that we are not just *goyim* anymore. We love the Torah and the Jewish nation!" explained Amanda. *Goyim* is a Hebrew term meaning "non-Jews," and in some Orthodox contexts it carries with it a derogatory "idol worshipper" meaning. As my dinner companions confided, the choice to leave Christianity and seek out Torah learning was not an easy one. They shared stories of excommunication from friends and family when they openly rejected their Christian upbringings. Amanda, the daughter of an evangelical pastor, related her own painful story of leaving Christianity:

I just knew in my heart that Christianity was false and I had to walk away. When I started to really dig and ask questions, things just didn't add up. There were too many inconsistencies between the Old and New Testaments. I felt disgusted by the idol worship I was raised with. But then I had to tell everyone we wouldn't be coming to Easter anymore. They thought I was crazy. That I was betraying them. . . . You know, I thought it would be easy just to make a clean break and throw away all the Christmas ornaments. But I still remember that day when I put everything in the trash. I just broke down crying. All of the memories. It is not easy just to throw away your whole culture. But you know it is false and that you are on a different path. A path to seek the truth.

The two other married couples at my table, all middle-aged professionals, narrated similar stories of abandoning their Christian identity and "idolatrous" customs and credited the Temple Institute with helping them to find a new spiritual community. They felt indebted to Rabbi Richman for his willingness to provide spiritual mentorship when (at that time in 2012) many Orthodox rabbis in the United States still remained wary of the Noahide movement, viewing it as suspiciously close to Jews for Jesus and Hebrew-Roots evangelicalism.

As dessert was served, the keynote speech was delivered over Skype by former Knesset member Moshe Feiglin from his office in Jerusalem. In 2012, Feiglin was one of the most outspoken political figures in Israel supporting the Third Temple movement, known for his frequent visits to the Temple Mount, which inflamed political tensions on the site. Feiglin first gained notoriety in the Israeli political scene in 1993 when he cofounded the Zo Artzeinu (This Is Our Land) movement to protest the Oslo peace process. He was subsequently accused of sedition by the government, and in 1997 he was sentenced to six months in prison by the Israeli Supreme Court. He continues to advocate for full annexation of the Palestinian territories and the offering of financial incentives to Palestinians to encourage their immigration to other Arab countries.

On the screen, Feiglin spoke excitedly about a spiritual revolution happening in Texas that was helping to fulfill the true purpose of the Jewish nation. He thanked the audience for being part of the divine plan and understanding that the mission of Israel in the world is to build the Temple. He reaffirmed to the Noahide audience that building the Temple was part of the commandment of *l'taken haolam* (fixing the world). The Temple was part of the cosmic order of the universe, and it had to be restored in order to bring peace and unity to all of mankind.

Amanda leaned over and whispered in my ear, "Isn't just so exciting what is happening?"

"What do you mean," I asked, caught off guard.

"You know the war and everything . . . it's the birth pains." Israel's current aerial assault on Gaza in response to Hamas rocket provocations, she meant, was a sign of the "birth pains" of an imminent messianic era. And at the center of this messianic world order would be the Third Temple, a "Temple for *all* the nations," as I heard repeatedly the entire evening. Later that night in the hotel I could not sleep. I was overwhelmed with questions: What kind of philosemitism was this? Had messianic Zionism created a new Judaic faith? Who were the Noahides?

The twenty-fifth anniversary gala in Dallas replayed in my mind for years as my research took me away from the United States to the front lines of the Temple movement in Israel. When an Israeli rabbi asked me to attend a Noahide wedding of two Filipino foreign workers in Jerusalem (2016), it reactivated my questions from the 2012 gala and initiated a new round of transnational fieldwork on the Noahide movement from 2017 to 2019 as I searched for more answers. Why had tens of thousands of people worldwide left the Christianity of their ancestors and dominant national cultures to embrace the Noahide faith?

Christian-Zionist support for the State of Israel dates back to the nineteenth century with the rise of *premillennial dispensationalism*: a Christian belief that the restoration of a Jewish nation in Israel is part of a chain of divine events leading up to the arrival of the Antichrist and the Great Tribulation, a worldwide period of war and disaster that will eventually usher in the Second Coming of Jesus.[5] For premillennialist Christians, the establishment of the State of Israel in 1948 and Israel's seemingly "miraculous" victory in 1967 provided definitive evidence that the premillennial eschatological timeline was playing out and the long-awaited "rapture" of true Christian believers into heaven, the anticipated mass conversion of Jews, and the return of Jesus to earth were approaching. As Susan Harding argues, the popularization of premillennialist ideas in twentieth-century America occurred alongside an important shift in conservative evangelical communities away from world withdrawal and a focus on individual salvation and toward direct engagement in political activism aimed at swaying both domestic and international policy.[6] In the 1970s and 1980s, American evangelicals increasingly saw themselves as agents of social change in a time of perceived "moral decay" (viz., feminism and liberalism) and founded political action groups aligned with the Republican Party.[7] Not only did they see supporting the State of Israel through political lobbying and fundraising as imperative for advancing the messianic timeline, but they also found more immediate gratification by viewing support for Israel as a way to contribute to the general welfare of America, another kind of "chosen nation" with a divine manifest destiny and a central role to play in redeeming humanity.[8]

Building on premillennial theology, influential evangelical preachers like Jerry Falwell and John Hagee further elaborated and popularized a "prosperity theology" that emphasized Genesis 12:3 ("I will curse those who curse you"), arguing that America's material and spiritual blessings were fundamentally linked to its support for Jews and the State of Israel.[9] For the majority of American evangelicals today, the exclusive Jewish right to the Land of Israel is a divinely instated and indisputable fact. According to recent surveys, 80 percent of American evangelicals agree that "God's promise to Abraham and his descendants was for all time" and 65 percent agree that "the Bible says God gave the land of Israel to the Jewish people."[10] As Daniel Hummel has argued, Christian Zionist motivations cannot be reduced to either messianism or political pragmatism but rather must be viewed as a "dialectic between religious belief and political action" as religious ideologies converge with broader material and political interests.[11] Specific geopolitical and economic interests, alongside a "shared loathing of Islam" within a clash of cultures narrative post-9/11, have helped unite Christian Zionists in America with the Israeli right wing just as much as symbiotic messianic desires.[12]

The Noahide–Third Temple movement alliance represents a distinct new stage in the evolution of messianic Zionism and its constitutive transnational interfaith alliances. For the gala attendees whom I met in Texas, who had been exploring the Hebrew roots of their faith for years and viewed Israel as having imminent messianic significance, it was not a far theological leap to embrace the concept of a Noahide "Gentile covenant" that is included in the Torah and part of a divine master plan. Like the conservative Protestant churches from which they depart, Noahides continue to conceptualize Jews as an ethnonational entity to which they do not have access. Rather than trying to be Jews, most Noahides embrace the idea that by attaching themselves to the Jewish people, they will achieve salvation and help to fulfill biblical prophecies. Behind both Christian-Zionist and newer Noahide conceptions of Judaism and the State of Israel is an emphasis on Jewish spiritual-racial exceptionalism as the key to unlocking universal redemption for all of humanity. However, in a significant departure from Christian-Zionist communities, the Noahide movement is unique in that it involves ex-Christians revoking their belief in the divinity of Jesus and submitting to Jewish Law largely through the use of internet technologies that connect them to rabbinic authorities based in Israel. I will return to examine these digitally mediated transnational spiritual connections after first addressing the historical and theological origins of the contemporary Noahide movement.

THE TEXTUAL AND HISTORICAL ORIGINS OF THE NOAHIDE FAITH

The concept of a "Noahide covenant" embedded in the Torah stands at the center of Jewish legal and theological attempts to explain God's relationship to non-Jews. According to the rabbinic tradition, a non-Jew is not obligated to convert to Judaism, only to follow the foundational moral laws given to the biblical Noah after the Flood. The Seven Laws remain incumbent upon all of humanity just as Jews are beholden to the 613 laws that fall under the Mosaic Covenant revealed at Mount Sinai. The Noahide Laws, derived through rabbinic exegesis of specific verses in Genesis, include the following:[13]

1. Do not deny God (Interpreted as a commandment to believe in the One God of Israel, thus prohibiting any forms of idolatry, including attributing divinity to Jesus).
2. Do not blaspheme God.
3. Do not murder.
4. Do not engage in illicit sexual relations.
5. Do not steal.
6. Do not eat from a live animal.
7. Establish courts / legal system to ensure obedience to said laws.

The Talmud expands on each of the seven, debating their proper order and applications.[14] The Noahide Laws postdate the existence of a Jewish commonwealth, and therefore it is important to read the Talmudic discussion as a hypothetical one, an attempt to establish a legal precedent for the *future* status of non-Jews in the Land of Israel when a Jewish kingdom will be restored in messianic times.[15] According to the rabbinic consensus, for non-Jews to live under Jewish rule in the Land of Israel they would have to qualify halachically as Bnei Noah (Children of Noah): non-Jews who observe the Seven Laws of Noah. Observance of the Seven Laws distinguishes a non-Jew as nonidolatrous and God-fearing, someone who by extension can be afforded the legal right to live as a *ger toshav* (resident alien) in the Holy Land of Israel alongside the Jewish nation. Through their elaboration in rabbinic discourse, the Noahide Laws became, according to David Novak, the "minimal prerequisite for naturalized citizenship in a Jewish state."[16] Yet even without the existence of a sovereign Jewish nation, rabbinic commentators in the Talmud still viewed the laws as the eternal moral foundation for humanity and a core component of the Jewish messianic agenda. Even if the Noahide Laws could not be fully enforced outside of a Jewish polity, the laws themselves continued to have an "a priori universal status" in Jewish theology.[17] As the descendants of the biblical Noah, all Gentiles are born obligated to these laws, but they must come to accept their obligation.

The extent to which the Noahide Laws were widely known or adopted by non-Jews in antiquity is an ongoing debate in contemporary academic and rabbinic scholarship with important stakes for those invested in the Third Temple / Noahide movements. Some Noahides and rabbinic mentors that I spoke with argued that the Seven Laws were accepted by actual Noahide subjects in antiquity and pointed to the archaeological and textual evidence of quasi-Jewish communities that existed in the Mediterranean. Jewish and Christian sources from the first to third centuries CE describe the presence of communities that adopted Jewish practices but not did not convert to Judaism, known collectively as the *sebomenoi* ("fearers of the Lord").[18] Flavius Josephus, a Roman-Jewish historian, commented on the existence of God-fearers living close to their Hellenistic Jewish neighbors, writing that "many of them [Greeks] have agreed to adopt our laws; of whom some have remained faithful, while others, lacking the necessary endurance, have again seceded."[19] Jewish sources refer to the God-fearers as their own category of pseudo-Jews, distinct from both Israelites and full converts, but, as Novak argues, it is unlikely that the doctrine of the Seven Laws, developed in rabbinic discourse of the second century, was already widespread in the Hellenistic period.[20] There is to date no definitive historical evidence to suggest that sebomenoi communities were following the Seven Noahide Laws as the foundation of their religious beliefs and identities.[21] However, according to some of my informants, the Noahide faith was not a "new religion" but a "lost tradition" once kept by the ancient God-fearers. Moreover, configuring the Noahide faith as a pre-Talmudic institution allowed some of my interlocuters to de-divinize and recuperate the historical character of Jesus by claiming that what we call "Christianity" was originally a messianic Noahide community and that Jesus was simply the first Jew to spread the Torah to Gentiles and bring them into the Noahide Covenant.

The Seven Noahide Laws, rather than predating Christianity, may have actually emerged in *response* to it. Following the rise of Christianity, rabbinic references to the sebomenoi disappear and there is a shift to Noahide Law as the basis for distinguishing between Jews and non-Jews.[22] As Novak suggests in his foundational work on the subject, this may be due to the fact the sebomenoi were among the first converts to Christianity, forcing rabbis to rethink Gentile participation in Jewish practices through a sharper concept of Bnei Noah that does not recognize quasi-Judaism and more clearly delineates which aspects of the Torah a non-Jew can adopt.[23]

In a clear rejection of quasi-Jewish practices, the Talmudic consensus advocates for prohibitions against the Bnei Noah performing Jewish *mitzvot* such as the observance of Shabbat, a commandment intended exclusively for Jews under Mosaic Law.[24] Non-Jews are forbidden from accessing the full canon of Jewish sources, as attempts to study Torah would be considered infringements on the spiritual inheritance of the Jewish people. According to some commentators, a non-Jew must limit their study to only the parts of the Torah that pertain to their inheritance (the Seven Noah Laws). Studying the Seven Laws was considered a *mitzvah* for Gentiles, an act for which they will receive spiritual reward.[25] Talmudic commentators thus sought to clarify the legal status of non-Jews while safeguarding the integrity of Jewish traditions, giving full access only to official converts and clearly separating Judaism from Christianity.

Today, the rabbinic understanding of Noahide Law is based primarily on the consensus developed in the Talmud and on the medieval commentaries of Maimonides, who further elaborated the concept in the twelfth century. In his *Mishneh Torah* (*Hilkhot Melakhim*),[26] Maimonides reaffirms the idea that Judaism does not demand conversion and compels non-Jews only to keep the Seven

Laws that were commanded to the biblical Noah: "Moses our Teacher was commanded by the Almighty to compel the world to accept the commandments of the sons of Noah. Anyone who fails to accept them is executed."[27] This injunction is typically not used to advocate for the murder of non-Jews but rather, as Eugene Korn explains, "pronounces axiological death."[28] It implies that all human morality stems from the Noahide Laws and failure to accept them is a failure to be fully human.

Maimonides establishes multiple classifications and levels of Noahide status in the *Mishneh Torah*. If non-Jews accept the Noahide Laws not on the basis of their own rational-moral judgments but instead on the basis of a wholehearted faith, because they believe in the divine revelation that occurred at Sinai, then their status is elevated to "Righteous of the Nations of the World" and they have a "portion in the World to Come" achieving salvation after death.[29] Only those who are Noahide on the basis of *faith* can go on to formally declare their acceptance of the Seven Laws in front of a rabbinic court and obtain the biblical status of a ger toshav, a non-Jew with the legal right to reside in the Land of Israel.[30] The category of ger toshav (resident alien) appears throughout the Hebrew Bible, where it references non-Jews who had certain rights and protections inside of a sovereign Jewish polity. While the Hebrew Bible does not explicitly mention that the ger toshav observed the Seven Laws, or that these laws were the legal preconditions for their protected citizenship, commentators like Maimonides, and indeed the contemporary Noahide movement, read the Noahide Laws back into the entire biblical text (into everything after the Flood) and view them as the code that all non-Jewish residents of the Land of Israel must have adhered to.

From this perspective, the ger toshav of the Hebrew Bible become proto-Noahides: righteous nonidolatrous Gentiles living alongside the Hebrew nation who serve as a template for the renewal of biblical categories of citizenship in the future Jewish polity to be reconstructed in messianic times.[31] Like the commentators in the Talmud, Maimonides engages with the Noahide Laws because they are integral to his eschatological blueprint: in the end of times, not only will the kingdom of Israel be restored, but a pure global monotheism will arise as Gentiles recognize the authority of the Seven Laws and the Torah and accept the oneness of God.[32] Just after clarifying Judaism's stance toward various categories of non-Jews in the *Mishneh Torah*, Maimonides describes the advent of the messianic era, rejecting the occurrence of supernatural miracles and emphasizing the practical restoration of Jewish sovereignty in the Land of Israel: "One is not to presume that anything of the ways of the world will be set aside in the Messianic era, or that there will be any innovation in the order of creation; rather, the world will continue according to its norms. . . . The sages said: 'There is no difference between the present age and the Messianic era but delivery from subjection to foreign powers.'"[33] According to Maimonides, reestablishment of Jewish sovereignty will usher in an era of peace when Jews will be free to study Torah and attain knowledge of their Creator to the full extent of human capacity and the one preoccupation of the entire world will be to know God as righteous Noahides.[34] Following his Talmudic predecessors, he reminds the reader that observance of the Noahide Code does not imply access to *Judaism* and reinforces prohibitions against the Noahide study of Torah and observance of Shabbat. His ruling places Noahides in a bind: they should avoid performing Mosaic Law commandments so as not to appear deceptively Jewish, but even though Jewish practices are off-limits, they should also avoid any ritual innovations that would amount to the creation of a "new religion."[35]

"We do not permit them to make a new religion," writes Maimonides, portraying the Noahide Code as purely a matter of internal belief.[36] Unlike Mosaic Law, the Noahide Code does not in fact require any ritual action, as observance of the laws relies only on intellectual reasoning and/or belief in the revelation of the Torah. Did Maimonides discount the human need for ritual life? Did he imagine that Noahides would be content with a purely intellectual pursuit of God? Writing about the Noahide concept as an ideal construct, Maimonides did not address the practical questions of Noahide identity and religious expression that would inevitably emerge as the Noahide concept shifted from theory to practice in the modern era.

While the Noahide Code remained a marginal conversation in Jewish thought of the medieval and early modern period, it reemerged in the writings of nineteenth-century rabbis vying for Jewish inclusion within the new nation-states of Europe. In an embrace of Enlightenment values, certain European rabbis utilized the Noahide Code to argue for the universality of Judaism and to contradict Christian claims that Judaism was an excessively particularistic religion that regards all Gentiles as immoral.[37] Rabbinic commentators living in Christian Europe tended to include Christianity as an example of a Noahide faith, viewing it as an acceptable form of monotheism that did not violate the prohibition against idolatry (Law 1), while commentators living in Muslim lands like Maimonides viewed Christianity as a form of idol worship and in violation of the code.

The writings on the Noahide Covenant of Rabbi Elijah Benamozegh (1822–1900) represent the first modern Jewish attempt to reactivate the Noahide concept and refashion it into a living faith identity. An Italian rabbi and a kabbalist, Benamozegh promoted the Noahide Laws as the future religion for all mankind: "We Jews have in our keeping the religion destined for the entire human race, the only religion to which the Gentiles shall be subject and by which they are to be saved, truly by the Grace of God, as were our Patriarchs before the Law."[38] This religion of humanity, "Noachism" as he terms it, dates back to the covenant that God made with Noah and has been "preserved by Israel to be transmitted to the Gentiles" at an opportune time.[39] The task of spreading the Noahide faith is in fact the ultimate purpose of Jewish existence outside of Israel. Benamozegh describes the Jews as God's "first born" nation with a special mission to guide the rest of "God's children" (non-Jews/Noahides) toward adoption of the Noahide Code. From this perspective, Jewish ethnoparticularism was established by God to facilitate a universalistic goal; Judaism is simply the "means of protecting and of realizing the authentic universal religion, or Noachism."[40] Benamozegh was not overly concerned with policing the boundaries between Jewish and Noahide practice but rather saw Noahidism as a way to unite the world under the umbrella of Torah. He explained that if Noahides wish to take upon themselves the idiosyncratic elements of Jewish Law and custom, they may freely do so.[41]

Under the spiritual direction of Benamozegh, French theologian Aimé Pallière (1868–1949) abandoned his path toward the Catholic priesthood and became the first known modern man to publicly adopt a Noahide identity. Discouraged from conversion to Judaism by Benamozagh, he took on the status of a Noahide to serve as a bridge between Orthodox Judaism and the Gentile world, promoting the Noahide faith among skeptical ex-Catholics like himself who had traded in the divinity of the church for Protestantism but were still struggling with the deification of Jesus.

In his autobiography *The Unknown Sanctuary*, Pallière takes us through his theological evolution. The unraveling of his Catholic faith began on the night that he, a young seminary student at the time, wandered into a Neila service during the conclusion of Yom Kippur (the Jewish day of atonement) in his native city of Lyon. The firsthand experience of passionate and collective Jewish prayer in the language of the Bible made him question the premise of replacement theology: "Fancy a young Christian, brought up in the naïve conception that the Old Testament has no mission other than preparation for the New which was definitely to replace it. . . . And now suddenly Israel appeared to me, still living its own life, with nothing to indicate the foretold decrepitude. . . . Israel has still the right to live. Israel lives."[42] The question of a *living Israel* became for Pallière "a germ implanted by Neila" that would grow stronger as he threw himself into the study of the Hebrew language and reexamined the scriptural proofs for Christianity.[43] He describes this process of Judaization as purifying his Catholic faith, "coming closer to the religion which was historically that of Jesus."[44] Pallière would eventually embrace the Noahide Laws and articulate a response to Christian replacement theology by positing the Noahide Code as the true universalistic messianic message of a Jewish Christ who never intended to abolish Mosaic Law.[45]

Pallière's autobiography gives us insight into the identity crisis that he faced while grappling with the fact that the Noahide Laws do not prescribe any particular religious expression. In his autobiography, he describes writing to Benamozegh and airing his concerns that Noahidism leaves him suspended in the boundary between Christianity and Judaism, without the clear identity, ritual life, or faith community that would be afforded to him if he were to complete a full conversion to Judaism—concerns that would reemerge again in my interviews with contemporary Noahides.[46] Pallière wonders whether he will ever be truly content with a purely "moral conversion . . . without expressing it in any form of religious practices."[47] Benamozegh assuages these fears by emphasizing the greater service to Israel that Pallière performs by forgoing conversion and becoming a Noahide apostle to the nations. Remaining outside of Mosaic Law will allow Pallière to preach to Gentiles and "bring about the final evolution of Christianity," using Torah truth to "correct" Christianity in three essential points: "the question of the Incarnation, the manner of understanding the Trinity, and the abolition of the Mosaic Law for the Jews themselves."[48] In his correspondence, the rabbi offered Pallière a chance to serve as an instrument of divine prophecy: "The future of the human race lies in this [Noahide] formula. If you will convince yourself of it, you will be much more precious to Israel than if you submit to the Law of Israel. You will be the instrument of the Providence of God to humanity."[49]

Pallière died in 1949 in the wake of World War II after becoming a prominent leader in the Zionist movement in France and serving as the vice president of the Jewish National Fund in Paris. His conversion to the Noahide faith and subsequent dedication to the Zionist movement attunes us to the early role of Noahide theology as supportive to Zionist political goals (the establishment and maintenance of a dominant Jewish-majority population in the Land of Israel) and the codevelopment of Noahide identity alongside Jewish religious nationalism. Pallière viewed Zionism as part of the destiny of the Jewish people, who by returning to the Holy Land and playing their role as God's chosen nation would help Gentiles around the world to realize their own destiny: to become Noahides and assist the Jewish nation in bringing messianic times.

During fieldwork interviews, rabbinic informants and Noahide leaders from the United States, Israel, Canada, and France often began their own narrations of Noahide history with Pallière, viewing his autobiography as a template for the modern Noahide spiritual trajectory. "When I read *The Unknown Sanctuary* I felt this real kinship with him. He was the first modern Noahide. What he experienced more than one hundred years ago, I experienced over the past decade," explained Jean-Michel, a French Canadian Noahide whom I interviewed in Montreal, the location of another growing Noahide community, in 2018. "I also grew up Catholic and then found Protestantism as an adult," he continued. "I threw myself into the study of Hebrew sources and took the next logical steps. I realized that Jesus was not God and the Torah contained a Gentile covenant that included me. After a very confusing and gut-wrenching period I finally had the answers I was seeking. My wife is still a Christian though. She just cannot let go of Jesus. But we manage together. She still goes to church but she agreed to take down the crosses that were hanging in our home."

While Pallière is most likely the first modern Christian to adopt a Noahide identity, and he did succeed in transmitting Benamozegh's teachings to a close circle of ex-Catholic friends, we cannot credit him with starting a "Noahide movement." For Pallière and his disciples, being Noahide amounted to an intellectual exercise, a sustained engagement in theological reasoning through scrupulous study of Jewish and Christian sources.[50] The true birth of Benamozegh's "Noachism," the Noahide concept transposed from rabbinic legal theory to a living religion, would begin only at the end of the twentieth century, and in contrast to Pallière's followers, it would consist predominantly of Christians coming from evangelical, Baptist, Messianic, and Seventh-day Adventist backgrounds.

NOAHIDISM AS A RELIGIOUS MOVEMENT

> In my youth, I was indoctrinated by theologians who had discarded their Jewish brethren. They ignored a body of knowledge, backed up with thousands of years of study by pious Jewish sages. These same theologians and pastors wanted the Jews to trade in their eternal Torah given to them by the Creator at Mount Sinai over three thousand years ago. They wanted the Jews to take that profound manual of sacred instruction, written in Hebrew (the Mother of all languages and the very DNA of human speech), and trade it in for a musty set of texts and doctrines cooked up in dank medieval monasteries.
>
> —Vendyl Jones, *A Door of Hope*

The contemporary Children of Noah movement first emerged in the American Southwest, where it found fertile ground following the proliferation of millenarian and Hebrew-Roots movements in the second half of the twentieth century.[51] According to Jeffrey Kaplan, who first investigated the Children of Noah as part of his comparative study of religious radicalism in America, the movement was born inside of a particular Christian "apocalyptic millenarian" milieu of the 1990s.[52] Apocalyptic millenarians, Kaplan explains, see themselves as "actors in the End Time drama" and share in a "Golden Age myth" whereby they are participating in the birth of a new and better world.[53] Belief in Jewish exceptionalism was a common component in the end-time dramas of apocalyptic millenarian groups, in both philosemitic and antisemitic varieties.[54] Throughout the 1990s, individual Protestant ministers coming out of the apocalyptic setting of the American Southwest began leaving Christianity and adopting a Noahide identity. Vendyl Jones (1930–2010), a former Baptist minister and self-fashioned biblical archaeologist who famously went looking for the Ark of the Covenant, is often credited with founding the Noahide movement in the United States.

Jones, also allegedly the inspiration behind the *Indiana Jones* movie character,[55] held a master's in theology from the Bible Baptist Seminary and studied archaeology at Bob Jones University, a conservative evangelical college. His lifelong pursuit of archaeology in Israel was driven by his belief that recovering treasures from the Second Temple would spark mass Jewish immigration to Israel and that such objects would be placed in the future Third Temple in Jerusalem.[56]

Jones was first introduced to the Noahide Laws in 1956 after resigning from the pastorate and beginning intensive Torah studies with an Orthodox rabbi in Greenville, South Carolina. As he excavated the Torah and attempted to purify his Christian faith from "pagan" influences, he began to discern a clear prophetic plan unfolding in Israel. God was still with his "first born," the Jewish nation that was regenerating in Israel, where the divine hand was actively guiding world history. Christianity, in comparison, was a stale and inauthentic imposter, a "musty set of texts and doctrines cooked up in dank medieval monasteries."[57] The Holy Land was calling, and in 1967, following his own premonition that Israel would soon fight a major war, Jones moved his family to Jerusalem and volunteered with the Israeli army. During the Six-Day War, Jones became acquainted with Rabbi Shlomo Goren (1917–1994), the religious Zionist founder of Israel's military rabbinate who later served as the third Ashkenazi Chief Rabbi and became one of the first national rabbinic figures to advocate for rebuilding the Temple. After the war, Jones continued to carry out excavations in the Qumran caves, funded and assisted by teams of international Christian volunteers. In 1988 Jones and his team claimed to have found the original "balm of Gilead" (a type of oil used to anoint Israelite kings), and in 1992 he allegedly discovered Second Temple incense. Jones recounts the praise that he and his volunteers received from Rabbi Goren during a visit to their field site: "Goren turned his gaze to the sixty or so dust-caked volunteers, 'What church are you from?' I told the rabbi that they were all from a variety of religious backgrounds. He turned to me saying, 'You have come to Israel looking for a treasure. You have already found a treasure. All of these people are truly a treasure. I cannot believe this. I think Mashiach has come!'"[58]

Through his budding friendships with religious Zionist rabbis like Goren, Jones laid the groundwork for establishing a transatlantic Third Temple movement–Noahide alliance. It is unclear exactly when Jones began referring to himself as a "Noahide," but he was using this term to self-identify in 1990 when he organized the first International Noahide Conference in Fort Worth, Texas, with the collaboration of rabbis based in Israel. Among those present at the conference were Rabbi Menachem Burstin, a representative of the Israeli rabbinate, and Rabbi Yoel Shwartz, considered the preeminent authority on the Bnei Noah subject and a leader of the "nascent Sanhedrin" project, an attempt to revive a rabbinic supreme court that existed in antiquity in preparation for the Third Temple and establishment of Jewish theocracy.[59] Also present was Rabbi Meir Kahane (1932–1990), who founded the militant Jewish Defense League in the United States and the ultranationalist KACH party in Israel in the 1970s. Kahane, who was assassinated a few months after the conference, was part of a first wave of Orthodox rabbis to form alliances with early Noahide leaders and ex-ministers like Vendyl Jones. In his keynote speech at the conference, Kahane connected the emerging Noahide movement with the unfolding of Jewish prophecy in Israel and the final redemption of mankind:

More than any people on this earth, you people are witnesses of the lord, for you people are those for whom the world was created. The people who witness that there is one God, omnipotent, all powerful, and there is none beside him. You people are making history, you people are bringing the world back to the purpose for which the almighty made it. . . . He who has eyes and ears to listen, can hear and see the coming of the Messiah. These are the days in which we live. We have seen miracles . . . he bangs on the door, he beats upon it, and he says open for me and I bring you redemption, and the key to that door is faith.[60]

Kahane's interest in the emerging Children of Noah movement makes sense in relation to his broader post-Zionist vision and particular spiritual-racial ideology that emphasized the sacred categorical distinction of the Jewish people established through their biblical covenant with God, a categorical distinction upon which Noahides build their own spiritual identity and notion of a separate (and subordinate) Gentile covenant in the Torah. Shaul Magid explains that Kahane often drew upon on a particular "grammar of racism" shaped by his upbringing in postwar America.[61] In his writings and public speeches, Kahane strategically mobilized a racialized discourse of Jewish difference that he invoked to push back against secular Jewish assimilation and uncomfortable associations of Jews with whiteness and white privilege and to reinforce the eternal nature of anti-semitism (i.e., Jews as history's ultimate victims).[62] Conservative American Noahides, coming out of Evangelical Christian churches, resonated with Kahane's racialized and biblically justified ideology of Jewish exceptionalism. They also aligned with his particular vision of Zionism as a Jewish "separatist movement" where Israel no longer relies on the support of other nations, but rather the nations come to *rely on* Israel as the gateway to redemption.[63] This power reversal was critical for Kahane in his program to defeat Jewish diasporic weakness, a degeneracy that he believed was perpetuated by the State of Israel's dependence on and capitulating attitude toward non-Jewish nations.[64] On November 5, 1990, seven months after his appearance at the first Noahide conference in Texas, Kahane was assassinated in Brooklyn by El Sayyid Nosair, an Egyptian American with connections to Osama bin Laden who later confessed to the murder of Kahane when he was arrested in connection with the World Trade Center bombing in 1993.

In the wake of his murder, Meir Kahane's followers and disciples dispersed, creating new initiatives and institutional homes through which they repackaged and proliferated Kahane's political teachings. The Temple Institute, founded by Rabbi Yisrael Ariel (a leader in Kahane's political KACH party), became one such home for Kahanist ideology nested just under the surface of an NGO dedicated to Jewish heritage, Temple education, and spreading Torah to "the nations." With a more legitimate and nonviolent public face, the Temple Institute gained access to state funding and international donors, becoming an important spiritual home and political bridge between conservative Christians abroad and Israel's messianic right wing.

In summary, the 1990 Noahide conference was a watershed moment, connecting the first generation of Noahide leaders, who had recently left or were in the process of leaving Christianity, with the rabbinic leadership they had been searching for—rabbinic leadership that shared in their anticipation of messianic times and, in the words of Kahane, could hear the messiah "banging on the door." In recognition of his work on the conference, Vendyl Jones received a blessing from Israel's former Sephardic Chief Rabbi Mordechai Eliyahu, who credited him with reviving the concept of Bnei Noah under the authority of the Chief Rabbinate of Israel. This endorsement from the Chief Rabbi illustrates why the Noahide movement cannot be brushed aside as a fringe phenomenon. The Noahide movement is an extension of religious Zionist political theology that is shared across a spectrum of Orthodox Jewish actors, from Third Temple activists who seek to transform Israel into a theocratic state to the very centers of Israeli state-sponsored rabbinic authority in the form of the rabbinate. Noahides validate the foundational tenets of religious Zionist theology, first articulated in the writings Rabbi Abraham Isaac Kook (1865–1935); they appear as living proof of Kook's claims that universal redemption flows from the restoration of Jewish sovereignty in the Land of Israel. Noahides help to transform Zionism from an ethnocentric project into one that can be performed in the name of all humanity, a universalist extension of Zionism that can be mobilized by diverse actors found everywhere from Israel's political margins to its religious, state-sponsored center.

During his lifetime, Vendyl Jones spoke regularly in synagogues and churches, offered Torah study classes in home, and hosted Shabbat meals, but he never formally led his own Noahide congregation despite believing that Noahides would go on to form their own communities. As is evident from his autobiography, he clung to the idea of seeing the Third Temple become a reality and, in pursuit of this vision, cultivated long-term friendships with rabbinic mentors from the Temple Institute including Chaim Richman. As I discovered at the Temple Institute's twenty-fifth anniversary gala in 2012, there are thousands of ex-Christians worldwide who now consider Rabbi Richman "their rabbi," and the Temple Institute has become one of the leading rabbinic organizations based in Israel to mentor newly forming Noahide communities.

Throughout the 1990s and early 2000s, ministers coming from Protestant churches continued to follow Vendyl Jones's early example, adopting the Noahide faith and allowing Orthodox rabbis to guide their studies—in some cases, bringing entire congregations along with them. In 1991, members of Emmanuel Baptist Church in Athens, Tennessee, tore down their steeple and recited a prayer for the removal of idolatry from the building, officially becoming one of the first Noahide congregations in the United States. The event made national news in a *Wall Street Journal* article with a headline that read "Tennessee Baptists

Turn to Judaism for New Inspiration: Christian Fundamentalists Seek Roots of Their Faith; There Goes the Steeple." The transformation of this Baptist community into a Noahide one was spearheaded by their minister, J. David Davis, whose own path to the Noahide faith included intensive theological investigation and a journey to the shores of the Dead Sea as a volunteer on one of Vendyl's quests for lost Temple treasures, culminating in his own close relationship with the Temple Institute.

Reverend David Davis came of age in rural Georgia in the 1960s, and after serving in the U.S. Navy, he earned a degree in theology from Tennessee Temple University in 1972. As a Baptist minister he embraced the Noahide concept after nearly two decades of rigorous theological investigation into the historical character of Jesus, a research obsession that ultimately led him to refute the virgin birth and the trinity and to identify with the ancient "God fearers" (sebomenoi). Davis's *Finding the God of Noah* (1997) is one of the earliest examples of what is now a growing genre of Noahide autobiography in which spiritual journeys from Christianity to Torah truth are narrated, either in print form as books or on websites, blogs, and Facebook posts. Davis's narrative exemplifies a common theological evolution that Noahides undergo as they search for the historical Jesus and begin to question core tenets of Christianity. It highlights the identity crisis provoked by a newfound knowledge of Jewish sources and the reclassification of Christianity as a form of "idolatry," an identity crisis that is resolved, Davis claims, only through the discovery of one's authentic, God-intended identity (Noahide).

When Davis began exploring the Hebrew roots of Christianity in the 1980s, which he refers to as an attempt to "sanitize" the New Testament, he came into Vendyl Jones's orbit and was recruited by Vendyl to help excavate the sacrificial ashes of a red heifer used in Temple purification rituals. While the digs in Israel did not yield the Temple objects needed to initiate a messianic era, they did expose Davis to Vendyl's disciples, who were further along in the process of extricating themselves from Christianity and convinced him that the trinity was a continuation of Roman paganism. After Davis returned from Israel, his faith began to fall part: "I was not a Christian in the technical sense, so who and what was I?"[65] The answer came in the form of a 1986 issue of the *Biblical Archaeology Review* that included an article titled "The God-Fearers: Did They Exist?" The article introduced Davis to the sebomenoi of antiquity, the Gentiles who lived during the period of Jesus and embraced Jewish customs: "They served the God of the Hebrew scriptures and studied with Jews, but there were two distinct economies in the same biblical environment," he wrote.[66] Davis would go on to discover the Noahide Laws in the rabbinic tradition and would come to identify with the God-fearers, finding in them an ancient model for the contemporary Noahide community: "The identity crisis was about to end. After thirteen years of searching, I now knew that I was a God-fearer."[67] Ready to accept the Noahide Laws, Davis found it difficult at first to obtain mentorship from Orthodox rabbis, whom he describes as "prepared to convert but not to teach the Torah path to gentiles." This would change, though, after the 1990 Noahide conference when ministers like Davis were introduced to rabbis coming from Israel who were eager to build connections with emerging Noahide communities. In his autobiography, he shares his memories of the conference and the official endorsement that it received from Chief Rabbi Mordechai Eliyahu.[68] In a response letter to the Chief Rabbi Eliyahu, Davis and his colleagues vowed to obey the Seven Laws and to respect the boundaries of Jew and Noahide: "We acknowledge and accept all that is required of us in Moses and the holy Prophets. We recognize the distinct difference that Hashem made between you, the people of Israel, and we, the nations of the world. And since God committed these oracles to Israel, we accept your authority and encourage you to accept the responsibility of teaching us the perfect will of God in our lives and conduct."[69]

The excerpt reveals an important aspect of Noahide ideology that clarifies why the majority of Noahides from the American Southwest have *not* sought conversion to Orthodox Judaism as they embrace a spiritual and racialized "difference that Hashem made" between Jew and Noahide. As Davis reiterates at the end of his book, "I have not converted to Judaism. I have converted to Torah."[70] This phrase would follow me in my fieldwork across continents. What does it mean to be converted to Torah but *not* Judaism? Noahides were converting to the Torah of their rabbinic mentors coming from Israel's religious far right. They now had a divine status and identity inside of the messianic Zionist project, no longer Christian financiers of the Second Coming watching from the sidelines as Jewish settlers reclaimed the Holy Land but rather active partners with the Jewish people, with their own Gentile covenant to fulfill.

Davis's conversion to the Torah of religious Zionism is evident in the final chapter of his book, where he recounts his first trip to Israel as a Noahide in 1991 to meet with leaders of the Third Temple movement. He identifies with pioneering Jewish settlers and the land annexing mission of religious Zionism when he decides to take a road trip across the "dangerous" landscape of the West Bank, asserting his "right to travel anywhere in the land of Israel."[71] As a Noahide and a "righteous Gentile" according to Jewish Law (and thus with the halachic ability to reside in the Land of Israel), he views the land as a combined Noahide and Jewish inheritance and imagines himself as participating in reclaiming it from Arab control. Davis recounts his ascent to the Haram ash-Sharif / Temple Mount in Jerusalem, which he visited with the intent to declare "by our presence and power, that this sacred area is once more a place of prayer for all people." "The Arab guards were quite agitated at our reading and praying," he writes. "One ran up and demanded to know whether we were Jews or Christians. I said neither: we are Bnei Noah."[72]

Just as Jews were returning to their biblical identity as Israelites, resettling the land with the aim of initiating a messianic era, Gentiles also had the opportunity to "return" to their biblical identity as Noahides and participate in the fulfillment of prophecy in the Land of Israel. By embracing the Noahide status in lieu of conversion to Judaism, Noahides reinforce ideas of Jewish spiritual-racial superiority and exclusive claim to the Land of Israel. Davis notes Rabbi Richman's enthusiasm for cultivating a Third Temple movement–Noahide alliance, explaining that Noahides were far better partners than previous evangelical backers of the Temple whose support "had nothing to do with love of the Temple of Hashem, but rather was aimed at fulfilling a Christian eschatological scenario."[73] Noahides were *kosher* Gentiles, dedicated to Jewish dominance in Israel and ready to submit to rabbinic authority, and the ideal partners for the Third Temple movement. As one Orthodox rabbi stated in an online editorial, Noahides constitute the Jewish people's one true "group of gentile friends," in contrast to Zionist evangelicals who have always had "hidden agendas" and "ulterior motives," namely supporting the State of Israel while simultaneously attempting to proselytize to Jews and convert them to Christianity in advance of the anticipated Second Coming of Jesus.[74]

Davis's spiritual journey exemplifies a trend that continued into the 2000s as Protestant ministers exploring the Jewish origins of their faith found themselves on the Noahide path. By the early 2010s, Noahidism had emerged as a distinct religious movement in the United States, under joint Noahide and Jewish rabbinic leadership with nascent physical congregations meeting for textual study and ritual observance. Children of Noah communities would continue to flourish in the United States and abroad during the second decade of the twenty-first century as the internet facilitated stronger connections between Noahide spiritual seekers, religious Zionist rabbinic leaders in Israel, and rabbis from the tech-savvy Chabad Hasidic movement who are also invested in Noahide proselytizing as a form of messianic activism.

Today there are dozens of rabbis who might all be placed along the ideological spectrum of religious Zionism participating in the production of Noahide books, media, and online courses. In addition to contributing to Noahide-led websites and organizations, Orthodox rabbis have also established their own organizations for Noahide outreach that include, but are not limited to, the Temple Institute in Jerusalem (under Rabbi Yisrael Ariel), the Brit Olam World Noahide Center (under Rabbi Oury Cherki), Ask Noah International and the Noahide Academy (both Chabad-affiliated), Gal Einei (under Rabbi Yitzchak Ginsburgh), Yeshiva Malchut Shel Chesed (Breslov-affiliated under Rabbi Shalom Arush), Jews for Judaism (led by Rabbi Michael Skobac), Outreach Judaism (Rabbi Tuvia Singer), and Yeshiva Pirkei Shoshanim (U.S.-based and Ultra-Orthodox). While these organizations differ in their specific legal interpretations (on, for example, varying levels of permissibility when it comes to Noahides participating in Jewish ritual life), they are motivated by a shared messianic and post-Zionist theocratic vision, a political theology that views Noahides as allies in the securing of Jewish sovereignty over the Land of Israel and the eventual rebuilding of the Temple.

Rabbis from the Chabad Lubavitch Hasidic movement also serve as some of the most influential sources of rabbinic authority driving the contemporary Noahide movement and the production of online resources in the twenty-first century, a move that follows Chabad's early embrace of the internet in 1993 as a mode of disseminating Hasidic teachings to the outside world.[75] Chabad's involvement in organized Noahide outreach dates back to the 1980s when the late Lubavitcher Rebbe, Menachem Mendel Schneerson, first began promoting the idea that Gentiles had a place in the covenant with God through observance of the Seven Noahide Laws. For the Rebbe, dissemination of the Noahide Laws was part of his messianic program, a step in the process of a global *tikkun* (rectification) that would unify mankind under a common moral code in preparation for an imminent messianic era. The Rebbe's desire to spread the Noahide Laws and outreach to Gentiles was part of his theological response to the horrors of the Holocaust. As he wrote in a letter in 1986, "Had these Divine Commandments been observed and adhered to by all the 'Children of Noah,' namely the nations of the world, individually and collectively, there would not have been any possibility, in the natural order of things, for such a thing as the Holocaust."[76] Only a universal social contract grounded in belief in one God could prevent human atrocities like genocide.

In a move akin to Elijah Benamozegh's vision articulated a century prior, Schneerson revitalized the Noahide Laws in his discourses, shifting them from an ideal legal construct to an implementable universal religion. He insisted that the diffusion of Noahide Law was an eternal Jewish *obligation* and one of the positive commandments given to the Jewish people at Sinai.[77] According to the Rebbe, God exiled the Jews so that they could convince humanity to adopt the Noahide code through verbal persuasion, carrying on a tradition of Jewish proselytizing that dates back to Abraham and Sarah, the first Jews who "disseminated Godliness among the Gentile nations."[78] Disseminating the Noahide code was how Jews accomplished their role as "a light to the nations" (Yeshayahu 42:6), uniting the world with God in the fulfillment of biblical prophecies: "For I will turn the people to pure language, so that all will call upon the name of God to serve Him with one purpose" (Zephaniah 3:9).[79] Delivery of the Noahide code to humanity would complete the process of "civilizing the world" according to divine will, and it was toward this end that the Rebbe provided specific directives to his followers to engage in Gentile outreach.[80]

In the 1990s and early 2000s, some members of the Chabad movement began to respond to the Rebbe's vision more actively by approaching political leaders and encouraging them to proclaim the universality of the laws. The Noahide Code resonated with conservative American politicians as it provided a biblical legal basis for outlawing abortion and homosexuality (Noahide Law 3 forbids murder, and Law 4 forbids "illicit sexual relations"). This occurred most notably in 1991, when the U.S. Congress designated March 26 as "Education Day, USA" and, in honor of the Rebbe's ninetieth birthday, signed a resolution (H.J.Res. 104) proclaiming the value of the Noahide Laws as the basis of all civilized society and the principles upon which the United States was founded.[81] In the years leading up to his death in 1994, the Rebbe continued to encourage outreach to political leaders from "superpower" countries like the United States who could help exert influence around the world.[82] For many Chabad followers, the Noahide Laws are considered the only moral code that can uphold justice on earth and will prove more effective than any forms of secular diplomacy in solving global conflicts, including the Israel-Palestine one. During a wave of violence in Israel (September 2015–January 2016), inflamed by tensions on the Temple Mount due to growing numbers of religious Jews on the compound, Chabad rabbis handed out flyers and paid for billboards proclaiming the importance of the Noahide Laws to Palestinians.[83]

Even as they began actively promoting the Noahide Laws in the 1990s, Chabad rabbis generally kept their distance from the ex-Christian ministers spearheading new Noahide communities in the American Southwest and were notably absent from the 1991 Fort Worth conference, where Temple movement rabbis were featured speakers. This stance reflects Chabad's own complex relationship with Israeli religious Zionism. As a Hasidic movement that remains anchored in the United States, Chabad stands outside of the particular history of Israeli religious nationalism and the religious Zionist institutions that became increasingly influential after 1967. Yet, as scholars of Chabad have noted, the late Rebbe affirmed a religious-Zionist ideology and took an active interest in the affairs of the State of Israel, maintaining relationships with Israeli political leaders and weighing in on national religious issues and state policies.[84]

While Chabad followers are typically not on the front lines of the Third Temple movement, those who live in Israel may still vote for religious nationalist parties and participate in religiously motivated settlement in the West Bank. Although their daily methods for bringing the messianic era may differ, Chabad shares in the larger vision of the Temple movement: in messianic times (believed to have already begun with the establishment of Israel), a Third Temple will be rebuilt and Israel will become a Jewish theocracy supported by Gentile nations who have embraced their true identity as Noahides. This messianic imaginary was often depicted in the form of artwork or murals in Chabad houses that I visited that were involved in Noahide outreach. For example, I photographed the mural depicted in Figure 3 in a Chabad center in Jerusalem. The prophesied Third Temple is suspended between the earthly and heavenly realms. It is positioned alongside the outline of a Jerusalem skyline, demarcating its final geographic location, but also adjacent to a depiction of Chabad's brownstone headquarters in Crown Heights, Brooklyn. Thus, we

FIGURE 3. A mural in a Chabad center in Jerusalem involved in Noahide outreach. It depicts the anticipated future Third Temple alongside Chabad's current headquarters in Brooklyn. (Photo by the author.)

see Chabad's diasporic messianism, established after the Holocaust and focused on strengthening Jewish observance outside of Israel, merging with a post-Zionist messianic vision of theocratic revival in the Land of Israel. The motif marks again the growing inroads that religious Zionism has made on Chabad communities in the decades after the Rebbe's death. It should also be noted that the Chabad emissaries most actively involved in Noahide outreach in the Global South, I found, were typically born and raised in Israel and thus had grown up inside of a religious nationalist milieu where messianic aspirations for Temple rebuilding and a theocratic state are widespread.

Rather than actively building Temple vessels, training Temple priests, or ascending to the Temple Mount, Chabad's messianic activism, in contrast to Temple activists, typically prioritizes forms of *soul work*: performing daily mitzvot, raising awareness of the Noahide Laws, and drawing secular Jews into the observant fold as a means of initiating the messianic era. Toward this end, Chabad rabbis are typically sent as emissaries to different countries to strengthen isolated Jewish communities and convince secular Jews to "return" to an observant life. Since the early 2000s, some Chabad emissaries have increasingly directed their energy toward the cultivation of Noahide communities, particularly in locations across the Global South where the Noahide movement is growing rapidly, and Chabad houses are often the only Jewish centers on the ground that can be accessed by spiritual seekers on their way out of Christianity.

Chabad rabbis are now among the key players working to reformat the Noahide concept, from the realm of ideal construct to communal identity, to meet the needs of Judaizing communities in Latin America, Asia, and Africa. This is accomplished through in-person classes on Noahide Law based in local Chabad houses along with the establishment of transnational virtual venues for Noahide education. The Noahide Academy, for example, is a Chabad-affiliated website that offers a selection of online courses. Through the academy's online bookstore, Noahide students striving to distance themselves from former Christian customs can purchase a Noahide prayer book that provides daily liturgies, variations on Jewish holiday observances, and lifecycle rituals such as weddings and funerals. The prayer book begins with the following admonition, reminding the reader to respect the boundary line between Jews and Noahides even as they give their Noahide status a religious expression: "The intent for these 'Suggested Prayers' is to provide home and communal prayers that are appropriate for Gentiles who follow the Torah based Noahide Code. Care has been taken that the prayers included here do not encroach on the spiritual heritage of the Jewish people, and there is no attempt to establish additional obligations for Gentiles, beyond the Noahide Code."

The Chabad rabbis whom I spoke with in Israel, who were involved in Noahide outreach, enthusiastically credited the internet with becoming a providential medium, one that was enabling the spread of Noahidism in advance of a messianic era. Now that Jews were freed from persecution and existential threats, they explained, Jews could finally share their Torah with all of humanity. According to my interlocuters, the internet had finally opened the gateway to a messianic era by serving as a means to disseminate the Noahide Code—what they considered to be an applicable and practical pathway forward for the final spiritual and moral cultivation of mankind.

DIGITAL NOAHIDISM, NOAHIDE PREACHERS, AND RABBINIC AUTHORITY

The rapid proliferation of Noahide communities in the twenty-first century on nearly every continent is profoundly linked to the advent of the internet. Virtual networks connect tens of thousands of individuals who are searching for Torah resources and rabbinic mentorship but are geographically isolated and/or unable to access Orthodox Jewish communities locally. In 2005, Ray Peterson, one of the original Noahide leaders from Texas, launched the Noahide Nations website, one of the first virtual platforms providing Noahide resources, online courses with Orthodox rabbis, and a training program for Noahide clergy who were starting up their own congregations. By 2016, Noahide networks and online centers for learning had grown significantly, providing spiritual seekers with opportunities for daily Torah study through blogs, online courses, YouTube videos, and Facebook groups available in English and increasingly in other world languages (French, Spanish, Russian, and Portuguese).

Today, digital platforms are extending Orthodox rabbinic authority into new geographic locations where questioning Christians have been gravitating toward the Hebrew origins of their faith for decades. In turn, a new class of digitally savvy Noahide preachers have appeared as religious authorities, bridging the gap between rabbinic mentors based in Israel and emerging Noahide communities on the ground. In lieu of Orthodox Jewish conversion, Noahide preachers model a new kind of *frum* (Yiddish for observant) Noahide lifestyle, one guided by Jewish Law and the eschatological vision of their rabbinic mentors.

The first organized Noahide communities that formed at the beginning of the twenty-first century were typically hybrid online/offline—based around a local congregation with a physical community center or "Noahide synagogue" but also conducting online outreach to a broader national or transnational Noahide audience. The Netiv Center for Torah Study, founded in 2010 in Humble, Texas, now includes five satellite locations in the United States and Canada and an influential website that reaches thousands of Noahides worldwide through podcasts and a YouTube channel. The flagship center in Humble offers regular in-person Torah classes, Rosh Hodesh (new month) gatherings for women, and a "Whiskey and Wisdom" Torah study group for men.[85] More recently, in 2021, Netiv launched an online initiative to build a comprehensive Noahide curriculum for "Torah-Observant Gentile Families" with content for pre-K- through high-school-aged children.

Netiv, Hebrew for "the path," identifies as a "non-affiliated orthodox Jewish outreach to non-Jews who want to learn Torah," firmly positioning itself under the authority of its rabbinic advisory board and reinforcing the idea of Noahidism as a subdivision of Orthodox Judaism. The website features content from Orthodox Jewish rabbinic advisors as well as the director of Netiv, Rod Reuven Bryant, a former pastor and army chaplain. In founding Netiv, Bryant has created a venue for Christians to engage in the rigorous study of Jewish sources and Jewish Law: "I often tell the rabbis who come to teach us not to act as if our people don't know anything. They're knowledgeable and sophisticated. If someone walks in and says, 'Has anybody ever heard of *Pirkei Avos*?' it would be embarrassing. These rabbis are blown away when a four-year-old boy quotes Rashi. The people who come here work very hard to acquire their knowledge."[86]

Bryant, who first became involved in missionary work at the age of sixteen and went on to lead a Texas megachurch, explains that he did not begin his spiritual journey looking for Judaism but rather stumbled upon it while teaching a course on church history: "We went all the way back to the Greek Orthodox and Roman Catholic Churches, and then all of sudden there was nothing there. We'd gone all the way back and we were still left with a huge question mark. . . . I started asking all sorts of questions, and as I began to fill in the blanks, it became painfully obvious that I had to get out."[87] His subsequent revelation of Torah truth, which he describes as being "Born Again, Again," made his work as a Christian minister unbearable, and he suffered two heart attacks from the mounting stress.[88] When Bryant and his wife discovered that they had Jewish ancestry, he finally resigned from his position in the church to embark on a conversion process. Like the first modern Noahide Aimé Pallière, Bryant was ultimately convinced to forgo Jewish conversion by a "big chacham" (respected Torah scholar) whom he met during a trip to Jerusalem: "He asked me if I was planning on converting and I said yes, because that was my intention at the time. 'God forbid that I should tell you what to do,' he went on, 'but I really think that you should remain a Noahide. You'd be much more of a help to both the Jewish and non-Jewish world if you don't convert.'"[89] Bryant now serves as strategic bridge between Jewish and Gentile worlds, ministering to thousands of other ex-Christians who have also "worked their way backwards" seeking the authentic origins of their faith and are now standing on the doorstep of Judaism.

In an online lecture from July 28, 2019, Bryant clarified common misconceptions of the Noahide movement for his followers, addressing accusations aimed at growing congregations like his own that Noahide was a "new religion."[90] For rabbinic mentors and observant Noahides who are beholden to Jewish Law, this accusation is deeply problematic as it implies that they are in violation of a halachic prohibition that forbids the creation of a new religion. The question of Noahide as a "religion" rather than a halachic status reflects the changing social life of the movement in the twenty-first century. The Noahide faith has grown beyond the small Torah study groups of the 1990s to become organized communities like Netiv with their own forms of religious expression. For many ex-Christians seeking to fill the gap in their experiential spiritual life since leaving their former churches, intellectual study of the Seven Laws is no longer sufficient. When Noahides create adaptations of Jewish prayers and lifecycle events (so as not to infringe on Jewish heritage and Mosaic commandments) they innovate a uniquely Noahide religious lifestyle and ritual practice. However, most Noahide leaders like Bryant remain adamant that Noahidism does not constitute a new religion.

"Noahide is not a Gentile religion for the non-Jew," Bryant reminds his audience in the lecture. "A Noahide's religion is Judaism and Torah. . . . My religion is Jewish, but I am not."[91] Bryant classifies himself halachically as a Noahide, as having the legal status of the righteous non-Jew, a status that is subsumed under Judaism, and therefore cannot be considered a "new religion." This line of reasoning naturally leads to the second common "misconception" that he addresses: the idea that Noahide amounts to a kind of second-class status within Judaism.

He acknowledges that newcomers often feel belittled when they first approach Orthodox rabbis and are told that they only need to keep the Seven Laws: "One of the things that we have all went through in our journey out of Christianity into Torah Judaism as either converts or righteous non-Jews is where is our place, what is our distinction, what do we do? . . . We are immediately told by the vast majority of good minded Jewish people: Just do the Seven and go to Heaven."[92] The patronizing rabbinic attitude is a "slam to the ego" for ex-Christians: "You feel like I am having to start all over, they think less of me, I don't have a religion, a community, a culture. I am out here all alone."[93] The most important thing, according to Bryant, is to begin the journey by calming one's desire to jump into Jewish practices and to "learn from a proper source," to seek Orthodox Jewish mentorship and slowly override one's Christian theological programming. "I didn't come into this thing because I wanted to be a Jew or wear a kippah or wear tzitzit . . . I came into this thing because I love God and I love Torah."[94] The goal, he implies, is not necessarily to be Jewish but to discover one's God-given identity according to the Torah.

The irony of Bryant's last sentence lies in the fact that, at first glance, Bryant is virtually indistinguishable from an Orthodox Jewish rabbi. In his YouTube videos he sits facing the camera in front of a library of Talmudic tomes. Dressed in a modest suit with a graying beard, glasses, and a black kippah, Bryant radiates normative masculine rabbinic authority. Even his speech is Orthodox-sounding, peppered with Hebrew words and halachic terminology in a Texan accent. He refers to God as "Hashem" and is careful not to say the full name of the Christian savior, referring to him only as "JC" (also a common Orthodox Jewish practice). This performance of rabbinic authority is characteristic of a new class of Noahide preacher/leaders like Bryant, digitally savvy middle men who often mediate between Orthodox rabbis and local Noahide communities.

Noahide preachers are typically college-educated, middle-aged males with previous theological training and pastoral experience. Noahide women play active roles in community building, organizing Noahide events, disseminating materials, preparing Sabbath celebrations, and educating children, but are largely absent from the ranks of religious leadership. Noahide men overwhelmingly serve as in-person preachers and online webmasters, responsible for delivering sermons and leading community prayers, mirroring the gender dynamics present in their former churches and in Orthodox Jewish communities. Leaders like Bryant strike a fine balance between replicating rabbinic aesthetics and affirming their status as pious Noahides who know how to respect the halachic boundaries that have been set for them. Bryant illustrates his piety and full submission to Jewish Law specifically through the act of *not observing*, urging his followers to refrain from Jewish-specific commandments such as the use of a mezuzah or the full observance of Shabbat.

In September 2019, Bryant made the front page of *Ami* (My nation; see Figure 4), a magazine catering to the Anglophone Orthodox Jewish community, and was featured in an article entitled "Frum Noahide: Why Does This Gun-

FIGURE 4. Cover of *Ami Magazine* from September 2019 featuring Noahide leader Rod (Reuven) Bryant. (Photo courtesy of *Ami Magazine*.)

Toting Non-Jew Wear a Yarmulke and Learn Gemara?" *Frum* is a Yiddish word that refers to a pious Jew but has recently been extended to label properly observant Noahides like Bryant, again illustrating the full transposition of the Noahide construct—a matter of internal faith according to Maimonides—to a form of Orthopraxis. In Jewish culture, frum status is signaled through one's mode of ritual engagement and observance of the law and, most immediately, through outward adherence to Jewish modest dress and fashion standards. The frum

Noahide demonstrates their piety, modesty, and respect for Jewish Law by adopting these standards and may use digital media to further their self-representations. A frum Noahide identity, cultivated through speech acts and correctly styled Orthodox dress and mannerisms, allows Noahide preacher-leaders to share in and extend the rabbinic authority of their mentors in online and offline encounters, becoming authoritative models for others in the process of leaving Christianity. As previous research on digital religion has argued, traditional forms of religious authority may be amplified in digital forums, specifically through the emergence of what Heidi Campbell terms the "new classes of religious authority" that have evolved online.[95] Frum Noahide preachers like Bryant have become subcontractors of Orthodox rabbinic authority, bridging the gap between Orthodox Jews and Hebrew-Roots Christians.

Scholarship on the topic of digital religion dates back to the early 2000s and in its first incarnation tended to emphasize the democratizing effect of the internet on religion. Through internet platforms, religion could be liberated from offline power structures and dominant faith doctrines, leading to new spaces of spiritual exploration and experimentation that would undermine traditional sources of religious authority.[96] Through digital Noahide resources, questioning Christians cultivate a novel spiritual subjectivity at the end of an often decades-long struggle with their faith. Thus, at first glance, the emergence of the Noahide faith seems to support the notion that digital religion functions as a creative and alternative "third space" of religion.[97] New forms of religious subjectivity and spiritual praxis emerge as questioning Hebrew-Roots Christians discover a faith identity online that captures their liminal positionality: Noahides are outside of Christianity, a part of Judaism, but not fully Jewish. Digital Noahidism arguably democratizes access to Judaism and Torah study for tens of thousands of questioning Christians worldwide. At the same time, the internet has the potential to simultaneously undermine and enhance traditional forms of religious authority.[98] Clergy members from a number of religious traditions have harnessed the power of social media and online social networks to enhance their legitimacy both online and offline, at times to censor and control the digital religious worlds of their followers.[99] As questioning Christians become Noahides and come under Orthodox rabbinic authority, their ability to freely explore and practice Judaism is still constrained by the rabbinic mentors who serve as gatekeepers by monitoring the online content of Noahide forums.

Previous research on Orthodox Judaism specifically has demonstrated the potential of the internet to both challenge and affirm rabbinic authority as increasing numbers of Orthodox internet entrepreneurs (e.g., religious women who have expanded their role by becoming online *yoatzot halakha*, or halachic counselors)[100] derive legitimacy through their offline affiliations with traditional male rabbinic authorities.[101] Likewise, digital Noahidism has enabled new forms of religious subjectivity for ex-Christians, who derive legitimacy through their associations with Orthodox Jewish institutions. Digital Noahide religion has effectively given rise to new classes of religious authority that exist online and mirror the attributes of traditional rabbinic leaders. Noahide preachers like Bryant embody Heidi Campbell's notion of RDCs (religious digital creatives), a new class of religious "digital entrepreneurs" who use their technological expertise to serve the religious organizations to which they belong.[102]

Digital entrepreneurs like Bryant extend the authority of their rabbinic mentors and gatekeepers while still carving out their own distinctive Noahide clergy positions. When Noahides serve as webmasters and communal preachers, they become proxies for Orthodox Judaism, bridging the spatial divide between Israel and locations abroad. Because the rabbinic leaders invested in the Noahide movement are primarily based in Israel and geographically far removed from their Noahide followers' daily lives, they depend on local Noahide preachers like Bryant to organize and implement offline community infrastructure—to give contemporary Noahidism a vibrant, living expression.

Hybrid online/offline Noahide communities like Netiv illustrate the authoritative modes of persuasion enabled by digital religion. Through encounters with frum Noahide preachers and rabbinic authorities online, Noahides are socialized into an Orthodox interpretation of the Torah and Jewish Law (halakha) as well as the particular religious-Zionist political theology of their mentors. Platforms like Skype and Zoom have even become virtual ritual spaces where aspiring Noahides can take a Noahide oath, vowing to forsake Christian "idolatry" and follow the seven commandments prescribed for non-Jews, taking these vows in front of a virtual rabbinic court (beit din) of three Orthodox rabbis based in Israel.

In summary, the internet has helped facilitate the convergence between individuals exiting Christianity with Orthodox rabbis. In turn, it has also enabled a novel form of faith-based diplomacy, one that builds on an older Christian-Zionist alliance, as ex-Christians come under the religious authority of rabbis from Israel's religious right wing and the Third Temple movement. Digital religion and online religious authority in this case have become powerful vectors of political theology, bringing participants into a collaborative project of world remaking where they can participate in transnational messianic alliances and begin living in the time of the Third Temple.

While previous research on digital religion has provided analyses of the discursive dynamics through which authority is constructed and conveyed,[103] the impact of local conditions and material inequalities on the authoritative potential of digital religion remains undertheorized. Even if we understand Noahidism as a case of collaborative spiritual exchange and transnational messianic allyship, it is, in certain contexts, still influenced by neocolonial dynamics.

To understand how and why Noahidism has grown most rapidly in locations across the Global South, we must consider the offline power dynamics in which

Noahide communities are nested and the power relations of Noahides vis-à-vis rabbinic mentors. As the following chapter will continue to illustrate, conditions on the ground that foreclose access to Jewish conversion in the Spanish post-colonies have helped to deflect spiritual seekers to Noahide resources online, channeling them into an arena of religious-Zionist rabbinic authority that welcomes them with open arms when local synagogues shut the door. But before turning to the ethnography in chapter 4, I want to conclude by addressing some of the missionizing dynamics that contour a transnational and digitized Noahide landscape.

JEWISH DIGITAL MISSIONARIES

"Wait . . . are you saying that Jews are proselytizing!?" This was a typical reaction I received when presenting my research in academic and Jewish community forums. Indeed, throughout the duration of my research for this book, I also struggled with the question of how to make sense of Orthodox Jewish rabbinic missionaries preaching the Noahide Code given Judaism's long-standing aversion to proselytizing. Moreover, the matter is complicated by the fact that we are not talking about winning converts to Judaism, but rather, Jews proselytizing *Noahidism.* While there is evidence of Jewish conversion taking place since antiquity, Jewish communities have historically refrained from actively and publicly proselytizing non-Jews for both theological and political reasons. As previously mentioned, many rabbis traditionally regarded Christianity and Islam as examples of established Noahide religions that already adhered to the basic moral code prescribed by the Torah. From this perspective, all "righteous Gentiles," including Christians and Muslims, already had a place in the "world to come" and there was no need to offer salvation to non-Jews by converting them to Judaism. Jews, in turn, often regarded themselves as a particularistic ethnosect, charged with a unique mission of guarding the Torah and Mosaic Law and were more focused on ensuring the transmission of Jewish traditions to their own descendants than gaining converts. Moreover, histories of religious proselytizing are typically linked to territorial conquest. Diasporic Jewish communities generally existed as religious minorities living under Christian or Muslim rule and operating in precarious modes of self-preservation, either forbidden from proselytizing altogether or simply not in a secure enough social position to actively spread Jewish theology or try to win converts among their non-Jewish neighbors.

Contemporary Noahide missionizing, on the other hand, *is* linked to a program of territorial conquest, albeit as a territorial project that is geographically displaced and occurring back in Israel/Palestine. The contemporary Noahide movement also replicates certain theological and political dynamics of "saving and civilizing" present in previous epochs of religious colonization. As this section illustrates, the movement reactivates and draws upon biblical-racial theories to classify humanity (as descendants of the Children of Israel or the Children of Noah) while mobilizing notions of spiritual-racial difference (between Jews and non-Jews) to justify a salvific national mission in Israel and messianic future for humanity. Furthermore, I wish to foreground the fact that the digital missionizing carried out by rabbinic mentors, based primarily in Israel and North America, is enmeshed in neocolonial power relations belonging to the Global North context in which they are situated.

Marla Brettschneider's research documented the interactions of Global North Jewish institutions, academics, and rabbis with Jewish-identified and Judaizing communities in sub-Saharan Africa.[104] She argues that while Jews have "long been situated as the Other within the global north" they unconsciously carry forward "aspects of historical Christian European modes of imperialism" in their interactions with Jewish communities in the Global South who often fall outside of the culturally normative and/or rabbinically grounded definitions of Jewishness that developed within Ashkenazi, Sephardic, and Mizrahi communities.[105] Moreover, as Brettschneider notes, the advent of the internet, and the new possibilities for connection that it has afforded Judaizing communities in the Global South who reach out to Jewish institutions in the Global North, has made it "nearly impossible to avoid falling in grooves, already dug, of outright colonial practices: of the 'civilized' and Jewishly knowledgeable imparting truths to the underdeveloped novice."[106] Global North Jews, historically subjected to persecution as a religious minority, have internalized Western narratives of modernity and civilization and often engage with Global South communities, even with the best of intentions, as culturally superior brokers of salvation and as privileged gatekeepers of Jewish identity.

In 2017, I returned to Israel to meet with representatives of a growing cohort of rabbis, coming from both Chabad and religious-Zionist streams of Orthodoxy, who were offering online courses and disseminating digital content for Noahide communities around the world via new website platforms, Facebook, and WhatsApp group chats.

The Noahide Academy, previously mentioned, is one prominent example of an Israel-based organization and internet portal through which some Chabad-affiliated rabbis disseminate Noahide teachings and mentor emerging Noahide communities from their homebase in Israel. This particular outreach website has the slick, professional appearance one would expect from an online university and interestingly lacks an overtly Jewish aesthetic (e.g., images of religious Jews, Hebrew text, or Judaica symbols).

The front page of the website features a photo of what appears to be a room of Caucasian college students, depicting the Noahide Academy as a virtual space that is academic, modern, and dynamic and specifically designed as a platform for English-speaking non-Jews.[107] According to its mission statement, the academy offers learning programs "to teach and guide Gentiles through the study and application of the Noahide Code in their daily lives." The online courses cover a wide range of topics, including introductions to the Seven Noahide Laws, proper Noahide prayer, the messianic era, Jewish mysticism, and Hebrew-language classes, with an average cost of about two hundred dollars per course. Some of the courses seem to be a cross between Jewish Law and self-improvement or wellness coaching, promising the life-changing results and positive emotional impacts that flow from knowledge of the Seven Noahide Laws. Courses are organized according to Noahide skill level, from beginner to very advanced, and include video and audio lessons, handouts, and quizzes; they culminate in the granting of a certificate of completion.

The website also highlights Noahide communities in the Global South and promotes the Noahide Academy's "North-South Campaign." The campaign allows Noahides in the Global North to send materials, such as prayer books, to Chabad-sponsored Noahide communities with fewer financial resources (notably all in formerly colonized countries of Africa, Asia, and South America), which are mentored by Noahide Academy rabbis but are not the primary audience for the website's online courses. The campaign aligns with another aspect of the academy's stated mission: to use the Noahide code to "transform developing countries" with the ultimate goal of promoting "universal access to Torah knowledge, personal empowerment and social stabilization within the coming years."[108]

When I last checked the Philippines page of the Noahide Academy's website in 2022, the stock photo that appeared did not come from any of the communities that I visited.[109] The image chosen to appear on the website dramatized and exaggerated the poverty of the community, engaging an aesthetic of Third World primitiveness that often appears in religious missionary literature and humanitarian aid campaigns. While most of the Noahide communities that I visited in the Philippines were indeed rural and disadvantaged to the extent that the academy's online courses and prayer books available for order would be out of their reach without financial assistance, most had access to food, housing, clean clothing, and education at the secondary level, with college-level study for more middle-class informants. The vast majority of my interlocuters, even the ones living in quite modest and rural conditions, had access to cell phones and an internet connection, which was not suggested by the website image. I was struck by the way the aesthetic of the Philippine page alongside the academy's stated mission to "transform developing nations" seemed to echo previous eras of religiously justified colonization in the Philippines. The Spanish conquest that brought Catholicism to the Philippines in the sixteenth century was carried out by Catholic priests who saw their work as a divinely ordained mission to "save and civilize." Likewise, the American occupation that brought Protestantism to the islands in the twentieth century sought to "uplift" Filipino natives and bring them into modernity. References to Filipinos as "child-like" were a common motif in U.S.

missionary reports,[110] connecting proselytizing to a process of maturity, personal intellectual, and spiritual development, themes that rabbis engaged in Noahide outreach also emphasized during our conversations.

One Chabad-affiliated rabbi whom I spoke with, Rabbi Cohen, reflected on how the internet had so profoundly influenced the growth of the Noahide movement in the Global South: "Access to the internet changed everything! All I have to do is open my smartphone and get on WhatsApp and I am in contact with Noahides all over Latin America and Africa every day." "But we [rabbis] are not trying to control them," he quickly clarified. "The main goal is to provide resources online, to identify and train leaders abroad so that they can build communities for themselves . . . as Jews it is our job to pass on insights in digestible ways so that humanity can grow spiritually."

I shared with him my feeling that Noahidism had become a new religion, especially now that it had taken the form of organized religious communities seeking theological and ritual direction from rabbis like himself. The rabbi immediately rebuffed my suggestion and insisted that Noahidism was *not* a religion but rather a biblical *category of humanity*, the natural and original monotheistic identity of all non-Jews that must be reconstituted in order to bring redemption. While Chabad-affiliated rabbis whom I spoke with explained that Noahides were part of the divine blueprint for humanity and have their place inside Jewish prophecy, some also reinforced the idea that they did not have access to *Jewishness*, lacking the upper levels of soul anatomy that are necessary to bring down advanced spiritual knowledge. It must be noted that the notion of an irreducible difference between Jews and non-Jews is an aspect of Chabad philosophy that was emphasized by the seventh Chabad Rebbe, Menachem Mendel Schneerson, as he encouraged his followers to implement a two-pronged proselytizing program aimed at bringing secular Jews back into Orthodox observance and Gentiles into the Noahide Code.[111]

As Elliot Wolfson has argued, this notion of an "ontological difference in the constitution of the Jew and the non-Jew, both physically and somatically" is often missed by academic scholars of the Chabad movement, who have tended to write about Chabad's emphasis on Noahide Law in an apologetic manner, arguing that it represents a "conciliatory attitude toward Gentiles" and a "weaking of traditional ethnocentrism" rather than seriously considering what is at stake in the way non-Jews are portrayed and the racialized undertones invoked in arguing for the spiritual hierarchy of Israel.[112] Wolfson contextualizes this particular strand of Chabad theology as part of the late Rebbe's reaction to the mass destruction of European Jewry and the subsequent relocation of Jewish refugees to America. In the wake of persecution and humiliation, internalized self-hatred, and rising pressures to assimilate to secular culture, the Rebbe may have felt the need to emphasize an ethnocentric notion of Jewish spiritual superiority as part of his efforts to draw secular Jews back into the fold and strengthen Jewish life.[113]

Chabad rabbis involved in Noahide outreach often depicted Jews as the active transmitters of divine knowledge and Noahides as passive recipients, invoking a material/spiritual binary to describe their divinely instated functions. According to this theological framework, Jews represented the spiritual realm and cognitive powers of the human mind, intended to act as transmitters of holiness and revelation and as intermediaries between humanity and God. Representing the mundane world, Noahides occupied the role of "civilizers" and "city builders," in the words of one rabbi, who take care of humanity's material needs but still require spiritual and moral cultivation—a process of individual salvation that was connected to a much larger cosmic rectification (including Israel's national redemption, the building of the Third Temple, and the coming of messianic times).

Today, digital Noahide missionizing continues to expand across the Global South and is not limited to Chabad-affiliated rabbis. The Israel-based religious Zionist organization Brit Olam: World Noahide Center has expanded its outreach to focus on growing Noahide communities across Latin America, Africa, and Asia. Netiv, a U.S.-based Noahide network, has expanded its outreach to Noahides in Latin America and in the Philippines in collaboration with Yeshiva Pirchei Shoshanim, an Ultra-Orthodox yeshiva based in Lakewood, New Jersey. Rabbi Chaim Richman (former director of international outreach for the Temple Institute) continues to provide Noahide education for emerging Noahide communities in India through his organization Jerusalem Lights. The contemporary Noahide movement was born in the United States in the 1990s through a convergence of Christian Zionists coming out of Hebrew-Roots churches with far-right religious-Zionist rabbis based in Israel. However, by the second decade of the twenty-first century, Judaizing communities in the Global South had clearly become the focal point and foremost arena of outreach for rabbinic authorities advancing the Noahide project.

Rabbis who had become invested in Noahide outreach were not forcefully imposing a new faith on foreign populations. Individuals on the edges of Christianity were actively seeking out rabbinic mentorship (primarily online) as they reconstituted their identity through the notion of descent from the biblical sons of Noah and their inheritance of a Noahide Covenant embedded in the Torah. The Noahide story, on the one hand, might be told as an internet success story, where digital technologies democratize Judaism, enabling non-Jews to explore Jewish teachings and seek out rabbinic mentorship when they are living far from Jewish communities. Yet digital spiritual exploration cannot be divorced from local conditions, power differentials between spiritual seeker and teacher, and neocolonial dynamics. Like previous epochs of religious colonization carried out by European colonial powers, the virtual proselytizing carried out by rabbis based in Israel is an extension of a messianic Zionist "providential theory of empire."

I borrow this phrase from Alfred Cave, who uses the providential theory of empire to describe the historical use of religion by expansionist nations to provide a divine purpose and moral justification for political domination.[114] According to Bruce Lincoln in his own work on religion and empire, cross-cultural and transhistorical projects of political conquest are grounded in a set of remarkably similar theological constructs: "reverence for a benevolent creator, a theology of election and vocation, a dualistic ethics, eschatological expectations, and a sense of soteriological mission."[115] Messianic activism in Israel employs its own Jewish versions of these constructs to sacralize territorial and demographic goals. For example, the ongoing Judaization of the West Bank and Jerusalem, the maintenance of a Jewish-majority population, and the preservation of exclusive Jewish right to the biblical Land of Israel—supported through the spiritual and political allyship of Christian (and increasingly Noahide) communities—are justified as the fulfillment of biblical prophecies and necessary steps toward the ushering in of a messianic era for all of humanity.

Noahide outreach, as a missionizing project that is both spiritual and national in nature, functions, in certain contexts, as a form of digitally mediated neocolonialism. The Noahide teachings that flow from centers of rabbinic authority in Israel and the United States through organizations like the Noahide Academy promise to, in the words of the Noahide Academy, "transform developing nations" by uplifting them with the Noahide Code. Rabbis and Noahides engage in comparative spiritual-racial judgements, drawing lines communally, theologically, and ritually between Jews and Noahides on the premise of innate genealogical and metaphysical spiritual differences, like the idea that Noahides and Jews possess fundamentally different kinds of souls, that I encountered in the Philippines (see chapter 4). In turn, some of the Noahides whom I spoke with had adopted a biblical-racial theory of humanity and had come to view themselves as the descendants of Noah's sons Ham and Japheth in need of spiritual enlightenment by Jews, the descendants of Noah's son Shem, believed to be the ancestor of the ancient Israelites, God's Chosen Nation.

The Noahide movement was characterized by my rabbinic interlocuters as a divinely ordained stage in humanity's spiritual evolution, part of a messianic process that includes the expansion of the State of Israel to its biblical borders and the rebuilding of the Third Temple in Jerusalem. Behind universalist claims of perfecting and uniting humanity, spreading a common moral code, and ushering in messianic times, there is a concrete territorial project that imagines a post-Zionist theocratic future for the State of Israel supported by non-Jews worldwide. This is the vision of Rabbi Oury Cherki, founder of Brit Olam: Noahide World Center, a physical center based in Jerusalem and a popular internet portal for Noahide communities around the world that provides access to a downloadable Noahide prayer book authored by Cherki as well as a Noahide declaration ritual available in sixteen languages. The declaration ritual involves a pledge form that Noahides can download (in their native language) and sign in front of a beit din, a rabbinic court made up of three Orthodox rabbis who witness the declaration act and also sign the document. According to the document, the Noahide vows to uphold the Seven Laws of Noah and declares aloud before the court their "allegiance to Hashem, God of Israel and King of the Universe, and to His Torah . . . I furthermore pledge to continue to uphold these laws in all their details, according to the Oral Law of Moshe under the guidance of the rabbis."[116]

Cherki, who previously studied under Rabbi Tzvi Yehuda Kook at the Merkaz Harav Yeshiva, is a rabbinic supporter of the Third Temple movement and a senior lecturer at Machon Meir in Jerusalem; Machon Meir is a large, influential, and relatively "mainstream" religious-Zionist organization in Israel that is connected to the settler movement and specializes in bringing secular Jews into Orthodox observance. In his writings, Cherki describes the Noahide movement as the "third stage of Zionism." In this third stage, following the establishment of the State (Stage 1) and the expansion of Jewish settlements in the West Bank (Stage 2), the Noahide movement extends the messianic process of Zionism to all of humanity. The Brit Olam website summarizes these stages for visitors, explaining that Judaism in diaspora could be focused only on internal issues of individual and communal life. Following the success of Zionism, of Jewish national revival and territorial conquest of the West Bank, the time has finally arrived for Judaism to deliver a "message to the whole of mankind," namely, by establishing Noahide communities and providing them with support. According to the website, Brit Olam is in contact with dozens of Noahide communities worldwide.[117]

Out of all the rabbis participating in Noahide proselytizing, Cherki is the most connected to the religious and political establishment in Israel, with ties to the right-wing Likud party (currently the largest party in the Israeli Parliament). In 2014, Brit Olam received official recognition and blessings from Israel's Chief Rabbi David Lau, and since then Cherki has facilitated Noahide declaration ceremonies in collaboration with members of Israel's state-sponsored rabbinate.[118] He views the Noahide movement not only as having spiritual and messianic significance but also as a national and geopolitical project. When we spoke in 2017, he was working with Tzipi Hotovely, then deputy minister of foreign affairs, on strategies to promote Noahidism and strengthen connections with Noahide communities abroad as part of Israel's diplomatic strategy. This was particularly salient in parts of the Global South, in Africa and Latin America, where philosemitic and Zionist trends were on the rise and evangelical political leaders were eager to build stronger relationships with the State of Israel. In 2021, as part of Rabbi Cherki's efforts to expand the global reach of Brit Olam, he announced the formation of a new strategic alliance between Brit Olam and two other prominent Noahide organizations, Yeshiva Pirchei Shoshanim and Netiv, both involved in Global South outreach. By presenting as a unified rabbinic front, rather than competing factions, the groups strengthen their religious authority and the status of Noahidism as a legitimate Torah pathway for Gentiles grounded in rabbinic consensus.

Messianic Zionism, as a mobile political theology, can also operate as a form of spiritual neocolonial influence that is decentered and deterritorialized, carried out through diverse digital channels and proxy-state organizations like Brit Olam that claim to be fulling the destiny of the Jewish nation. As new Noahide communities proliferate across the Global South, aided by rabbis based in Israel, the actual act of land conquest and physical intervention is geographically displaced (occurring back in Israel/Palestine). Through digitized messianic landscapes, Jewish ethnonationalism in Israel takes a transnational detour through spiritual communities on other continents.

At the same time, thinking about Noahidism and messianic Zionism from a framework of spiritual neocolonialism is certainly complicated by the fact that the "colonizing nation" here is, in a sense, a *future theocratic state* that does not quite exist but manifests in the present through the work of real and virtual publics. Third Temple activists, rabbinic authorities, and Noahides collaborate on and co-constitute a vision of biblical revival through internet-mediated relationships. The "state" here is a speculative design, the blueprint of a possible future, that the act of design brings into being in a meaningful way by eliciting affective states and emotional attachments in the designers. Like Third Temple activist Yehuda Etzion, who created professional architectural plans for an expanded Jerusalem and rebuilt Third Temple, Noahides whom I spoke with from different national contexts also saw themselves as creative messianic actors. Living out new Noahide subjectivities meant playing an active role in revitalizing biblical categories of being, an act of future-scaping that was helping to materialize a Third Temple messianic reality. More immediately, being Noahide meant participating in transnational Zionist allyship and a form of faith-based diplomacy that supports religious Zionist actors in Israel.

In summary, Noahide subjectivities and developing communities remain tethered to a project of Jewish ethnonational dominance and biblical revival on the ground in Israel. The Noahide movement effectively universalizes religious Zionism, imbuing Israeli biopolitical strategy with additional layers of sacred eschatological meaning that travel globally, influencing spiritual communities around the world and the creation of new religious subjectivities. This, I would discover, was the case in the Philippines, home to one of the largest Noahide communities in the world, where messianic Zionism had become a powerful resource for postcolonial spiritual reinvention.

4 · "RIGHTEOUS AMONG THE NATIONS"

A Case Study of Noahide Communities in the Philippines

By 2015, the most developed Noahide communities worldwide in terms of numbers, synagogues, and ritual life were located in the Global South. In contrast to North America and Europe, where Noahide communities are smaller and tend to exist as informal networks of families and friends rather than large, organized congregations, Noahide communities in Latin America, Africa, and Asia exhibited a different pattern after entire churches transitioned collectively to the Noahide faith. In most cases, this transition took place under the direction of a congregation's (former) Christian minister who had adopted the Noahide faith while receiving spiritual guidance from rabbinic mentors based in Israel and/or Chabad emissaries operating locally. This, I would discover, was the case in the Philippines, home to one of the largest Noahide congregations in the world: around three thousand members with at least fifteen synagogues on six different islands during the time of my fieldwork.

The following ethnography contextualizes the adoption of Noahidism in the Philippines in relation to localized power dynamics and postcolonial religious histories. How exactly does one make the transition to Noahidism in the Philippines? How do entire families come to abandon their belief in the divinity of Jesus and *live as Noahides* in this devoutly Christian country? What is the relationship of Noahides in the Philippines, and Global South more broadly, to remote and virtual forms of Orthodox rabbinic authority? This chapter provides initial answers to these questions, drawing on participatory observations and interviews conducted with men and women in their early twenties to sixties who transitioned out of Christianity over the past decade. It reveals the critical role of the Noahide preacher in mediating between virtual rabbinic mentors and offline communities. At the same time, it exposes some of the tensions that have emerged as Noahides find themselves caught between the idealistic expectations of remote rabbinic mentors, who guard the boundaries between Judaism and Noahidism, and a growing desire for augmented ritual life and access to Judaism on the ground. One of the reasons Noahidism has grown most profoundly in the Global South, I discovered, is due to the geographic obstacles and economic inequalities that often block widespread access to Orthodox Jewish conversion in these locales. When avenues to conversion are foreclosed, the Noahide movement becomes a viable alternative, affording Judaizing Christians access to rabbinic authorities, a divinely instated and Torah-based identity, and an active role to play in Israel's messianic destiny.

While the extension of Noahidism into the Global South represents a form of digital missionizing, it is a spiritual exchange that is not unidirectional and whose outcome is not determined. The Noahide movement and messianic political theologies more broadly have become powerful transnational motors of spiritual reinvention as Christians in the Spanish postcolonies adopt new religious subjectivities and, increasingly, demand access to full Jewish conversion.

RELIGIOUS DIVERSIFICATION IN THE PHILIPPINES

Noahide conversion in the Philippines is a multigenerational family affair and one that is reflective of broader social conditions: namely a loosening of the Catholic hegemony and a growing climate of religious exploration, where it is not uncommon for families to move through multiple churches together in a single generation. According to Aurora, a forty-year-old mother from Mindanao, "Noahide is successful because we make time for religion here in the Philippines. It is natural to discuss God with our family and friends in our free time. We speak and debate openly. We change churches. Everyone is looking for the truth, to get closer to God."

Indeed, spiritual conversations are infused into urban landscapes in the Philippines. Shop windows, trucks, and iconic jeepneys (shared taxis made from modified cars) function as advertisements for religious options, displaying biblical quotes, Catholic imagery, or announcements for new Protestant and Evangelical denominations. Noahide messaging also appears as part of the city spiritscape. For example, a jeepney owned by a Noahide family displays a bumper sticker that reads, "Noah wants you to keep the 7 Laws!" and advertises the asknoah.org website as well as Chabad.org on its front window (See Figures 5 and 6).

Previously colonized by Spain, the Philippines remains an 80 percent Catholic-majority country with the third largest Catholic population in the world after Brazil and Mexico. Since the 1990s, there has been a burgeoning of new religious and messianic movements in the Philippines offering spiritual alternatives to the dominant national Catholic faith.[1] The literature on religious diversification in the Philippines indicates that the decline in institutional Catholic affiliation does

FIGURES 5 AND 6. Noahide Jeepney with a bumper sticker that reads, "Noah wants you to keep the 7 Laws!" (Photos by the author.)

not correlate with a decline in religiosity itself, as Catholic youth in particular are drawn toward the experiential spirituality and political engagement available in Pentecostal and Evangelical churches.[2] When it comes to spiritual exploration beyond locally accessible Christian and Muslim options, the widespread availability of the internet, especially through low-cost cell phones, has enabled Filipinos to obtain information about Jewish beliefs and practices and to come in contact with rabbinic mentors promoting the Noahide faith.

Recent interest in Hebrew-Roots Christianity and Judaism is bound up in the Philippines' long and complicated history of colonialism and religious conversion. Judaizing movements have been on the rise in the twenty-first century across the Spanish postcolonies, where Christian communities are adopting Jewish practices and/or pursuing Jewish conversion, identifying as "lost Israelite tribes" or as the descents of Sephardic Jewish converts to Catholicism (*conversos*),[3] with varying degrees of success in gaining recognition from the larger Jewish world and the State of Israel.[4] Scholars have linked these trends to spiritual, economic, political and subjective factors, including a desire for status elevation, identification with Jewish histories of persecution, and narratives of redemption that motivate a desire for inclusion in the messianic future of Israel. While there exists a substantial literature on Judaizing trends across the Spanish postcolonies of Latin America, Judaizing communities have yet to be examined, to the best of my knowledge, in the anthropological or sociological literature on the Philippines outside of this account. In the meantime, scholarship on conversion to Christianity and Islam in the Philippines helps contextualize the growth of Noahidism in the country and informs our understanding of the social and political changes driving religious exploration in the Philippines in recent decades.

The diversification of Christian denominations in the Philippines, which now pose a significant spiritual and political counterforce to centuries of Catholic hegemony, dates back to the end of the nineteenth century during the U.S. occupation (1898–1946), when Protestant organizations interpreted U.S. political control over the Philippines as a divine sign to begin proselytizing Filipinos.[5] American missionaries quickly followed in the wake of military forces establishing Protestant congregations including Methodist, Protestant, and Seventh-day Adventist churches that developed locally into Filipino-led churches that either remained affiliated with Protestant umbrella organizations in the United States or evolved into breakaway churches operating under their own national religious authority.[6] The relatively quick success of Protestantism in the Philippines has been attributed to the gap in spiritual leadership left by the withdrawal of Spanish Roman Catholic orders during the U.S. occupation, the success of publicly staged debates between American missionaries and Roman Catholic priests, and Filipinos' newfound access to Bibles and Christian literature through contacts with Protestant missionaries who worked to promote literacy and social reform. During the Spanish colonial period Filipinos were often forbidden from possessing Bibles, and such an act was punishable by law.[7]

Before American missionaries arrived in large numbers, new Protestant denominations, born in the Philippines and founded by Filipinos who dared to defy Spanish authority and engage in Bible study and interpretation, had already begun to reshape the religious landscape. For example, Filipino theologian Nicolás Zamora, whose father was incarcerated in Spain for reading the Bible and questioning the authority of the Catholic Church, founded La Iglesia Evangelica Metodista en las Islas Filipinas in 1909. Zamora's congregation was one of the first autonomous Protestant churches in the Philippines and, moreover, refused to submit to the control of American Methodist missionaries. In 1914, Felix Manalo (a former Catholic who traversed Methodist and Seventh-day Adventist churches) founded Iglesia ni Cristo, now the third largest religion in the Philippines (after Catholicism and Islam); a nontrinitarian church with a revivalist messianic ideology, Iglesia ni Cristo views itself as the prophesized reestablishment of the "original" church of Christ in the Far East at the end of times.

Islam, which first arrived in the Philippines in the thirteenth century and is most prominent in the southern islands of Mindanao and the Sulu Archipelago, has also experienced rapid growth in the second half of the twentieth century through a movement popularly referred to as Balik-Islam (return or returnees to Islam). Since the 1970s, when Muslim-Christian tensions reached a critical point in the Philippines following the formation of the Moro Islamic Liberation Front (a Muslim separatist movement seeking independence in Mindanao), it is estimated that two hundred thousand Filipinos converted from Christianity to Islam. Like Judaizing communities in the Philippines (both Noahides and those seeking Orthodox conversion), members of Balik-Islam resist a conversion narrative and instead assert that they are "returning" to the "original" religion of their ancestors from which they were separated due to the historical forces of imperialism.[8] According to Teresita Cruz-Del Rosario, conversion to Islam is imagined not only as return to a state of spiritual purity but also as a reclaiming of historical sovereignty and a reversion to "pre-colonial time and space" when the Philippines "was an organic part of the Indo-Malay world" before this sovereignty was interrupted by Catholic colonization.[9] From a theological perspective, returnees also argue that Islam is the "natural religion" into which man is born, similar to how Noahides view the Seven Noahide Laws not as another "manmade religion" but as the "natural" or "original" covenantal identity for all Gentiles, who are believed to have descended from Noah's sons Ham and Japheth.[10] This idea of returning to the pure and precolonial religious past of one's ancestors became even more salient in my interviews with Filipinos who had broken away from the Noahide movement to pursue Orthodox Jewish conversion. During my fieldwork, I met with aspiring converts who asserted that they were in fact the descendants of Sephardic Jews forced to convert to Catholicism in Spain during the fifteenth century who later resettled in the Spanish colonies including the Philippines (cases I return to at the end of this chapter).

Judaizing Noahides and Balik-Islam converts in the Philippines both attest to a widespread social phenomenon of religious shifting and spiritual exploration. Researchers found that 67 percent of Balik-Islam members had at least one experience of denominational shifting within Christianity before joining Islam.[11] In the thirty interviews that I conducted with Noahides in the Philippines, all of my interviewees reported trying one or more Protestant denominations, typically those with an emphasis on reclaiming Hebrew roots and adopting Jewish rituals, before arriving at the Noahide faith. Additionally, research on Balik-Islam has emphasized the impact of migration on religious conversion in the Philippines as Filipinos working abroad in Muslim countries convert to Islam. Around 2.2 million Filipinos currently work abroad and send remittances home, a critical part of the country's economy and a pathway to socioeconomic stability and mobility for many families.[12] For migrant workers facing precarious conditions while living abroad in Muslim countries, for years or decades at a time, conversion to Islam provides an important social and spiritual network that enables them to better navigate the material and emotional demands of overseas life.[13] While the majority of foreign homecare workers in Israel come from the Philippines,[14] I personally encountered only two Filipino couples in Israel who had become Noahides while working in the homes of Orthodox Jews in Israel, although there may very well be many more. The vast majority of my informants in the Philippines were first introduced to the Noahide faith in their home country after transitioning out of Messianic and Seventh-day Adventist congregations. Some informants reported that they were interested in seeking overseas work permits specifically for Israel as a result of their engagement in the Noahide movement, but the outcome of their efforts have yet to be documented or quantified.

Exposure to and interest in Judaism in the Philippines can be situated within a larger postcolonial context of religious shifting, one influenced by patterns of transnational missionary activity and global migration that pushes back on notions of religious conversion as radical rupture, instead revealing conversion to be a gradual process providing forms of social and economic capital as global wealth inequalities restructure family dynamics and national economies. While Noahide disavowal of the divinity of Jesus and submission to Orthodox rabbinic authority is, on the one hand, a significant theological departure from their Christian origins, Noahide theology also remains consistent and compatible with the messianic-Zionist imaginaries that were permeating my informants' former churches and spiritual lives for decades. Before they had heard the word "Noahide," my interlocuters' lives and spiritual journeys had already been influenced by traveling political theologies that center Jews and the land/State of Israel as vehicles of salvation and had already come to view Zionism as part of a divinely ordained messianic process.

NOAHIDISM IN THE PHILIPPINES

"It is not easy to confront people who are very bright in the New Testament. After my father's death, I went everywhere where our brethren are located to spread the message of Bnei Noah [the Children of Noah] to them. There were lots of debates but eventually they accepted that there is only one God. Hashem," explained Jeremiah, a Noahide preacher and one of the spiritual leaders guiding the community in the Philippines. Jeremiah was officiating a Noahide wedding in a village on the island of Cebu where seven Noahide families lived in housing clustered together, a short distance from their local *barangay* (village) center. The Noahide faith is now a registered religion in the Philippines, and Noahide communities on different islands can conduct legally recognized wedding ceremonies and Noahide baby "dedications" that have taken the place of baptism ceremonies. The wedding that I was invited to witness was held in the community's synagogue, a one-room concrete house that is kept immaculately clean for Sabbath worship. Worshippers sit facing a rear window that orients their prayers in the direction of Jerusalem. Flags of Israel and the Philippines and a laminated poster listing the Seven Laws of Noah emblazoned over a graphic of Noah's Ark hung on either side of the front door. The community, I soon discovered, considered themselves as having the status of "righteous among the nations," a living manifestation of Maimonides' twelfth century legal ruling: "Anyone who accepts upon himself and carefully observes the Seven Commandments is one of the *righteous of the nations of the world* and has a portion in the World to Come" (Mishneh Torah, Kings and Wars 8:11).

I arrived the morning of the wedding, and as would occur in the other Noahide communities that I would later visit, I was greeted like a celebrity. For most of the villagers, I was the second Jew (and the first Jewish woman) whom they had ever met in person, with the first being a Chabad rabbi who previously visited the community. With nervous excitement, the wedding guests approached me and asked if I would pose for pictures with them. "A real Israelite woman!" exclaimed one of the guests as she wrapped her arms around me and positioned her selfie stick. She then posed by smiling and pointing one index finger upward to proclaim her belief in the "One God," a uniquely Filipino Noahide substitution for the V-sign pose that is common across Asia. Another family requested blessings for themselves and their three small children, lowering their heads slightly to signal that I should place my hands on them and give a benediction. It took me a minute to process their request.

What happens when you become the desired redemptive body for your informants? Did this not replicate previous colonial dynamics of anthropologist as white savior? However, my interlocuters were asking me to participate, and I felt uncomfortable denying their requests. To refuse to bless them would also be a refusal to participate on their terms, reducing me to yet another academic perpetuating one-way knowledge extraction. I was hoping to theorize with them and cultivate horizontal relationships as much as possible. But what exactly did I owe them in return? I was a walking remnant of the biblical Jews whom they admired, a piece of the living Israel that they had been seeking for decades as Hebrew-Roots Christians inside a Catholic majority culture. The fact that I was deeply uncomfortable with playing this role was now irrelevant. I slowly recited the "Birkat HaKohanim" from memory: "Yevarekhekha Adonai Veyishmerekha.... May the Lord bless you and guard you. May the Lord shine his face upon you and be gracious to you."

I had come to the wedding eager to witness firsthand the new Noahide rituals that had been crafted by local Noahide leaders in collaboration with virtual rabbinic mentors based in Israel. The ceremony began with a procession of close relatives and honored guests, called one by one into the synagogue as klezmer music played through loudspeakers. The men wore kippahs, and the women wrapped their hair in colorful headscarves, adopting a style that is common among married Orthodox Jewish women. The bride and groom, a couple in their early twenties, stood under a wedding canopy fashioned from an Israeli flag. Together they lit seven candles symbolizing the Seven Noahide Laws, a reminder of God's original covenant with mankind and the Noahide inheritance.

The groom recited a variation on the Jewish marriage pledge: "Behold, you are betrothed unto me according to the Laws of Moses as they relate to Bnei Noah, the Children of Noah. I pledge to honor, respect, and maintain you. I assume all of the responsibilities incumbent upon a loving and faithful husband, and I pledge to lead my life according to the Torah of Moses as it is related to the Bnei Noah."

The bride responded, "I pledge to honor and respect you. I assume all of the responsibilities of a loving and faithful wife, and I pledge to lead my life and build our home according to the Torah's Noahide Laws, so it will be a sanctification of God's Name in the world."

As the celebratory meal commenced outside, I was ushered to the sidelines and given a seat overlooking the festivities. Aware of the dietary laws that Jews follow, and wishing to demarcate and respect my Jewish status, the community did not attempt to offer me any of the cooked food but graciously placed at my table a supply of coconuts, bananas, and mangoes freshly harvested from the fruit tree groves that surround their home. I took advantage of the down time to speak with community leaders to get a better sense of how the Noahide faith travelled to the Philippines, where it has grown to approximately three thousand members spread across the central and southern Bisaya-speaking islands and the northern Tagalog-speaking islands. The particular network of Noahide communities under Jeremiah's pastoral care, I learned, were largely former members of the Sacred Name Believers, a Seventh-day Adventist breakaway sect.

The Sacred Name movement began in America in the 1930s with Sabbath-keeping Christian churches. In addition to adopting Jewish rituals, the movement emphasized the practice of vocalizing the Hebrew tetragrammaton (the four-letter name of God found in the Torah that Jews do not pronounce) as "Yah-weh." Jeremiah explained to me that his father had been a Sacred Name preacher and had already begun making changes, steering his brethren away from the New Testament and toward Jewish observance of the Sabbath, the New Year, and Passover. After his father's death, Jeremiah took over, traveling to different islands and converting his father's communities to the Noahide faith. To denounce their former Christian faith, followers collectively burned their Christian books after first cutting out the names of God from the pages and burying those pieces according to Jewish tradition.[15] Some members reported partaking in a *mikveh* (Jewish ritual bath) purification ceremony to mark their final departure from Christianity. While immersing privately in a river or ocean, they asked God to forgive their previous sins of idol worship.

At first, Jeremiah explained, he struggled to find trustworthy Jewish resources to steer the group away from Christianity in the wake of his father's death. "We studied everything," he explained. "And we would also go and debate Christians to spread the Seven Laws." I would later witness one of these polemics firsthand during a second round of fieldwork when Jeremiah brought myself and my husband (who was traveling with me) to a Messianic church conference with the hope of using live Jews as theological fodder. "These are *real* Jews," he explained to the conference pastor. "And they do not believe in Jesus or pronounce the name of God." Winning theological debates with Protestant Hebrew-Roots ministers, especially messianics who believe in the divinity of Christ and claim to be practicing Judaism, was one of the ways that Noahide preachers in the Philippines gained converts and strengthened their positions as religious authorities representing "authentic Judaism." A turning point came in 2008, Jeremiah explained, when, aided by the connective power of the internet, he was able to access his first copy of *The Divine Code* (2011) and initiate online relationships with rabbinic mentors from the Chabad-affiliated Ask Noah International website that was providing support for emerging Noahide communities at the time.

The Divine Code is a popular and often cited book by Noahide leaders that elaborates all applications of the Seven Noahide Laws according to a Jewish legal framework. Written by Rabbi Moshe Weiner in Hebrew and edited by Rabbi Michael Shulman, both Chabad-affiliated rabbis, the book is available for purchase online on Amazon. This 655-page book, endorsed by two Chief Rabbis of Israel, was considered by many of my interlocutors to be the most authoritative and comprehensive explanation of the Seven Laws to date, often described to me as the "*Shulhan Arukh* for Noahides." The *Shulhan Arukh* (literally "Set Table") is the most widely accepted complication of Jewish Law, written by Joseph Karo in the sixteenth century.

While Jeremiah has built relationships and received training from different competing rabbinic organizations involved in Noahide outreach, such as Yeshiva

Pirchei Shoshanim and Brit Olam, he explained that he had more recently chosen to limit his loyalties to Chabad. Varying halachic opinions and changing ritual instructions from different rabbinic sources were bringing confusion to his followers, and these changes threatened to erode his credibility, which hinges on his ability to transmit lessons directly from a verifiable rabbinic source—lessons that he translates and delivers to his followers in their native dialect during annual in-person visits and weekly online sermons. Community members trusted Jeremiah to lead them away from the false teachings of Hebrew-Roots churches peddling "fake Judaism" and respected the fact that he had devoted his life to correcting his father's mistakes, bringing the community along with him after he discovered the Noahide truth. Jeremiah's authority was rarely questioned in my interviews with community members under his pastoral care. On only one occasion, an elderly male member of the community pulled me aside to inquire, "I need to ask you . . . where does he get his authority from? Do you know his rabbis personally? . . . Does the Jewish world know who we are?" I understood this exchange as indictive of the fissures of doubt that eventually emerge in digitally mediated religious movements. Jeremiah's legitimacy as a middleman and his ability to "stand in" for remote Orthodox rabbis could be called into question. Other community members might have been asking themselves similar questions but did not feel comfortable voicing them aloud to me.

Noahide communities in the Philippines have their own gendered, classed, and intergenerational power dynamics. Married middle-aged men typically stepped into the role of Noahide preacher, leading discussions of the weekly Torah portion and communal prayers in the synagogue (selections of Psalms read aloud collectively in English from the Noahide prayer book provided by Ask Noah International). Women, I found, were deeply engaged in Torah study and forms of Noahide worship alongside men, but it was generally not acceptable for women to act as preachers or ritual leaders in the synagogue.

While middle-class urban dwellers were typically fluent enough in English to explore Noahide teachings on their own and read supplemental information about Judaism online, others, especially those without higher education or English fluency, relied on traveling Noahide preachers for theological and ritual instruction. Some Noahides lived in more rural areas, meaning they had limited or irregular access to the internet, which impaired their ability to study Jewish sources on their own, an issue often compounded by varying levels of English fluency. Diego, a community member who had in fact received higher education and was fluent in English, reflected on his own personal limitations:

> The only resource person for me is Jeremiah. I first met him when he was coming to the community once or twice a year. And then the information I got was oral, not by text. So studying Judaism for me as a Noahide at that time, and even until now, the material and information is very, very limited. Living here in this isolated

place it is hard to connect to the internet, there is little cell service. There are a lot of things that I want to know regarding Judaism and Noahide. That's the problem. How can I get information?

Diego also hinted at the inadequacy of the new Noahide rituals handed down by rabbis based in Israel: "Personally, I will say we need more ritual. It is not enough, just the Seven Laws. What do I do to bury my dead? For the birth of my baby? If you ask me in my heart, I want to be converted [to Judaism]. I feel that being a Noahide is just for today." Other informants reiterated concerns regarding the vagueness of their new identity, *Jew-ish* but not Jewish, and the ritual vacuum they faced after leaving Christianity that seemed to require constant improvisation.

Anthony, a Noahide from Manila, expressed similar sentiments:

> When you first become a Noahide you feel like you are in a strange place. Okay, I am not a Christian anymore but I am also not a Jew. How should I explain this to people? What do I tell the kids? How should I practice my faith? When my mother passed away we didn't know what to do. The family wanted to have her embalmed but this is forbidden according to Jewish Law. In the end we put *Bat Chava* [Daughter of Eve] on her grave with a Jewish star according to the Jewish custom. She always prayed to one God even when she went to the Catholic church so she was basically Noahide without even knowing it.

While families expressed gratitude for new Noahide ritual resources, like the prayer books coming from rabbis in Israel, some community members still had the sense that Noahide was uncharted territory. They were unsure how to navigate the question of raising children and being Noahide in the Philippines where Christianity is deeply embedded in national culture. "I was not sure if I could participate in Christmas with my friends," explained one woman. "I did not want to violate one of the Seven Laws and participate in that idolatry." Noahides were struggling to live their new faith and relate to their friends, neighbors, and colleagues in a country where Judaism is still relatively unknown.

I asked families if they feared persecution as a Jew-ish minority in a Catholic country and received mixed responses. Some individuals had experienced harassment from family or neighbors when they chose to leave Christianity and had concerns that this harassment might increase as Noahide synagogues became more prominent in the country. Others brushed my concerns aside and related with pride the Philippines' history of rescuing Jews during the Holocaust, President Duterte's ex-wife's Jewish ancestry, and their country's warm relations with the State of Israel as evidence that Noahides would not be seen as a threat. In general, the Noahides that I spoke with indicated to me that they were supportive of Duterte's controversial administration, marked by his support for the extrajudicial killing of drug users, and one young man even suggested that Duterte might himself be a Noahide in hiding: "He made a comment that the trinity was nonsense and he said there is one God, so some Noahides think he is actually a hidden Noahide," he explained. Noahide support for Duterte in the Philippines hints at the ways in which the global politics of Noahidism / the Third Temple movement converse with the national politics of Noahide communities. Messianic Zionism not only structured the ways in which my informants thought about Israel and its salvific mission in the world but also colored the ways in which they interpreted their local political reality. This came across in casual comments that some Noahides made to me about their Muslim neighbors and the ongoing siege of Marawi City that was being carried out by an ISIS-affiliated separatist movement during the time of my visit. Some community members drew parallels between Israel and the Philippines, equating all Muslims in the Philippines with the one violent group responsible for the Marawi siege. One Noahide woman from Mindanao, Maria, made the following comment while we were discussing local politics: "We feel very close to the Jewish people and Israel because we are also dealing with Muslim terrorists in the Philippines. We are also struggling against this evil." Maria understood Israel and the Philippines as dually engaged not in conflicts over sovereignty with religious and ethnic minorities but in sacred battles for the triumph of holiness against forces of "evil" in the world represented by the Muslim "Other."

A heavy rain began to fall. As the wedding guests dispersed, I was ushered into one of the homes to continue interviews with married couples from the community. I caught a glimpse of the Noah's Ark poster again and was struck by the thought that Filipino Noahides might have a personal relationship to the story of the Flood. The Philippines, as a Pacific island nation, is beset by natural disasters. Regular flooding, caused by heavy seasonal rains, typhoons, and tsunamis, is worsened by ongoing deforestation and development that erodes soils, causing devastating landslides. Like the biblical Noah, my interlocuters viewed themselves as "righteous among the nations"—a small minority who had found the one true God while living among "idolatrous" neighbors in a country where the flood waters were always threatening to rise. Jeremiah made this connection, between idolatry and divine punishment, as he continued to relate the history of the community: "It is sent from God. I believe that most of the calamities here [in the Philippines] are because of the sin. Because of the presence of the cults here. They are worshipping their ancestors, their grandparents, asking for help, asking for blessings. They worship their dead."

After sunset the local families gathered for an evening Torah study, a tradition whenever Jeremiah visited their community. They again donned their Jewish-style hair coverings out of modest respect for the sacred material to be discussed.

I was invited by the community to observe and record the lesson for my research purposes. Jeremiah opened his laptop and began his sermon in English so that I could follow.

"Okay, what makes them different than us?" he asked. "What makes the Jewish people different from us? In the eyes of Hashem, we are equal. Because we are all human. But there is a special people and a chosen people by Hashem, because they were the only country, the only race who easily accept the Torah." He segued into a Kabbalistic discussion of the components of the soul. "So what are the components of the soul; do you remember?"

The adults responded in unison: "Nefesh, ruah, neshamah, hayah and yehidah."

"As we all know, only three we have," he replied. "And the five levels of soul are intact with the Jewish people. So we don't need to convert because we have our own path." Noahides, he explained, have only the first three levels of the soul, corresponding to a lower animalistic nature, while Jews have the remaining three spiritually elevated levels. Consumed with prayer and hundreds of *mitzvot*, he continued, Jews operate on a spiritual level that cannot be comprehended by Gentiles.

A similar depiction of soul anatomy appears in the *Tanya*, a canonical work of Hasidic philosophy written at the end of the eighteenth century by Rabbi Shnuer Zalman, the founder of Chabad Hasidism. The Tanya makes the distinction between the "divine soul" of the Jews and the "animal soul" of "idolatrous nations"; according to Zalman only Jews possess a divine soul, which allows them to "uplift their animal soul and transform it into a vessel for holiness."[16] The hierarchy of soul anatomy developed in the *Tanya* is a distinct feature of Chabad Hasidic philosophy and not representative of Jewish theological consensus. While the Tanya draws on the widely accepted messianic eschatology of Maimonides (addressed in chapter 3), who offered a universalistic vision of redemption and argued that Jews and non-Jews have an equal capacity to attain knowledge of God, the *Tanya* also develops these ideas in more ethnically exclusive directions, including a spiritual-racial typology that differentiates between Jews and non-Jews.[17]

Elliot Wolfson explains that Chabad Hasidism's particular emphasis on the irreducible difference between Jews and non-Jews was inspired by biblical depictions of ancient Israelites as the "Children of God" or as God's "firstborn," who as the nation chosen to receive the Torah are believed to have an "indigenous bond" with the divine essence.[18] The notion that Jews are somehow intrinsically holier than non-Jews represents a minority stream within Judaism, a religion that is largely opposed to racial division and racist ideologies. This minority opinion can be traced back to the eleventh-century writings of Jewish poet and philosopher Yehuda Halevi. As Menachem Kellner has argued, it is important to remember that when Halevi first articulated these ideas, he was writing in a context where Jews were a despised and persecuted people, subject to cycles of expulsion and violence at the hands of more powerful Christian and Muslim kingdoms, and thus, Kellner concludes, Halevi's emphasis on Jewish spiritual-racial supremacy and innate connection to God can be read as a defense mechanism intended to enhance the morale of his community.[19] While authoritative Jewish philosophers including Maimonides continued to disavow such ideas throughout the Middle Ages and modern era, notions of Jewish supremacy have more recently resurfaced and gained traction in certain post-Zionist theocratic circles in Israel. For example, the 2009 book *Torat HaMelekh* (The King's Torah), authored by two disciples of Rabbi Yitzhak Ginsburgh (a prominent advocate for Third Temple building, Jewish monarchy, and Noahide outreach), advocates for Jewish racial and spiritual supremacy. The book caused public outrage in Israel when it became clear that such ideas could be used to incite and justify violence against Palestinians.

Diego interrupted: "So meaning, we are just the same as an animal?" Jeremiah clarified: "Actually we have an animal soul because we are focused on material things. It is very hard for us to compare to the Jewish people; we are nothing compared to them. We are dust."

I was starting to panic. Where was he going with this? Did he pick this particular topic specifically because I, a Jewish woman, was present? What if I were asked to respond? If I were to question Jeremiah's hierarchical theology, I would be accusing him and his followers of false consciousness, of being duped by some inauthentic version of Judaism, implying that there is a stable or singular one to begin with. To make any claims that my understanding of Judaism was somehow superior might have thrown me back into the colonial arrogance of anthropology in the first half of the twentieth century, in addition to being a direct challenge to the Noahide leader's authority and the fragile trust that Jeremiah had built with his community as they followed him out of Christianity and into the unchartered waters of the Noahide faith. Instead of speaking up, I gazed into my notebook, avoiding any eye contact with community members that might reveal my discomfort. I wrote in my notes, "Why would anyone want to join a religion where they are told that they are dust?"

The question continued to haunt me, and a few days after the wedding I decided to return to the Noahide village to spend more time with the families living there and learn more about their individual spiritual journeys. It was not uncommon for Noahide families to move through multiple denominations before arriving at Noahidism. "We have been like ten different religions since I was a kid!" explained Gabriella, a college student in her early twenties whom I spoke with during the wedding ceremony. "We started as Catholics and then my parents kept changing churches. We were Evangelicals, and Seventh-day Adventists, then different kinds of messianic, and finally Noahide," she explained.

If I wanted to understand the community's particular Hebrew-Roots evolution and their "return" to a Noahide identity, Angelica told me, then I needed to visit Beit El (Hebrew for House of God), the cave-synagogue at the top of a nearby mountain where some Noahides previously lived during their time as Sacred Name Believers. I had already bonded with Anjelica during the wedding in the Noahide village. A vivacious and outspoken matriarch of the community, she was one of the first women to disrupt the starstruck manner of engagement with me, joking around and warmly caring for me like a daughter.

We woke up just after sunrise to begin the ascent up the mountain. As we set out on the path, Anjelica offered a blessing for our success: "Barukh Hashem! [Hebrew for Thank God] This morning we have to climb the mountain, may Hashem guide us! Hashem you have to protect us in coming to the cave. Barukh Hashem, my life in this cave was amazing." Anjelica's infectious energy and constant reminders of gratitude for life motivated me during the exhausting two-hour vertical hike. Her husband went ahead of us, using a machete to clear a path through the overgrown forest. A few of the village mothers and their children joined us for the expedition, singing Hebrew songs that they learned from YouTube videos as we climbed the mountain.

When we arrived, I collapsed, asthmatic and drenched in sweat, onto the cold floor of the cave, where I gazed up at words "Beit El" still visible in fading white paint on the rock wall. The cave opened into an impressively large cavern where the Sacred Name congregation previously met and worshipped and then branched off into smaller rooms where individual families lived before moving out and building their own homes. Anjelica began the tour by explaining that she first came here as a young missionary in 1984 after rebelling against her Catholic parents and joining the evangelical nontrinitarian Church of God during its "peace and love crusade." At this time, she explained, the Church of God was helping the government to fight the New People's Army (an armed guerrilla wing of the communist party in the Philippines) in Mindanao. Anjelica was sent with a small missionary contingent to the cave to establish a new outpost of the Church of God.

In the early 1990s, Jeremiah's father arrived at Beit El and brought the Church of God missionaries into his Christian Kabbalah / Seventh-day Adventist sect called the Sacred Name Believers. He instructed the families to build homes nearby and transformed the cave into a Sabbath worship space. Anjelica reminisced, "He brought us the Torah. He taught us the Hebrew alphabet and sacred names [for God] and other lessons from Israel. We were always worshipping on Friday afternoon and Saturday in the morning and afternoon. We did Shabbat here. On Friday afternoon we would gather all kinds of foods. We had to cook first. By sunset on Friday we finished all the cooking for the sabbath day and then we did not make a fire."

Another community member, Josephine, a mother in her forties now living in a nearby city, reflected on the times that she visited the Beit El cave for Sabbath celebrations as a child growing up in the Sacred Name community:

I remember growing up as a Christian until I was five, and then we changed to a Jew-ish religion led by Jeremiah's father. I loved him and saw him like an angel. Every word he said, I believed it was true. He was very kind and his face looked like a picture from the Bible with a long beard and a cane and a hat with Hebrew writing. Like a character from Moses's time! We used a Christian bible, but we changed the name of God, and we had a special costume for prayer, long white robes like from the bible. . . . Now the costume is changed. And the way we pray is different. Before it was one God with a son, so we still spoke about Jesus. Jeremiah said that Jesus was his father's mistake. We trust him.

Josephine's memories of Beit El again highlight the extent to which Judaizing currents had already permeated Christian communities in the Philippines, decades before the arrival of Noahidism and the new relationships with overseas rabbis facilitated by the internet. If Noahidism had successfully taken root, the missionizing efforts of Orthodox rabbis were only one side of the story, and arguably their success was facilitated by a particular crisis of Protestantism unfolding on the ground. Communities like the Sacred Name Believers were receiving the Noahide message after decades of grappling with their Judaizing faith. For decades they had been drawing closer to the Torah and trying to make sense of their own identity in the boundary zone between Christianity and Judaism.

Anjelica walked around the cavern collecting plastic bags and broken bottles left by recent visitors and commented, "You know, I was one of the caretakers of this place, in honor of my pastor. It was my job to clean this place . . . you wouldn't believe how beautiful it used to look." To this day, she carries on her work as a sacred groundskeeper for the new Noahide synagogue in the village, making sure that visitors respect the space and prepare themselves before entering to pray. "Before you go to the synagogue you have to clean your body. You have to take a bath and dress up. You have to enter in the front door by the Seven Laws and read them. Then you enter the synagogue and you listen to the presence of God," she explained to me.

We sat in silence together in the cave while the children played. Finally, Anjelica began to tearfully sing one of the songs from her past, from her Sacred Name Believers or Church of God days: "In the years I live for self alone, no need to have a savior, hopelessly I wandered on, then comes the dawn and I behold His loving face still watching over me and He has fled through my tears, through my tears I see Zion's gates unfolding, there will be no more tears. Through my tears I see Zion's gates unfolding, through the cloud, that there will be no more tears." Here in Beit El, at the top of a mountain in the Philippines, Anjelica had been yearning for Zion, tapping into a transnational imagination of Israel's biblical past and a utopian vision of its future redemption.

We returned to the village to rest. We had bonded, I hoped, during the hike when the community saw me covered in dirt and sweat, a more humanized version of the devout and spiritually elevated Jews that Jeremiah had described in his "levels of soul" lecture a few days prior. The sermon was still weighing on me, and I was waiting for an opportune time to bring it up with the families. Diego finally broached the topic that evening after the children had gone to bed and some of the adults from the community were sitting outside sharing a pungent jackfruit. "There is something on my mind. I want to ask you what you thought about the sermon the other night. Do you believe we have an animal soul?" Diego inquired.

My initial attempt at neutrality ended, and I quickly become emotional: "Look, honestly, I never heard this idea growing up as a Jew in America. I was shocked when I heard this, and it hurt me to listen to it."

"But where is this written? Do you know where he got this?" Diego pressed.

"I think it comes from a certain stream of kabbalistic and Hasidic teachings, but not every Jew agrees with this. I was not raised this way. . . . Many rabbis, like Maimonides, argue that Jews and non-Jews are equally holy. I do not believe I am higher than you. I mean if anything you are higher than me spiritually. The way you are devoted to your spiritual journey, the synagogue you built, your faith it is impressive."

Diego cut me off. "It's okay. Don't worry, Rachel, you don't have to get upset. You are a Jew. You are one of the chosen people. You are superior. This is not a problem for me."

"Yes, in general in the Noahide community we believe that the Jew is higher than us," added one of the other men present. I rambled for a few more minutes, attempting to cite authoritative rabbis who do not hold to the level-of-soul theology, already slipping back into the scholarly imperialism I wanted to avoid. Maybe I was trying to "save" them with my liberal Judaism, but I also could not remain silent and tacitly condone the teaching. My interlocuters were asking me to reveal my own interiority just as I had asked them to do in their interviews. In the end, my words had some ameliorating impact. After I left the village, one woman, who had been present during the evening conversation, sent me a message thanking me for my candid words. "It's like you removed a thorn that was in my foot," she wrote.

Regardless, I knew I had crossed a line by openly refusing to play the role that Jeremiah probably expected of me and by contradicting his teachings. I feared that he would cut off contact. This would eventually happen during my second trip to the Philippines, but for the time being we parted ways in 2017 with a warning. As we sat together for a final interview in a coffee shop, he alluded to my conversations with the community in his absence after I asked him about the possibility of full conversion to Judaism for the brethren: "Convert? How can they convert? They cannot even afford a candle for Shabbat. . . . That is why we explain that Jews and Noahides have two separate paths but headed in the same direction," he explained motioning upward to the heavens. I believe Jeremiah was worried that if I continued to ask questions about conversion, deflecting attention away from the refrain that Noahides had "separate but equal" roles to play in the divine plan, I might be putting lofty and unattainable thoughts in the minds of the brethren. His comment was a wake-up call, attuning me to the economic disparities that blocked Jewish conversion and positioned the Noahide faith as a viable alternative for Judaizing communities in the Global South. At the same time, if the community were to convert somehow, it would mean the end of his leadership. Any members who became Orthodox Jews—the only stream of Judaism they consider valid—would need to resettle in Jewish communities under the direction of an Orthodox rabbi. Jeremiah would no longer be able to lead them, a task that he had told me on multiple occasions was performed in honor of his father, who made him vow to keep the community together after his death.

I left my first fieldwork trip to the Philippines anxious that our relation might be broken and that I might be denied access to Noahides communities upon return. I was pleasantly surprised in 2018 when I reached out again and informed Jeremiah of my plans to return, this time accompanied by my husband. He responded eagerly, explaining that the presence of my husband would help strengthen his followers in Mindanao. Jeremiah had seen pictures of my husband on Facebook. With his beard and kippah, he matched the aesthetic of Orthodox religiosity that the community was used to seeing in YouTube videos of their rabbinic mentors. Jeremiah's religious authority depended, in part, on his ability to procure observant Jews for the community, to prove that his connection with the religious Jewish world extends beyond the internet. My husband's presence as a visibly religious man would have this effect. During our trip, some informants insisted on referring to my husband as "rabbi" despite our attempts to clarify that he did not in fact have any ordination. On more than one occasion, men would grab hold of my husband's *tzitzit* (ritual fringe garments) and quote Zechariah 8:23 to us: "In the end of times the nations will take hold of the Jew by the hem of his robe and say, 'Let us go with you, because we have heard that God is with you!'" As we visited different Noahide communities, my husband was frequently requested to lead Torah study sessions or speak about halachic issues with Noahide men, whose preoccupation with my him often worked strategically to my advantage. While my husband spent his time alone with male members of the community, I was able to meet privately with the women, who could now speak more openly with me about topics like marriage, childbirth, and their relationship to Jewish laws pertaining to women's modesty.

Sarah is young Filipina woman who became a Noahide in her teens following the conversion of several family members. Her Facebook profile lists her name in Hebrew as Sarah Bat Noah (Sarah, a daughter of Noah), an increasingly common practice by Noahides on social media coming from the Philippines and other countries. I sat with Sarah one Friday afternoon while she played a song for me on her iPhone composed in the Bisaya dialect by Jerome Pagalan Suson, a former evangelical singer who released the video in 2015 after publicly declaring himself a Noahide.[20] The explanation beneath the YouTube video described the now yarmulke-wearing Jerome as "a former composer of some Christian/pagan songs" who had "composed his first song for Hashem." (Hashem, literally "the Name," is a common way to refer to God in Orthodox Jewish culture.) As we listened, Sarah translated the song into English for me:

God of Avraham, Isaac, Yaacov.
Your laws are my guide in this life.
You are the one I am longing for.
Your commandments are my guide.
That I will learn from you. I adore you.
God of Avraham, Isaac, Yaacov. Barukh Adonai Elohei Yisrael (Blessed are You
   Lord God of Israel)
I will only pray for you. In the path of our life.
There is no other God except you. You alone Hashem only you.

The song was a declaration of faith from the newly converted. It told a story of one man's awakening to the God of Israel and eternal commandments of the Torah, finally severing the singer's connection with his "idolatrous" Christian past. We sat in front of Sarah's community synagogue, a one room concrete building painted in blue and white. At the time of my fieldwork, this Sarah's Noahide community consisted of about eighty people from fourteen different families living in close proximity to one other. The synagogue, constructed in 2005, is one of eight Noahide synagogues on the Philippines' southernmost island of Mindanao.

A group of ten women, including teens and grandmothers, gathered around Sarah and me as we traded songs. Sarah attempted to teach me Jerome's song in Bisaya, watching with a beaming smile as I broke my teeth on the pronunciation, attempting to replicate the "ng" sound in the dialect. "Teach us Jewish songs!" a grandmother requested. I chose a simple niggun, a wordless Hasidic melody, and taught it to the group in a call-and-response style. Some of the women took out cell phones and recorded me. For the majority of the community, my husband and I were the first Jews whom they had met in person even though Judaism occupies a virtual presence in their daily lives through the circulation of Facebook content and YouTube videos created by rabbis for Noahides.

I was curious about the women's relationship to Noahide media online. This particular Noahide community was rural and lower class but not impoverished. Adults carried cell phones and seemed to be able to access a signal strong enough to stream videos. Since English is taught as a second language in the Philippines, most villagers under the age of forty, especially those with a high school or college education, were fluent enough to easily understand English-language media covering Jewish topics. I asked the women which rabbis they liked to watch when they study Torah online, especially when Jeremiah was not present in the community to lead them in lessons. "We want to be close to the Jewish people. To learn from them, to improve our lives and get close to God. I personally love to watch videos of Rabbi Skobac and Rabbi Tuvia Singer, they help us to debate family and friends and explain why Christianity is false," explained one young mother.

"When I am at the university and I have a good internet connection I love to watch Rabbi Alon Anava, especially his teachings on spirituality and modesty. I am trying to dress more modestly now, like Jewish women. Rabbi Anava explains that women who walk in shorts take on the sin of those who look at her," Sarah explained.

"Anything about reincarnation and redemption . . . or what it will be like in messianic times when the Temple will be built. I love videos from Rabbi Richman and the Temple Institute," explained another woman in her thirties. The women continued to name online personalities, all Orthodox rabbis belonging to a religious-Zionist demographic in Israel.

It is important to clarify which online Jewish worlds the women were in fact accessing when they said that they were "studying Torah online." Noahide media is often thematically connected to the political ideology of Israel's religious right wing and the Third Temple movement. This media is selectively curated and circulated by rabbis and local Noahide leaders who manage Facebook groups and WhatsApp chats for Noahides. Search engines like YouTube also effectively limit exposure to particular Jewish political and theological visions, linking together related videos that channel Noahide seekers into a rather narrow zone of religious authority. The more videos they watch, the more circumscribed their digital Judaism becomes—more firmly entrenched inside the authority of a religious-Zionist worldview, where political events in Israel are interpreted through a biblical prophetic lens.

"You seem to spend a lot of time online learning from Jews in Israel who are very far away, but have you ever thought about visiting the local Jewish community here in Manilla?" I inquired, referring to the small Orthodox Jewish community of approximately seventy families living in the capital city, which does occasionally assist local Filipinos in Jewish conversion. The Orthodox synagogue in Manila, Beth Yaacov, is a Sephardic synagogue that was built in 1962 by Syrian Jewish expatriates who relocated to the Philippines from Brooklyn for their work in the international fabric trade. The synagogue now caters mostly to expatriate Israeli and American Jews along with a small number of Filipino converts, residents of metro Manila who come from upper-middle- and upper-class homes. Occasionally the community flies a *beit din* (Jewish rabbinic court consisting of three rabbis) to the Philippines from Israel in order to conduct an

Orthodox conversion for a cohort of aspiring converts who have completed years of study and preparation. This is an expensive process as the conversion cohort must raise funds and cover airfare expenses for the rabbis.

The women seemed a bit startled by my suggestion. "It is very far, very expensive to go there. And even if we go there, we heard it is difficult to get in," explained one woman. I would later hear stories from Noahides in Manila of their inability to physically enter the synagogue, which stations armed guards at its front gate, carefully regulating who can enter due to security concerns about potential terrorism as well as past experiences of Christian missionaries posing as potential converts. In 2019, I spoke with one of the Jewish ex-pat leaders of the Beth Yaakov community about these concerns and he explained: "We get requests every day from Filipinos expressing interest in the community. But we had bad experiences in the past with missionaries trying to get in the front door so today we are more careful and we ask for recommendations from someone inside the community. We get all kinds of emails. Lots of claims of about Spanish last names and people who believe they are descended from Sephardic Jews who came from Spain."

The history of Judaism in the Philippines dates back to the sixteenth-century Spanish colonization, when crypto-Jewish merchants who had experienced forced conversions to Catholicism and persecution during the Spanish Inquisition sought new lives in the Spanish colonies, where they could covertly practice their faith behind closed doors.[21] The first openly Jewish community was established during the U.S. occupation, when American Jewish expats, primarily servicemen traveling with U.S. military forces and business entrepreneurs, began arriving in the first decades of the twentieth century along with Jewish refugees fleeing the mounting persecution in Europe that led up to the Holocaust. The American Jewish community in the Philippines worked closely with business and political elites in the Philippines to rescue and offer asylum to nearly one thousand European Jewish refugees in Manila, a program cut short by the Japanese invasion of the Philippines (1941–1942), during which the synagogue in Manila was destroyed. Following the arrival of the Syrian Jewish expats from New York, the Orthodox synagogue and community center in Manila was reestablished and remains the primary locus of Jewish life for both Sephardic and Ashkenazi Jews living in the Philippines.

But to enter the synagogue gates, an aspiring convert must have a prior connection to someone in the Jewish community who can vouch for them. I had heard stories about Noahides who previously tried to enter the synagogue seeking conversion assistance but had been turned away at the door for lack of connections. This history may have contributed to Jeremiah's discouraging attitude toward Jewish conversion and led to his forming close ties with internet rabbis promoting Noahidism, who were eager to provide resources for his already sizeable community of followers.

In addition to the synagogue in Manila, at the time of my fieldwork there were three Chabad houses in the Philippines catering primarily to American expats and Israeli tourists. During my visits, I met with Chabad emissaries who were reportedly struggling to keep up with daily requests from Judaizing Filipinos looking for Jewish mentorship. "Every day we get emails. 'Show us light' and stuff like that. They are so hungry for Torah," explained one Chabad emissary. In response to the demand, Chabad houses in the Philippines had implemented weekly or monthly learning sessions for questioning Christians and newly affiliated Noahides, where they introduced attendees to the Seven Laws and permissible forms of Noahide observance and prayer. Notably, the three Chabad houses that I visited during my fieldwork in the Philippines were not affiliated with Chabad International, the American-based organization overseeing and assigning emissaries to specific locations. Rather, they were Israeli representatives affiliated with the messianic wing of the movement located in Israel, which views the deceased Lubavitcher Rebbe as the promised Messiah and await his return. While spreading awareness of the Noahide Laws is critical for the emissaries and they view the growth of Noahidism in the Philippines as fulfilling the prophetic vision of the late Rebbe, they are also careful to maintain strict boundary lines between the Noahides whom they mentor and the Jewish expats and tourists that they serve. According to reports from both Chabad emissaries and Filipino/a informants, Noahides who attended weekly Noahide lectures were discouraged from attending Shabbat services and ritual gatherings specifically for Jews for two reasons; first, according to Chabad, the performance of Jewish-specific mitzvot outside of the Seven Laws is forbidden to non-Jews; and second, there were concerns that such mingling might lead to intimate relationships between Jewish men and local non-Jewish women—forbidden according to Jewish Law. In short, access to Judaism via Chabad houses in the Philippines was limited to Noahide-specific study sessions and gatherings and not meant to be a venue for conversion assistance.

Even if aspiring converts managed to enter and begin attending services in Beth Yaacov, where conversion is technically possible, relocation to Manila to live and convert with the local Orthodox community, which is located in the most expensive part of downtown Manilla, was far beyond the financial means of most Noahides. Orthodox conversion is a lengthy process that requires the potential convert to immerse themselves inside of a Jewish community and live in walking distance of the synagogue for Shabbat observances. In effect, the local socioeconomic barriers to accessing Judaism were further propelling Judaizing Filipinos into a digital Noahide landscape.

During the course of my fieldwork, I met with three families that had managed to navigate both economic and social obstacles and complete an Orthodox conversion through the Beth Yaacov synagogue in Manila. Notably, they were upper-middle to upper-class families and thus able to live in walking distance of

the synagogue for Shabbat and take jobs that did not require working on Saturday. They were also college-educated, giving them advanced English-language
skills that enabled them to easily study Jewish texts translated into English during conversion classes. In addition to social class, gender played a role in accessing Orthodox conversion. I also spoke with four Filipina women who had
married expat American Jewish or Israeli men living in the Philippines. Their
husbands were able to mobilize financial resources and/or communal Jewish
connections to facilitate the conversion process, which is often not straightforward, as aspiring converts may endure long waiting periods before a rabbinic
court will advance their files.

My questions about conversion created an awkward energy in the group. Sarah
and the other women from the community broke away from our circle in order
to begin preparations for the Noahide Seventh-day celebration that would begin
at sundown. A group of young men set up loudspeakers and began to stream
Hebrew music as they organized playlists on their phones for the evening. Noahides from surrounding towns began to arrive and assist with preparations. The
women emerged in new outfits that conformed to Orthodox standards of modesty: skirts or dresses to the knee and sleeves to the elbow, with colorful scarves
to cover their hair. They greeted newly arriving guests not with the Jewish "Shabbat Shalom" but with the phrase "Happy seventh day," meant to clearly reinforce
the boundary between Jews and Noahides. Jeremiah and his rabbinic mentors
from Chabad maintain that it is forbidden for Noahides to observe the Jewish
Shabbat, as it is a commandment that was specifically given to the Jewish people
at Mount Sinai. Because Noahides cannot observe a Jewish Shabbat, the community utilized a special Noahide prayer book designed for their own "seventh
day" of rest, a ritual structure that, interlocuters explained, was intended not to
infringe on Jewish spiritual inheritance.

Just before sunset, a group of young women from the community initiated
the evening ritual by lighting seven candles representing the Seven Laws of
Noah. The candle lighting was followed by the song "Woman of Valor" (Eshet
Hayil) that is also sung on Friday nights at the Jewish Shabbat table. This was
one of the Jewish rituals that Noahides *were* allowed to perform on their seventh
day, community members explained, as it was not a commandment given to the
Jewish people under Mosaic Law. "Woman of Valor" is a poem of praise that
comes from the Book of Proverbs (31:10–31) and is traditionally sung by Jewish
men to show appreciation for the mother of the family and her domestic labor
performed during the week. During the Friday night meals that I observed in the
Philippines, a recorded Hebrew version of the song was played through speakers
attached to a phone. As the song played, Noahide families gathered around their
mothers and embraced them. The upbeat table song that Jewish families sing on
Friday nights was transformed into a devout prayer and climactic moment of the
Noahide seventh-day ritual. On Saturday morning, the seventh-day ritual con-

tinued with communal worship in the synagogue. Noahides on different islands typically gather in their local synagogues and collectively recite selected psalms from their Noahide prayer book before tuning into a Facebook livestream sermon delivered by preacher leaders like Jeremiah.

While an organized ritual life had clearly been established within Noahide communities, my interlocuters were adamant that Noahide was *not* a religion. "It is more of a lifestyle than a religion . . . or maybe like a status," mused one mother from the community. "It is how Judaism and the Torah want a Gentile to live, but that is totally different from a *religion*," her husband added. These comments reflect the ideological influence of rabbinic mentors who understand Noahide Laws as a universal form of divine "natural law" that supersedes all "manmade religions." Rabbinic informants likewise disavowed comparisons of the Noahide movement to a religion (this would imply that they are guilty of violating Jewish Law, which forbids the creation of a new religion). Noahide, I was told repeatedly, was simply a "legal status" for the "righteous Gentile."

I spoke with a Chabad emissary who worked with the Noahide community in the Philippines. During our interview in 2018, he acknowledged the Noahide community's desire for ritual guidance but still insisted that Noahide was *not a religion* but rather a "way of life" that does not actually require any ritual innovation. If the Noahides who attended his Torah classes chose to adopt rituals, he explained, that was purely voluntary and reflected a natural human need: "Being a Noahide doesn't demand ritualistic patterns but we also cannot deny them of human patterns. For instance, a baby is born. You celebrate it. A boy reaches a certain age, you celebrate that. Marriage, you celebrate that." But these "voluntary" Noahide rituals were fundamentally different from the Jewish *commandments* that require Jewish daily worship and holiday observances. The rabbi elaborated, "In Judaism [ritual] doesn't come to fulfill a need. It's a commandment from God. With Noahides there aren't any commandments that will tell you: On Friday August 25th you do a certain thing. There isn't something like that, so if there are any ritualistic patterns to that way of life it would be voluntary, to fulfill a certain need." According to his theological framework, Noahides follow natural and logical human needs and Jews follow divine illogical commandments. He emphasized the idea that Jews and Noahides had two distinct roles to play and that each would be judged by God according to how they had performed their given mission: "Each person has his own responsibility. That must be made clear to them [Noahides], first of all so they don't feel inferior, and second so they don't look for ways to express and resemble something else. Even a Jew who comes to sacrifice before the Temple and wants to be as close as possible [to the holy of holies] . . . even he must give the sacrifice to the Cohen [Temple Priest], and the Cohen will sacrifice." Noahide is to Jew as Jew is to Temple Priest. I had heard this refrain before during my interviews in Israel with Third Temple activists. Everyone had a place and a role to play in the divine order, and this order was critical for the coming messianic era when a Jewish priesthood would be revived, the Temple would be rebuilt, and the Gentile world would recognize their "true identity" as Noahides.

But the question remained, why would anyone want to join a religion where they are told they are "dust"? I came back to this line in my fieldnotes for months. What exactly did Judaizing Christians in the Philippines gain by adopting a Noahide identity? On a practical level, it was clear from my interviews that Noahidism had become a viable alternative when Orthodox Jewish conversion was out of reach. But this alone could not account for the success of Noahide preachers in bringing thousands of individuals out of Christianity, and the general pride and contentment most interlocuters reported toward their Noahide identity. Joining the Noahide movement had given my informants a profoundly meaningful identity and a biblical inheritance. Noahidism had become a spiritual container, one imbued with Orthodox Jewish legitimacy, that could hold them after they fell out of Christianity. Noahidism provided a home after the beliefs they had been raised with (e.g., the trinity and the divinity of Jesus) had been overturned as they drew closer to the Hebrew roots of their faith. Being Noahide meant becoming a transnational "Temple builder" and working in partnership with Israel toward the fulfillment of messianic prophecies. In other words, Noahide identity added metahistoric and eschatological meaning to my informants' lives, operating, I argue, in a manner analogous to previously documented cases of "lost tribe" identities. As previous research has demonstrated, lost tribe claims have flourished because they serve a variety of spiritual and political needs in postcolonial contexts, specifically as communities seek to liberate themselves from legacies of Christian colonialism.[22] Noahidism also serves spiritual and political needs and moreover, like lost tribe claims, has gained traction through the reactivation of biblical-racial theories, whereby biblical categories (e.g., the Children of Noah and the Children of Israel) are used to classify humanity.

NOAHIDISM AS "LOST TRIBE" ANALOGUE

In circulation since antiquity, the myth of the Lost Tribes refers to the ten Israelite tribes of the Northern Kingdom who were sent into exile in the eighth century during the Assyrian conquest. According to Jewish prophecies in the books of Isaiah, Jeremiah, and Ezekiel, the ten tribes will be gathered again in the Land of Israel along with Jewish exiles (descendants of two tribes of the Southern Kingdom of Judea) following the advent of messianic times. Mentioned only twice in the Hebrew Bible in the Book of Kings, the Lost Tribes took on a greater significance in the Jewish postbiblical literature where, Zvi Ben-Dor Benite suggests, they served as a historical precedent and theological resource for understanding the "lost condition" of Jewish life in diaspora following the destruction of the Second Temple.[23] He notes that Josephus attested to the existence of an "immense multitude" of Lost Tribes waiting somewhere beyond the Euphrates, the literal end of the world according to Greco-Roman cartography of the time.[24] In Jewish and Christian sources, the tribes were often described as superhuman, imagined, Benite writes, "at the edges of the earth or beyond its boundaries . . . associated with the end of time, the end of the world."[25] Sought after for centuries by explorers, missionaries, anthropologists, politicians, and more recently geneticists, they have been "located" on nearly every continent.

Christopher Columbus, for example, famously claimed to have discovered the lost tribes in the Americas, using lost tribe theory to correlate his geographical discoveries with biblical history and imbue his missions with eschatological meaning.[26] The messianic motivations driving lost tribe discoveries were later conjoined with the political goals of modern nation-states, most prominently in the histories of Britain, the United States, and Israel. Identifying colonial subjects as "lost tribes" imbued British imperial expansion with salvific prophecy-fulfilling implications and set the stage for twentieth-century British interests in restoring the Jews to the Holy Land that culminated in the Balfour Declaration of 1917.

Beyond the specifically eschatological function, lost tribe mythology, much like the Hamitic Hypothesis of the nineteenth century (explained in the introduction), enabled the Western world to make sense of difference and develop racial categories during the colonial encounter. Edith Bruder, in her study of lost tribe communities in Africa, writes, "The existence of the Lost Tribes in an unknown location represented a tool that provided the means to qualify and name both the incomprehensible and the fearsome . . . from Africa to America, it was a critical element in the construction of the biological and cultural past for countless people."[27] Lost tribe theories were used to write histories for the colonized in accordance with a biblical metahistory of humanity, histories that also effectively categorized one's relative degrees of whiteness and civilization. Lost tribe narratives were later internalized in the postcolonial era and served as reracializing founding mythologies for communities across the Global South.

The Bnei Ephraim, for example, a community of Madiga untouchables in Andhra Pradesh, claim to belong to one of the lost ten tribes of Israel and wish to "repatriate" to Israel.[28] According to Yulia Egorova and Shahid Perwez, who examined the Bnei Ephraim case, the lost tribe narrative became a form of "Jewish liberation theology" that elevated the status of the community.[29] The exclusivity of Jewish identity offered this untouchable community a rooted and sacred history, a Jewish story of suffering and redemption that the authors claim "mirrored their own condition of discrimination."[30] In another example, the Lemba, a South African ethnic group, were identified as a possible "lost tribe" by nineteenth- and early twentieth-century missionaries who noted that their food taboos, ritual slaughter, and circumcision practices resembled Semitic practices—connections that were subsequently incorporated into the Lemba's own autoethnography.

Lemba claims to Israelite descent were later strengthened and gained international attention in the 1990s when a DNA study revealed Y-chromosome connections to a Jewish population outside of Africa.[31] As Noah Tamarkin argued in his recent ethnography documenting the "genetic afterlives" of the Lemba DNA research, the use of scientific epistemologies to validate and privilege the Lemba's Jewish ancestry over other genetic ancestors as well as the normative definitions of Jewishness imposed by scholars and Jewish institutions coming from the Global North are often at odds with the Lemba's more polymorphic self-understanding as Black Jews. The Lemba view themselves as part of global Jewry but also as ethnically distinct and indigenous to South Africa.[32]

In another prominent international case, the Bnei Menashe, an ethnic group from northeastern India, claimed to belong to the biblical tribe of Menashe.[33] The community was officially recognized as a "lost tribe" by the State of Israel in 2005 and relocated to religious settlements, where they play an important political and demographic role for the state by increasing the Jewish population in the West Bank. To date, seven thousand Bnei Menashe have converted to Orthodox Judaism and immigrated to Israel with the support of Shavei Israel, a religious-Zionist NGO that supports lost tribe repatriation. As the case of the Bnei Menashe demonstrates, full access to Judaism and assistance from the State of Israel is possible, *if* one can stake their claims in a story of Jewish biological descent that serves state interests. A "lost tribe" narrative becomes a desirable form of political currency for Israel, one that allows the state to further its own territorial goals, which are legitimized through a performance of indigenous Israelite return to the land. As Yulia Egorova has argued in her analysis of the Bnei Menashe case, by embracing Orthodox Judaism and reinforcing the political agenda of the Israeli state, the Bnei Menashe were able to successfully "override their racial otherness" and in turn have gained recognition and absorption into the Jewish majority in Israel.[34] In other words, Jewish Orthopraxis becomes a conduit for national inclusion in Israel when religious conversion is directed toward the biopolitical goal of maintaining a Jewish majority.[35] The case of the Bnei Menashe reveals the intricate interplay of race and religion as postcolonial communities adopt Jewish practices, claim Jewish identities, and/or seek official conversion and recognition from the State of Israel.

Lost tribe identity, however, has its limits. Not *every* Judaizing community in the Global South can claim to be a lost tribe. This is where the Noahide movement becomes most salient, as it functions in an analogous way to lost tribe claims, both in its theological appeal to questioning Christians in postcolonial contexts and in the way that it still supports the political, territorial, and messianic goals of religious Zionism. The Noahide movement effectively extends a form of lost tribe identity to the entire world: now anyone who rediscovers their "lost" Gentile covenant and biblical identity might be reinscribed into Jewish metahistory as the Children of Noah. Like lost tribe narratives, the Noahide faith writes an ethnohistory for postcolonial communities, rescripting their past in relationship to the biblical forefather Noah and his covenant with God in order to provide a more certain future, often in the face of a pervasive lack of social mobility. Diego, who had spent years separated from his family while working overseas (an economic necessity for 11 percent of the population in the Philippines), commented, "I am Noahide because I want to know how to live better. . . . How should I provide for my children and treat my wife? Sometimes I do not have enough money for bread. I want to know the Jewish answers. I want to know the wisdom of the rabbis. I want to know my purpose."

The embrace of Jewish ethnohistory by diverse communities across the Global South has been explained by some researchers as a response to a widespread postcolonial condition in which indigenous religious traditions have weakened and there is an experience of fractured or weakened identity.[36] Similar dynamics are noted in the testimonies and ethnographies of "crypto-Jews," Latinos claiming to be the descendants of Sephardic Jews who were forced to convert to Catholicism during the Spanish Inquisition. Many Sephardic converts came to settle in the Caribbean and Latin American in the fifteenth century, continuing to practice Jewish rituals in secret, such as the lighting of Shabbat candles on Friday nights, following Jewish food taboos, and performing kosher animal slaughter.[37] Since the 1970s, there has been a growing movement of Latinos claiming crypto-Jewish status based on Inquisition records that contain family names, deathbed confessions of Jewish ancestry by grandparents, and traces of Jewish rituals still performed by family members. Some historians and sociologists have cast doubt on the authenticity of crypto-Jewish claims, arguing that the movement is a result of "ethnic self-hatred" in Latino communities or by pointing to genetic tests to contest claims based on oral family traditions.[38] As Jonathan Freedman reminds us, because crypto-Jewish identity was, by necessity, transmitted orally and in secret (for fear of persecution), it cannot be verified using institutional or congregational records and thus remains "fundamentally unverifiable" and "epistemologically unstable."[39] The question of conclusive evidence aside, what is striking is that narratives of Jewish descent have taken hold across the Spanish postcolonies because they provide profound cultural and spiritual meaning in a mestizo milieu. Claiming Jewish descent has the ability to add metahistoric and eschatological meaning to one's sense of alterity.

The Noahide movement can be situated within this broader transnational landscape of postcolonial Judaizing trends. Like contemporary lost tribe and crypto-Jewish claims, embracing descent from Noah and a Noahide identity allowed my informants in the Philippines to acquire dignity and elevate their own status. While some Noahides may see themselves as inferior to Jews, their Noahide status felt spiritually elevated relative to their "idolatrous" Christian neighbors. Being Noahide meant gaining acceptance and validation as a "righteous Gentile" by rabbinic authorities, access to holiness and salvation through a covenantal

relationship with God enshrined in the Torah (the Seven Laws of Noah), an intimate (albeit virtual) relationship to the State of Israel, and increased access to
forms of Jewish wisdom and mystical knowledge (Kabbalah) valorized in my
informants' former churches. Maintaining relationships with religious Jews, in
particular male Orthodox rabbis, provided significant spiritual and social capital
for Noahide preacher-leaders and arguably even endows economic capital on
Noahides who end up assisting rabbis or working for Noahide organizations. Perhaps most profoundly, being Noahide meant playing an active role in shaping the
future of Israel, in the realization of biblical prophecies and the anticipated conclusion of Zionism (i.e., Temple rebuilding and the initiation of a messianic era).

THE LOOMING CONVERSION QUESTION

According to most of my informants, Noahide was "just a lifestyle" and "not a
religion." It was a part of Judaism, but Noahides were not Jews and shouldn't try
to become ones. Informants would repeat these lines, but I wondered if they
were they really confident in the logic. How did Filipino Noahides explain *what*
they were to neighbors and friends? How did Noahide children explain their
faith to teachers at school when they refused to participate in Christian holidays?
"I usually just say Adventist," explained one grandmother. "It is too hard to
explain Noahide. When people hear that they think Noa-*hide*, like something
hidden like a cult. At least when I say Adventist they know not to serve me pork."
Filipino Noahides had left Christianity, adopted Jewish lifestyles in terms of
kosher food, clothing, and prayer, and observed Noahide versions of Jewish holidays, but they were not Jews. While the majority of my informants stated that
they were happy to be Noahides, to live a Jew-ish life but not convert, I did
encounter dissenting voices along the way. For some, embracing a Noahide lifestyle and identity was not a final destination but rather a waystation on the road
to Jewish conversion and full inclusion in the ethnonational body of Israel, an
initial step toward becoming one of the "Children of Israel."

During my time in the Philippines, some Noahides confided that the new
rituals they had been given seemed like watered-down versions of the "real Judaism" they longed to access. Eli and Rebecca, a newly married couple in their
twenties, explained their decision to break away from the Noahide movement .
When I met with them in 2019, they were pursuing conversion with the Orthodox Jewish community in Manila. They acknowledged that this move was
enabled by the fact that they came from middle-class backgrounds and were able
to afford to live within walking distance of the Beth Yaacov synagogue. Rebecca
explained, "I first learned about Noahides online and then I started going to
Chabad classes [for Noahides], but studying the Seven Laws just felt too limiting.
The whole focus was on what we could and could not do in Judaism," explained
Rebecca. Eli added,

I also ended up at Chabad for a while because my first initial attempt to enter Beth Yaacov did not go well. I had recently left the Messianic church, and I was still wearing the messianic style kippah and tzitzit so when one member saw me he called me an "idolator" and said I was still worshipping Jesus . . . but eventually I just couldn't live with the uncertainty that is Noahide. I want to be certain that my children will be Jews, with a clear path and inheritance. But everything for Noahides is pure speculation. Everything is in flux and the future is unknown.

At the time of our interview, the couple was regularly attending services and classes at Beth Yaacov and in the process of saving money to travel abroad in order to complete their conversion in front of a rabbinic court. In the future, the couple hopes to make *aliyah* (immigrate) to Israel and raise their children there.

Reyna, a Filipina woman in her forties, lamented to me that Noahide identity was beginning to feel like a "glass ceiling," like Noahides were "purposely being held down" and discouraged from Jewish conversion: "Some of us are saying we want more. We are asking: why can't we be Jews? But they [rabbis] are saying only seven commandments, it is enough for you." According to Reyna, most Noahides in the Philippines would prefer to convert if they had the ability. Reyna had previously traveled to Israel on a tourist visa with the intention of staying and completing an Orthodox conversion. However, after arriving in Israel, Reyna's petition for a visa extension for the purpose of pursuing conversion through the Israeli rabbinate was denied, and she returned home to the Philippines disheartened. Conversion candidates coming to Israel from developing countries are frequently denied visa extensions for the purpose of conversion for fear that they are exploiting conversion to gain access to citizenship and economic benefits.[40] Reyna, having experienced weekly Shabbat observances while living in Jerusalem, explained that she no longer felt fulfilled by Noahide rituals: "I do not know where I belong now, and I am stuck. I cannot afford to move to Manila to convert, but I do not feel like a Noahide. My soul is crying, longing to be Jewish, to keep Shabbat . . . sometimes I wonder . . . if they went and converted the Bnei Menashe in India and brought them to Israel, why can't they do the same for us?"

At the end of my second visit to the Philippines, I decided to track down a breakaway community that was rumored to be "really practicing Judaism" even though they had not officially completed a conversion process and did not have an overseeing rabbi. Jeremiah spoke disapprovingly of the group and claimed they were "stealing the Torah and keeping Shabbat like Jews," an act that is considered a violation of Jewish Law by some rabbinic mentors and Noahide leaders. I contacted the breakaway community's leader, Yisrael Ben Chaim (a chosen Hebrew name), and we arranged a meeting at his synagogue in Mindanao. The extension of my research to the breakaway community would prove to be my final misstep with Jeremiah, who cut off communication with me following my visit to the group. I could only speculate on his reasons since he did not respond to any of my messages after the incident. One community member, a Noahide woman who had been part of the Sacred Name Believers since childhood and knew Jeremiah well, offered some insight: "By going there as a Jew, it was like you were giving them a stamp of approval." This approval flew in the face of teachings that condemned groups that overstepped Noahide ritual boundaries and began practicing Orthodox Judaism. My visit to the community threatened to reignite interest in the taboo topic of Jewish conversion.

The breakaway community, I came to find out, not only was practicing Orthodox Judaism but also had justified their departure from the Noahide community and their adoption of Orthodox Jewish practices by leveling up their place within Jewish ethnohistory. They were not Noahides but crypto-Jews claiming descent from the Jewish converts who arrived in the Philippines with the Spanish Empire, and they were ready to return to the faith of their ancestors.

I arrived on a Sunday morning as the community was setting up for morning prayers. As soon as I entered the synagogue, I was greeted by twenty men dressed according to Ultra-Orthodox Jewish fashion with black suits, white button-down shirts, fedora-style hats, beards, and *peyes* (Hasidic style side curls). The women were also dressed according to Ultra-Orthodox modesty standards with long skirts, shirts sleeves to the elbow, and scarves covering their hair. Using an Orthodox prayer book, the community recited Shacharit, the morning prayer service, in transliterated Hebrew using melodies that they had learned from videos online. They prayed facing Jerusalem, with Yisrael leading the men in the front and the women standing behind in rows. After morning prayers concluded, I sat down with Yisrael as he recounted his spiritual journey.

Yisrael's advanced mastery of English enabled him to study English-language translations and explanations of Jewish scriptural and rabbinic sources on his own, bypassing the mediation and translation typically provided by Noahide preacher-leaders like Jeremiah to their often less fluent congregations. I was impressed by Yisrael's self-taught knowledge of Jewish philosophy, halacha, and mysticism. He had grown up in a devout Catholic home and dated the beginning of his spiritual exploration to his philosophy major in college. In 2008, Yisrael joined a Christian Kabbalah group and became involved with a Messianic church, but left when he discovered that the group was stealing money from worshippers, promising to reveal the "secret name of God" in exchange for payments. Distrustful of Messianic churches demanding money for salvation and still longing for Torah knowledge, he began researching Jewish sources online, watching YouTube lectures by rabbis targeting questioning Christians and prospective Noahides. Yisrael recounted a climactic moment in his spiritual research when, in 2010, he fasted for seven days and spoke with God: "I said, 'Who are you! Reveal yourself! We want to worship you the way Israel worships you.'"

During this period of intense prayer and research, Yisrael gathered together members from his former "Kabbalah cult," as he now calls it, and together they formed a new community, one dedicated to the study of Torah and Jewish customs, a decision that led to the severance of ties with his Catholic family who could not accept his decision to leave Christianity and deny the divinity of Jesus. From 2012 to 2013, Yisrael identified as a Noahide, but after attending a Noahide convention in the Philippines he felt that studying the Seven Laws was too limiting. After working abroad in Saudi Arabia, he was able to return to the Philippines and initiate his own synagogue, using money that he saved to print Orthodox Jewish prayer books from PDFs online and to purchase "Jewish garb," including the suits and black hats that his community wears.

Today, Yisrael has about thirty people regularly attending Shabbat services and weekly classes in his home/synagogue, where he also translates and transmits what he has learned on his own also utilizing Facebook livestreaming to reach followers who cannot attend in person. His followers are committed to upholding an Ultra-Orthodox Jewish lifestyle under his guidance. He hopes that his community will eventually convert but feels anxious about contacting rabbis and asking for help for fear they will "try to keep him a Noahide." "We want to be Jews. We want to convert. At the moment we do not have a rabbi so we are just doing the best we can to study, to learn and practice as much as we can. And we pray that someone will help us. We know that even if we cannot be converted in this lifetime what we are doing is a *tikkun* for the soul and maybe the conversion will be for the next life," he explained to me.

Yisrael was well aware that it would be difficult to find a sponsoring rabbi or Orthodox Jewish organization willing to convert the community. Still, he was determined to continue studying and adopting Jewish practices using internet resources to the best of his ability. Even if the community was unable to convert, the act of striving for correct halachic observe was in his mind a tikkun, an act of repairing the soul and a worthy endeavor, one that elevates the soul to a higher level of holiness in preparation for the next life. We discussed the Kabbalistic concepts of tikkun (rectification) and *gilgul* (reincarnation) that had shaped his understanding of conversion, which he used to further explain his departure from the Noahide community. He emphasized the idea that potential converts exist because they have Jewish souls reincarnated into non-Jewish bodies. Yisrael believes that his own ancestors were Spanish conversos, Sephardic Jews forcibly converted to Christianity during the Spanish Inquisition who fled to the Spanish colonies including the Philippines, where they continued to practice a form of crypto-Judaism in secret. His intense longing for Jewish conversion, Yisrael believes, is a reflection of his soul's desire to return to its Jewish source, an individual act of reparation that contributes to a greater cosmic tikkun leading up to messianic times.

I remained in contact with Yisrael after my departure from the Philippines, and a few months later he informed me that he had reached out to Shavei Israel, the Israeli NGO that had played a key role in the conversion and immigration of the Bnei Menashe from India to Israel. Shavei Israel continues to work with Latin American communities claiming descent from Spanish conversos, referred to alternatively as the Bnei Anusim or Marranos, through its Spanish-language Conversion and Return Institute based in Jerusalem (a program approved by the Chief Rabbinate of Israel).

In his letter to Shavei Israel, which he shared with me, Yisrael introduced himself as the descendent of Sephardic Jews and explained that other members of his community also claimed this heritage:

> We know that the majority, if not all, of our forefathers were of Jewish Sephardic roots. Our grandfathers were mestizos (half Spanish, half Filipino), and their surnames are well to be found in the Sephardic surnames. . . . From the depth of our souls—we are Jewish. Outside appearances hide our true self, aided by generations of *galut* [exile] from those first Jewish conversos and marranos who escaped Spain and death. . . . Our ancestors cheated death by becoming Marranos and Jewish Conversos, and b'ezrat Hashem [God Willing]—through the light of Torah Kedusha [holy Torah] and Am Yisrael [the People of Israel], we rediscover who we are.

In the letter, he goes on to describe thirteen additional points of evidence for the community's hidden Jewish ancestry, highlighting the remnants of Jewish rituals still practiced by parents and grandparents, including mikveh immersion, Friday afternoon candle lighting, and ritual handwashing upon waking in the morning.

To date, there is extremely limited historical research on the Sephardic conversos who fled the Inquisition and resettled in the Philippines as Spanish colonizers; that which exists was largely authored in the first decades of the twentieth century when the American occupation of the Philippines ignited some interest in the topic among American historians.[41] The question of scant empirical evidence aside, I am not concerned with verifying Yisrael's claims to Jewish descent. Rather, for the purposes of this account, I am interested only in their narrative power, how theories of converso heritage add metahistoric and eschatological meaning to my interlocuters' lives.

Yisrael's community is one example of a former Noahide community that has "leveled up" their Noahide status and demanded further recognition and inclusion into the sacred history of Israel and covenantal relationship with God. In his letter to Shavei Israel, Yisrael draws on genealogical descent claims to reposition the group from the category of "Children of Noah" to "Children of Israel." The question of spiritual-racial identity that is at stake is further highlighted in the letter when Yisrael references the struggles of his community to reclaim their Jewish ancestry in the Philippines: "brothers of the same faith . . . few and scattered across the Philippines, who have managed to reclaim their Judaism in this very low and dark place, in the Far East, stuck in the *klipot*." In addition to utilizing the Kabbalistic concept of *klipot*, which refers to impure forces in the world that conceal holiness, Yisrael describes the position of his community in the Philippines in such a way that feels reminiscent of colonial tropes of the Far East as lowly, degenerate, and unenlightened. Being Jewish is a status that distinguishes his community in both religious and racialized terms. Jewishness confers a spiritual superiority that differentiates the community from "idolatrous" or "pagan" Christian neighbors. It also reinscribes them inside of the Jewish ethnonation, represented by the State of Israel and authenticated by notions of blood-based Jewish kinship.

The letter underscores the co-constitutive nature of race and religion as reracialization occurs through modes of religionization (the adoption of Orthodox Judaism in this case). Former Noahide communities like this one may now be counted among the many Judaizing communities worldwide that are challenging our conceptions of race and ethnonational boundaries in the digital age through identity projects that draw variously upon religious, mythological, genealogical, and genetic science research. Similar to Yisrael's community, I encountered other "breakaway" groups during the course of my research on global Noahidism. In Mexico, for example, former Noahides families, who had broken away from large Noahide congregations, had similarly begun practicing Orthodox Judaism together in small groups even if they had not yet secured a pathway to official conversion. Some of these families in Mexico were also claiming Sephardic heritage and basing these claims variously on Sephardic last names, oral family traditions, and/or the results of genetic testing kits performed at home.

As this account has illustrated, postcolonial projects of spiritual-racial reinvention are often driven by messianic political theologies that travel through digital mediums. This is evident in particular in the conclusion of Yisrael's letter, where he emphasizes that immigration to Israel, with the aim of participating in a messianic process and the eventual building of the Third Temple, is his group's end goal and driving motivation: "We cannot be fully Jewish outside the land of Israel, and above all we have to obey the mitzvah to possess and dwell in the land of Israel. . . . Please bring us back home. . . . We have succeeded in returning and keeping to our Jewish roots and traditions. As one people we will succeed in rebuilding Jerusalem, gathering our other lost brothers, in rebuilding the Third Temple and we will welcome our righteous Messiah."

At the completion of my research, Yisrael was still waiting for a response from Shavei Israel regarding his community's request for conversion and immigration assistance. Contestations over Jewishness—specifically, who can be recognized by Jewish institutions and rendered eligible for immigration to Israel under the Right of Return law—are shaped by racial and religious ideologies that influence forms of gatekeeping by political and religious actors in Israel who have the power to legitimate conversions and the identity claims of Judaizing communities across the Global South. It remains to be seen whether Yisrael's community and their claims to Sephardic ancestry will be legible and deemed compatible with the interests of Israeli state actors who desire non-Jewish allyship but not necessarily expansive access to Orthodox Jewish conversion in the Global South.

CONCLUSION

The Children of Israel, the Children of Noah, and the "End of Judaism"?

"This is the end of Judaism," Rabbi Hoffman told me as he guided me through an archaeological site outside of a West Bank settlement where, he explained, ancient Israelites once prepared olive oil for use in the Second Temple. Hoffman is an Orthodox rabbi based in Israel and a rabbinic mentor for growing Noahide communities around the world. He asked me about my recent trip to meet with Noahides in the Philippines. I told him about the community's wariness toward acting "too Jewish" and the new, specifically Noahide rituals the community had developed in collaboration with rabbinic mentors from Chabad. "I personally do not care if Noahides take on Jewish customs and rituals because we are finished with Judaism. We are trading this religion of exile for our true Israelite identity. Those rabbis who say that Noahides cannot act like Jews just haven't realized this yet, that the exile is over," Hoffman explained, alluding to his religious Zionist colleagues' more permissive stance compared to Chabad, one that allows for Noahide participation in a fuller range of Jewish ritual practices including holidays and circumcision.

According to Rabbi Hoffman, Judaism was outdated, equated with Jewish exile and the absence of national life—a condition that Rabbi Oury Cherki, another prominent Noahide mentor from the religious Zionist camp, likens to physical death. In one online article intended for Noahide audiences visiting the website of his organization Brit Olam, Cherki describes Jewish life in diaspora from the second century through the twentieth as a ghostly "disembodied existence" of the "Jewish spirit beyond the grave," characterized by Jewish intellectual production but lacking in any of the meaningful material/political achievements that define influential nations. Cherki writes, "For Jews in exile, Jewish life is reduced to culture alone. Like a disembodied spirit, lacking life and breath, it is taken up entirely by its own ideas and humors. It is a life that cannot be called real."[1] From his perspective, the creation of the State of Israel brought about the end of a physically defunct and lifeless Judaism by "resurrecting the Jewish national body from the dead" and transforming spiritualized (dead) Judaism into materialized, resurrected Israelitism. Cherki's emphasis on the reincarnation of national and individual bodies as the corporeal substrates for an imagined future messianic order further reveals how the very presence of *physical bodies*, especially in expanding West Bank settlements, serves as empirical evidence of divine sanction for a political project of territorial control.

As we toured the ruins, Rabbi Hoffman painted a picture of Israelite life during the time of the Second Temple: "They took the oil straight from here to the Temple in Jerusalem where it was used for sacrifices and candle-lighting. It is possible that the oil used in the miracle of Channukah was made here because they found a very old can of oil." After he showed me a cave containing the ancient olive presses, we paused on the edge of a hilltop, watching as the sun set over the Palestinian city of Ramallah. "For centuries the Hebrew nation has been running from place to place and now most of the nation has returned so the first part of the prophecy has been fulfilled," he continued. "And the rest will be fulfilled too. But I am not sure how God is going to organize it because those people [Palestinians] are not going to vanish in one day, but for sure this is going to be a full homeland of the Hebrew Nation. . . . Peace will only come when the Palestinians accept to be Noahides. Then everyone will be equal and everything will be in its place."

A homeland of the Hebrew nation. The end of Judaism. Noahides. Everything in its place. The rabbi was again alluding to the post-Zionist theocratic vision shared by Jewish Third Temple activists and many Noahides—to the "final stage of Zionism" articulated by Brit Olam founder Rabbi Cherki.[2] In this vision, the Noahide movement extends the messianic processes initiated in Israel with the creation of the state and Judaization of the land outward to all of humanity as non-Jews embrace their Gentile covenant within the Torah and identify as the Children of Noah. For Cherki, the activation and contemporary embodiment of Israelite and Noahide subjectivities are codependent. Just as Noahides needed Jewish ethnotheocracy in Israel to transform the concept of Bnei Noah from a textual philosophical/legal construct to a living spiritual community, Jews needed Noahides in order to finally exit exilic Judaism, to be fully reincarnated in the land as a Hebrew nation. Taken together, the renewal of animal sacrifices by Temple priests in training, pilgrimage to the Temple Mount in a state of bodily purity, Noahides declaring their faith in front of a virtual *beit din* (rabbinic court) on Zoom, territorial conquest and the expansion of Jewish settlements in the West Bank constitute a matrix of theological, material, and embodied practices that participate in Jewish indigeneity making in Israel and the imagined conclusion of Zionism.[3]

To examine Jewish messianism ethnographically, I discovered, was to traverse a landscape of mutually reinforcing ideological and material strategies in

Israel that enable Jewish ethnonationalism and territorial conquest, strategies ranging from explicitly messianic efforts to secular ethnocratic legal frameworks to the mundane security functions of the Israeli state apparatus. As Lorenzo Veracini reminds us, settler-colonial political projects typically work toward achieving "supersession," whereby the settler attempts to become more native than the local people both morally and epistemically. Becoming part of the land according to imagined biblical-racial categories of being functions as one of the means by which settler colonialism in Israel/Palestine effectively "obscures the conditions of its own production," concealing daily dynamics of exclusionary ethnonationalism and territorial annexation.[4] Within this matrix, the particular kind of "supersession" that theocratic post-Zionism proposes is both territorial *and* theological, a messianism that not only desires Jewish demographic domination over "Greater Israel" but also sees Judaism outside the Land of Israel as obsolete and replaceable.

At the same time, I learned that to study messianic Zionism in the digital age was to acknowledge that the vision of biblical revival Rabbi Hoffman shared with me that day now circulates far beyond the Temple Mount, West Bank settlements, and religious-nationalist institutions in Israel. As images and discourses of the Third Temple travel the world from Texas to the Philippines, passed along through websites, YouTube videos, and Facebook posts, they continue to reorganize theologico-political sentiments, inspiring the emergence of new religious subjectivities, influencing geopolitics and transnational messianic alliances, and shaping the way spiritual communities interpolate political developments by reading them through biblical prophetic lenses and providential national narratives.

On December 6, 2017, in the midst of my research with global Noahide communities, former U.S. president Donald Trump announced that the United States would officially recognize Jerusalem as the capital of Israel and relocate the American embassy from Tel Aviv to Jerusalem. The announcement ignited the production of internet memes declaring Trump a harbinger of the Third Temple who would finally give Israel the green light to commence building plans on the Temple Mount and usher in the messianic era. On Facebook, Temple activists in Israel and Noahides around the world began circulating a photoshopped picture of President Trump next to the future Third Temple superimposed on the Temple Mount.[5] Other internet memes and articles expanded on the prophetic meaning of the embassy move, suggesting that Trump was a *gilgul* (reincarnation) of the Persian king Cyrus the Great sent by God (once again) to complete the rehabilitation of the Hebrew nation in the form of a renewed biblical kingdom.

The ancient King Cyrus is venerated in the Hebrew Bible, credited with freeing Jewish captives from Babylon and helping to rebuild the Second Temple.[6] Trump, like Cyrus, was a non-Jewish (and morally suspect) politician unwittingly chosen to advance God's divine plan for humanity, evidenced by his willingness to recognize Jewish sovereignty over all of Greater Israel including the Temple

Mount.[7] Israeli prime minister Benjamin Netanyahu equated Trump with Cyrus: "In the long sweep of Jewish history there have been a handful of proclamations by non-Jewish leaders on behalf of our people in our land: Cyrus the great, the great Persian King, Lord Balfour, President Harry S. Truman, and President Donald J. Trump,"[8] thus locating Trump within a lineage of non-Jewish political leaders who aided in the national redemption of the Jewish people. For religious Jews, Noahides, and evangelicals abroad these were not sympathetic Gentile allies but instruments of God, selected to help actualize prophecy and move the messianic timeline forward.

Interestingly, the comparison of Trump to Cyrus originated not in Israel but rather with evangelical leaders in the United States. It was evangelical writer Lance Wallnau who first made the comparison in 2016, when Trump was a presidential candidate. While appearing on Pat Robertson's Christian Broadcasting Network, Wallnau argued that Trump had been given a divinely ordained mission to restore Christian America in advance of the messianic era and the Second Coming of Christ, a mission that for many premillennial evangelicals is contingent upon support for the State of Israel and the rebuilding of the Temple.[9] In the 1970s and 1980s, influential American evangelical preachers including Jerry Falwell and John Hagee popularized a "prosperity theology" that emphasized Genesis 12:3 ("I will curse those who curse you"), arguing that America's welfare and its material and spiritual blessings were fundamentally linked to its support for the State of Israel.[10] The migration of the Trump-Cyrus comparison from an American evangelical context to its embrace within religious and right-wing Israeli political circles exemplifies the multidirectional circulation and collaborative transnational construction of political theologies that shape the ways that history is narrated and futures are imagined.

The Trump administration's subsequent involvement in the United Arab Emirates–Israel peace deal was similarly interpreted through a prophetic Third Temple paradigm. On September 15, 2020, Israel and UAE signed a normalization agreement, now referred to as the Abraham Accords, making UAE the third Arab country to formally open diplomatic relations with Israel, a move that was preceded by years of covert military and intelligence cooperation between the counties. As political commentators were quick to point out, language in the normalization agreement suggested that the status quo on the Temple Mount / Haram ash-Sharif might be altered. The plan, which states that "people of every faith should be permitted to pray on the Temple Mount / Haram ash-Sharif," seemed to create an opening for the formal recognition of Jewish prayer on the Temple Mount, violating the status quo agreement with the Waqf that allows Jewish visitation but forbids open prayer. As one commentator remarked, the language transformed the site into a "shared Jewish-Muslim holy site" and set the stage for a physical division of the compound similar to the division of the Tomb of the Patriarchs in Hebron.[11] The subtlety of the wording was not lost on Temple

activists based in Israel and Noahides abroad, who saw the peace deal as herald-
ing a new era of support for Jewish claims to the holy site and a critical stepping
stone toward the rebuilding of the Temple and the completion of the Zionist
project. In celebration of the deal, Facebook posts by Third Temple activists
called on Emiratis and Bahrainis to "come and pray with Jews on the Temple
Mount."

One of my primary objectives in developing this account has been to use ethnographic methods to expand the study of religious Zionism beyond the geographic space of Israel/Palestine. Moreover, in addition to emphasizing geographic
plurality, it was my intention to broaden the scope of who is included in the
anthropology of Jews/Judaism. Only by paying attention to those on the margins of Judaism can we begin to grasp the porous and shapeshifting boundaries
of messianic Zionist landscapes in the digital age. Including non-Jewish Noahides in a study of Jewish messianic activism greatly expanded my field of vision,
enabling me to reconsider the very boundaries of Judaism in the twenty-first
century, as Noahide communities are part of Judaism but do not identify as *Jewish*. At the same time, I note for the reader that many people who identify as
Jewish are excluded from the theological topography of the Third Temple movement that views the Noahides as essential. For my informants in Israel, the inclusion of Noahides in their messianic vision came at the cost of entirely excluding
more liberal and secular Jews whose Jewishness is thus rendered illegitimate for
them. At the end of the day, boundaries are defined by both what you include
and what you exclude.

It is my hope that this account will be useful for ethnographers of religion
who might continue to develop approaches to an "anthropology of political theology": attending to mobile political theologies in conjunction with the material
realities that shape the textured lifeworlds of religious actors and elaborating on
the intersectional raced, classed, and gendered positionalities of messianic actors.
Such an approach resists collapsing messianic actors into homogenous and one-
dimensional "extremist" or "fundamentalist" categories that also obscure their
ideological hybridity.

Producing an anthropology of political theology requires the careful excavation of universalizing messianic political theologies to reveal the localized power
dynamics that make their global proliferation possible. Toward this end, chapter 2 situated the Third Temple movement within broader power dynamics in
Israel: forms of state violence, gendered and intergenerational dynamics, that
remain underexamined in the historical and anthropological literature on religious Zionism in Israel that continues to focus on male rabbinic elites. Through
sacrificial reenactments and Temple Mount pilgrimage tours, increasingly diverse
Jewish participants live in the time of the Third Temple through embodied and
affective experiences, participating in a processes of spiritual-racial reinvention,
of "nativizing" the self and state, reviving an Israelite identity with the aim of

materializing a theocratic post-Zionist future. Chapter 2 also rendered visible some of the modalities through which messianic political theologies collude with state power in Israel. Messianic activism in Israel is not antithetical to liberal Zionism and the biopolitics of the contemporary Israeli state but rather functions as a supportive appendage to them. Third Temple activists, including Temple Mount pilgrimage guides, function as proxy-state actors, hybridizing messianic and liberal ideologies to support expansionist territorial policies and Jewish ethnonational dominance.

What originally began as research focused on biblical revival activists based in Jerusalem grew into a seven-year project tracking the globalization of Third Temple political theology, an endeavor that led me to the Children of Noah movement, a new transnational Judaic faith whose emergence and evolution are narrated throughout chapters 3 and 4. As in my ethnographic work in Israel, applying an anthropology of political theology approach to the study of emerging Noahide communities in multiple national contexts required careful consideration of the ways in which traveling biblical-racial ideologies intersected with localized power dynamics as Noahides, in the process of exiting Hebrew-Roots Christianity, came under the influence of rabbinic mentors primarily based in Israel. Documenting the advent of Noahidism exposed new territories of messianic and missionized religious life, rendering visible those who sit at Judaism's racial and economic margins vying for inclusion in the sacred history of Israel either as the "Children of Noah" reclaiming their "Gentile covenant" within the Torah or as the "Children of Israel" seeking pathways to Orthodox conversion and immigration to Israel. As chapter 4 in particular demonstrates, the fluid geographical boundaries of the internet have extended Orthodox rabbinic authority and disseminated religious Zionist ideologies most profoundly in places where locals have limited access to Jewish individuals or institutions on the ground.

In the hope that I have not painted an overly deterministic or unidirectional picture of Noahide proselytizing by Orthodox Jewish rabbis, I remind the reader that the Noahide faith is also taken up, negotiated, and altered from the perspective of communities on the ground coming out of an often decades-long journey of theological investigation and religious shifting. Even as digital channels extend forms of rabbinic authority to new locales, the Noahide faith might eventually upend barriers to Jewish conversion in the Global South as Noahides speak back to rabbinic centers of power and exert their own influence on the Orthodox Jewish world.

In addition to my fieldwork in the Philippines presented in chapter 4, comparative research that I conducted with Noahide communities in Latin America, for example, revealed similar frustrations with Noahidism and growing demands for conversion assistance. In 2019, I conducted fieldwork in Mexico, where Noahide communities can now be found in at least twenty different cities and towns and number around two thousand members nationally. Like Noahide groups in the Philippines, most of these communities were under the direction of former evangelical preachers turned Noahides who were themselves receiving remote mentorship and resources from Israel-based rabbis and/or local Chabad houses. During our conversations, Mexican Noahides emphasized what they saw as underlying issues of racial and economic discrimination that had prevented them from attaining Orthodox conversion locally and, by extension, had contributed to the rapid growth of Noahidism across Latin America since 2015.

I note for the reader that Jewish conversion is a contested topic in Mexico and across Latin America due to the far-reaching impact of the Syrian Jewish *takanah* (edict) that not only bans conversion but denies converts and their children membership in the Jewish community. First issued in 1935 by the Syrian Jewish community in Argentina with the aim of preventing assimilation and intermarriage, the edict was subsequently adopted by prominent Syrian Jewish communities based in New York and Mexico and reaffirmed again in 1946, 1972, and 1984.[12] The edict, which is upheld to this day by Syrian Jews and affiliated Sephardic communities across Latin America, not only bans conversion but also denies converts and their children membership in the Orthodox Jewish community. If they wish to convert, Latin American Noahides typically must either relocate to the United States or complete an Orthodox conversion program online with a rabbi based in Israel. The online option is an expensive route (around seventy dollars per month per person for a year plus the cost of flying in a rabbinic court from Israel to carry out the conversion) and is one that is entirely out of reach for the economically disadvantaged. Even if Mexican Noahides do manage to convert, most cannot afford to live inside of the Jewish community in Mexico City to be within walking distance of a synagogue on Shabbat. Reminiscent of the Jewish ex-pat community in Manila, the majority of Orthodox Jewish institutions in Mexico happen to be located in some of the most expensive and exclusive neighborhoods of the capital city.

Financial barriers aside, Noahides from Mexico City who were actively searching for conversion assistance reported that they had trouble physically accessing Jewish spaces in the country. "When they see a dark Mexican face they just close the synagogue door on you," Hadassah, a twenty-one-year-old college student, commented to me. Hadassah became a Noahide with her parents in 2017 but had more recently completed an Orthodox conversion through an online program and was now living with a community of former Noahides who had converted and established their own autonomous Orthodox Jewish community outside of Mexico City. Even if Noahide families manage to finance a conversion, they must still contend with local issues of racial discrimination and economic inequality that limit their integration into established Ashkenazi and Sephardic Jewish communities in the country. These barriers to entry have led to the creation of independent convert communities like the one Hadassah is now part of. In their own enclaves, Mexican converts who have left Noahidism for Orthodox Judaism in the past few years have established synagogues, religious schools for children, *mikvaot* (ritual baths), and kosher restaurants.

"As soon as they found out I was a taxi driver, I felt they wanted nothing to do with me," explained Jose, another Noahide man in his twenties and a former Seventh-day Adventist, who explained to me that he had, on multiple occasions, attempted to speak with rabbis in Mexico City's Polanco neighborhood to inquire about a conversion process. Jose wished to convert but did not have the funds to join the online study group that Hadassah had utilized. At the same time, he reported that he was increasingly uncomfortable with the Noahide movement in Latin America. He felt that Noahide was becoming a "new religion" with its own liturgies and ritual innovations. "I want real Judaism," he said to me. Other former Noahides who had broken away from the Noahide movement in Mexico to pursue conversion similarly related their skepticism to me: "Noahide has become a poor man's Judaism." "It is the medicine the rabbis are giving us to try to calm us down so we do not ask to convert," explained informants.

Daniel was another former Noahide, originally from Trinidad, whom I spoke with in Canada following his conversion to Orthodox Judaism in 2019. He candidly and succinctly explained to me his theory of why Noahidism had taken off in Latin America and in locations across the Global South: "This is absolutely about having the financial resources [to convert]," Daniel explained. "That point is crucial. It is extremely difficult to uproot and move to another country. . . . Based on my experience, most [Noahides] would choose to be Jewish if they could but they remain stuck. No one wants to start something new. Given the choice they would choose to become Jewish."

It remains to be seen whether the Noahide movement will continue to proliferate, successfully incorporating a growing number of Judaizing Christians who find themselves in the borderlands between Judaism and Christianity, or whether it will ultimately give rise to increasing demands for Orthodox Jewish conversion and inclusion, a development to which centers of rabbinic authority in Israel and abroad will have to respond. Moreover, it also remains to be seen how global Noahides will respond to the growing entanglement of the Temple movement with the Noahide cause. While the vast majority of Noahides whom I spoke with expressed political views in line with Israel's religious right wing, I did encounter a few dissenting voices among North America Noahides. A few Noahides expressed concerns that certain rabbinic mentors based in Israel treated Noahides as geopolitical pawns for Zionist interests. Such an approach, they explained, belittled the serious spiritual questions and identity crises that Noahides leaving Christianity were trying to navigate. "Of course, I support the State of Israel," explained Nicole, a Noahide from Canada. "But the primary motivation for me is not about Zionism," she emphasized. "This is about figuring out who I am and what I believe now that I have left Christianity. Maybe someday we will convert, but for some of us that is too complicated or just not an option. For example, my husband does not want to leave Christianity, so I cannot convert because I do not want to divorce him. So right now, I am just asking that the rabbis take us seriously as Noahides who have chosen the path of Torah."

THE POLITICAL STAKES OF MESSIANIC ZIONISM IN THE DIGITAL AGE

My overarching argument throughout this book can be summarized this way: Messianic Zionism, as a traveling political theology, allows for the interaction and merger of religious systems, paradoxically enabling liberating modes of spiritual empowerment alongside patterns of neocolonial spiritual influence. Since antiquity, the biblical story of Noah and his sons has been manipulated to derive racial categorizations that have, in turn, become highly flexible theologico-political tools, used variously in projects of enslavement and political conquest and, more recently, in postcolonial spiritual and racial transformation.[13] To this day, biblical-racial constructs continue to energize a collaborative Jewish-Christian-Noahide messianic imagination, enabling my Jewish and non-Jewish interlocuters to refashion spiritual and national identities, to reimagine ancestral pasts, and to dream of alternative futures.

I highlight again for the reader that in tracking contemporary mobilizations of biblical-racial ideologies, I am not suggesting that the Bible or the Jewish tradition itself is inherently racist. Racial categorizations are not in fact "biblical" but rather represent the *imposition* of modern political ideologies back onto the Bible—attempts to ground contemporary racialized ideologies and ethnonational political projects in divine providence. Nor are ideas of Jewish and Noahide spiritual-racial difference and messianic-Zionist ideologies more broadly characteristic of a Jewish theological consensus. The Jewish tradition is replete with countertraditions attesting to the equality of Jews and non-Jews, all descended from the primal human pair described in Genesis and created in the image of God. While the notion of Jewish "chosenness" certainly exists in the Hebrew scriptures, in the sense that the Children of Israel were singled out to observe certain commandments that others were not required to, most rabbinic commentors have not tried to connect scriptural depictions of chosenness to notions of innate Jewish superiority over non-Jews. Throughout the Hebrew Bible and the books of the prophets, Israelites are frequently portrayed as fallible human beings, repeatedly judged by God and condemned for a lack of virtue when they fail to exhibit righteous behavior. The postbiblical rabbinic literature repeatedly affirms the equal and infinite value of every human life, Jewish and non-Jewish. Moreover, there exist to this day ample theological challenges to Jewish ethnonationalism and political Zionism from across the Jewish religious spectrum, from secular to Ultra-Orthodox thinkers coming from Ashkenazi, Sephardic, and Mizrahi communities.[14]

Just as spiritual-racial theories fuel messianic and political imaginaries, this work has attempted to underscore their material and political stakes, for the future of both Judaizing communities in the Global South and individuals back on the ground in Israel/Palestine, where ethnotheocratic ideologies continue to inflame cycles of violence and inhibit the establishment of a just peace for Israelis and Palestinians. As chapters 2 and 3 in particular demonstrated, beneath their universalistic claims of perfecting and uniting humanity, the Third Temple / Noahide movements are connected to state-sponsored projects of territorial conquest and have gained broad-based political and economic support from Israeli politicians as well as religious legitimation from authoritative members of the Israeli rabbinate (including the current Ashkenazi Chief Rabbi David Lau and Sephardic Chief Rabbi Yitzhak Yosef). In 2016, Chief Rabbi Lau publicly expressed support for the rebuilding of the Temple and for Noahide outreach.[15] In the same year Chief Rabbi Yosef gave a controversial sermon that was later aired on national television in which he stated that only non-Jews who accepted the Noahide Laws should be allowed to live in Israel.[16] I mention these examples to emphasize for the reader once more that the Third Temple movement, which began as a marginal religious faction in the wake of the attempted Al-Aqsa bombings by the Jewish Underground in the 1980s, has made significant inroads into the Israeli religious and political establishment.

I sit here writing this conclusion in July 2021 at the end of yet another cycle of reciprocal violence in Israel/Palestine. Tensions began mounting in early May 2021 surrounding the pending evictions of Palestinian families from the Sheikh Jarrah neighborhood in East Jerusalem, where Jewish settlers have been working to seize properties and Judaize the neighborhood for two decades. The crisis erupted into violence on May 7 when Israeli forces stormed the Haram ash-Sharif compound using tear gas, rubber bullets, and stun grenades. After issuing an ultimatum to withdraw Israeli forces from the compound, Hamas and Islamic Jihad began launching rockets into Israel, which in turn prompted a renewed campaign of Israeli airstrikes on the Gaza Strip. Inside Israel, widespread riots and protests quickly ensued, leading to intercommunal violence as Jewish residents were attacked by Palestinians and vice versa.

The overlapping of these events with Jerusalem Day, a controversial nationalist holiday that celebrates Israel's capture of Jerusalem in the 1967 war, further exacerbated tensions. On Jerusalem Day, thousands of religious-nationalist youth take part in an annual march through the city. It is a provocative display of national pride and one that symbolically lays claim to Jerusalem as the exclusive capital of Israel. The youth typically march through Palestinian East Jerusalem toward the Temple Mount, but due to mounting protests on May 9, 2021, the march was redirected by Israeli police to the courtyard in front of the Western Wall, just below the Haram ash-Sharif / Temple Mount compound. Facebook livestream videos captured the youth, packed into the Western Wall Plaza, euphorically singing "Remember Me Please" (Zachreini Nah), a song that transforms a passage from the Hebrew Bible into a chant demanding divine vengeance on Palestinians by substituting the biblical word "Plishtim" (Philistines) for "Palastin" (Palestine). Here again contemporary ethnonational categories are retroactively fitted back onto the biblical grid for the purposes of specific political aspirations. "Then Samson called to the LORD, 'O Lord GOD! Please remember me, and give me strength just this once, O God, to take revenge of the Philistines, if only for one of my two eyes' (Judges 16:28)."

In the background of the video footage that subsequently went viral online, Palestinian protestors could be seen clashing with Israeli police in front of the Al-Aqsa Mosque, where a tree had also caught on fire, creating the distinct impression that Al-Aqsa was being consumed in flames as the religious Jewish youth sang ecstatically from their location below about divine retribution. The footage had an apocalyptic aura, and as it circulated online, it escalated transnational excitement (and fears) that Israeli annexation of the Temple Mount was imminent.

Will Judaism once again become a religion of sacrifices and a priesthood? Was my research, as Rabbi Hoffman suggested, documenting the beginning of the "end of Judaism" as Jews and Noahides worked toward a shared vision of biblical revival? For Jews, this would imply the end of a rich ritual and textual tradition forged through the *dislocation* of the Jewish people from the Holy Land and in the absence of a physical Temple. It would mean the end of a tradition sustained through centuries of diaspora by a continuous desire to connect with divinity from anywhere in the world through the observance of daily prayer and *mitzvot*. As much as I hope this account will be inspiring to anthropologists of religion attending to transnational spiritual landscapes, it is also my intention to leave my Jewish readers with critical questions regarding the political influence of religious Zionism in the twenty-first century and Jewish ethnonationalism in Israel/Palestine.

Gershom Scholem, in his canonical 1971 essay *The Messianic Idea in Judaism*, predicted that a crisis that would eventually emerge if messianic Jewish thought were applied to the nationalist project unfolding in Israel in a practical manner. Will Judaism be able to survive, Scholem mused, if its latent messianism is transposed onto a "concrete realm" and mobilized for the "utopian return to Zion"?[17] Or will diasporic Judaism perish in the process (as some of my interlocuters so eagerly hoped it would)?

It remains to be seen whether annexation of the Temple Mount and the building of the Third Temple will in fact be the finale of Zionism, or whether alternative visions of joint Jewish and Palestinian belonging to the land and equal protection under the law will triumph. Historically, even before the advent of political and religious Zionism, there has arguably always been a tension between the literal and symbolic poles of Temple theology running through Jewish thought. A sixth century midrash (rabbinic commentary) imagines the Temple as ultimately transcending the physical space of the Temple Mount in Jerusalem and the entire world as a future macroscopic House of God. According to these more universal Temple visions, the task of humankind is to make the world an abode for divinity through righteous actions. "Rabbi Kohen, brother of Rabbi Hiyah bar Abba said: 'Just as the Divine Presence is found in the Temple in Jerusalem so will the Divine Presence fill the world from one end to the other. That is what is written: "May the whole earth be filled with His glory, amen and amen"' (Midrash Esther Rabbah 1.4)."

Following the destruction of the Second Temple, rabbinic leaders created prayer and ritual substitutes for the Temple's sacrificial services. It is unclear whether the rabbis viewed these substitutes as temporary (ritual placeholders until the building of a Third Temple would be possible) or whether they sought to fundamentally transform Judaism, rendering Temple services unnecessary.[18] Although Jewish liturgy continued to memorialize and preserve a longing for the House of God in Jerusalem, rabbis have also clearly warned of the danger of focusing too much on rebuilding the material Temple. In the eighteenth century, Jewish mystic Rebbe Nachman provocatively asked, "How can you pray for the Temple's rebuilding when you yourself continuously destroy it? Many are those who cry over the material Temple when they should really cry over their own inner ones instead."[19] As Rebbe Nachman suggests in this commentary, attention to Temple physicality at the expense of elevating the individual soul through prayer and good deeds is such a grave violation that it is akin to "continuously destroying" the House of God.

When I reread Rebbe Nachman's words, I am left wondering what tools the Jewish tradition itself might provide to counter ethnocentric and potentially violent visions of biblical revival and Temple physicality. What might an alternative political theology of the Third Temple look like? Could ancient Jewish notions of the entire world as a "Third Temple" motivate a radical ecological ethics or a greater concern for global wealth disparities? Maybe the Third Temple is already nascent inside of us, in our untapped abilities to build a truly sustainable and equitable planetary Temple home. I do not have answers to these questions, but I do know that such a project can only begin by returning to our sources, to the textual spaces where diverse imaginations of the Temple have always lived. Indeed, as Dalia Marx notes, in the Talmudic period rabbinic commentators went so far as to argue that acts of redistributive justice and loving kindness were not only considered to be of equal value to the animal sacrifices offered in the Temple, but were deemed superior: "Rabbi Eleazer stated: Greater is he who performs charity than [he who offers] all the sacrifices, for it is said, 'To do charity and justice is more acceptable to the Lord than sacrifice (Hos 10:12).'" (Sukkot 49b)[20]

Ultimately, by resisting characterizations of my informants as fundamentalists or extremists, and instead attending to the intersections of messianic political theologies with secular and liberal ideologies, this account has consciously steered away from positioning religious actors or religion itself as "the problem." Secular national ideologies, the very products of imperial encounters, that historically emerged in tandem with Europe's messianically driven colonial projects of the seventeenth through twentieth centuries continue to function not as antidotes to political exclusion but as deceptive masks for racial and economic inequalities within the modern nation-state.[21] We cannot simply look to secular liberalism as the obvious antidote to religious extremism. As much as religion has the ability to oppress, I still believe it equally has the potential to liberate. If this work circulates beyond the academic community, perhaps to religious communities, it is my hope that it will also provoke new engagements with Jewish sources themselves, with mystical and metaphysical interpretations of the Temple dating back to antiquity, which might provide inspiration and alternative imaginings of what it means "to rebuild the Temple speedily in our days."[22]

ACKNOWLEDGMENTS

First and foremost, I wish to express my sincere gratitude for all my interlocuters over the past decade, Jews and Noahides alike, who participated in my anthropological research, and candidly shared their spiritual journeys with me, with the desire to build bridges of understanding. I am particularly indebted to Noahides in the Philippines and in Mexico who so graciously and generously hosted me in their communities, dialogued with me, challenged me, and taught me so much. Although I cannot name all my interlocuters here, please know if you are reading this, that I am forever changed because our paths crossed. I see the world with more complexity and compassion because of you. It was my honor to bear witness to your stories and I remain inspired by your love of Judaism.

The completion of this book would not have been possible without a lifetime of love and support from my family. I am grateful beyond words to my parents, Debra and Jeffrey Feldman, for raising me in a home that modeled intellectual curiosity, for believing in me, and always supporting my academic studies and creative endeavors. Thank you, Mom and Dad, for generously pitching in with childcare during times that I had to travel for research in recent years.

My life partner, Yitzhak Glasman, has stood by my side since the beginning of my fieldwork in Israel, following me and this project around the world, and even jumping in as a research assistant at times. Yitzhak, you have always been my best and most lovingly honest critic and your input over the years helped immensely to bring this book to life. I am so grateful for your support and for our two beautiful children, Refael Nachman and Zimrah Cadem. Thank you for always encouraging me and lifting me up when I needed it the most. I wish to also express my gratitude to the rest of my immediate and extended family, in the United States and France, who have cheered me on for years.

I feel incredibly fortunate to have received excellent and generous mentorship during my doctoral studies at the University of California, Davis, during which the ideas in this book first took shape. I wish to express my sincere gratitude to my doctoral committee—Suad Joseph, David Biale, and John Hall—as well as the Anthropology Department at UC Davis for providing me with the resources and support to become an anthropologist and for opportunities to grow as a lecturer when I returned from the field. I am indebted to Suad Joseph for her phenomenal guidance in the fields on anthropology, gender studies, and Middle East studies. Suad, your commitments to scholarly rigor and ethical engagements in the field continue to inspire me and influence all the work that I do as a researcher and teacher. A special expression of gratitude is also due to my mentor, David Biale. David, thank you for working so closely with me on the historical and Jewish theological aspects of my doctoral research during my time at Davis. It was my great honor to be able to learn from you and discuss Jewish ideas with you. Your mentorship gave me the confidence I needed to work with Jewish primary sources as part of my scholarship and helped set me on my trajectory to become a professor of Judaic Studies.

I wish to express my gratitude to Nurit Stadler for welcoming me as a visiting graduate student in the Department of Sociology and Anthropology at Hebrew University from 2014 to 2016. Thank you for supporting my research, providing excellent feedback, and for connecting me to a wonderful community of scholars in Jerusalem during the time of my fieldwork. I am also indebted to the mentorship of anthropologist Smadar Lavie, whose critical feedback greatly enhanced my first publications after returning from the field. Smadar, thank you for always pushing me to think about the racial and gendered dimensions of my research on religious Zionism. Your work continues to provide an important model for me of the power of feminist scholarship to illuminate complexities on the ground in Israel/Palestine.

I must also acknowledge my peers at Davis, especially all the participants in Suad Joseph's Middle East seminar, who provided me with valuable feedback on my early writing experiments. I am grateful for the long-term friendships that were forged during my graduate studies. Especially to Tory Brykalski, Gabi Kirk, Anne Perez, Emily Schneider, Shira Schwartz, Lea Taragin-Zeller, Ariel Hendelman and Rebecca Bailin: thank you for supporting my research since its early stages when the project that would become this book first began to take shape. Ariel Hendelman, please know that meeting you "in the field" was truly an intellectual and spiritual gift. Thank you for always being a safe and honest space to explore the most difficult Jewish questions or sing a healing niggun. Tory Brykalski, I am grateful for your many years of intellectual and emotional support, for your willingness to play with ideas, and to traverse the intersections of anthropology and theology with me. This project is indebted to our many passionate conversations at Davis and across time zones.

I must also acknowledge Lia Tarachansky, a brilliant scholar and filmmaker, who played an important role in the evolution of this book. Lia, our years of intellectual and creative collaboration helped me enormously to refine my arguments and to consider the ethical and political stakes of the stories I was telling. On a few different occasions, Lia and I combined forces in the field, working side by side to capture the globalization of the Third Temple / Noahide movements through combined ethnographic research and documentary film work. While a few excerpts from our joint fieldwork made their way into this book, most is still forthcoming in our collaborative digital humanities project on messianic Zionism. Lia, I look forward to working with you in the coming years, to continue thinking about how to decolonize research, and to continue telling the stories we bore witness to together.

I am likewise indebted to everyone who generously provided feedback on book chapters during various stages of development, including my anonymous peer reviewers and scholars Michal Kravel-Tovi, Adryael Tong, Adam Shapiro, Jane Saffitz, and Annette Aronowicz. Your feedback was invaluable, helping me to nuance and greatly enhance my central claims. A big thank-you is also due to Omer Hacker, Tal Janner-Klausner, Yona Elfassi, and Mohannad Nairoukh, who acted as research assistants in Israel/Palestine, assisting me with work that either made its way into this book or other related journal articles. Thank you for accompanying me, for helping me with interviews and/or archival materials, and for sharing your valuable insights along the way.

The completion of this book would not have been possible without the support of the Religious Studies Department at Franklin and Marshall College. Thank you to my dear colleagues Stephen Cooper, SherAli Tareen, David McMahan, and John Modern for believing in me and hiring me just out of graduate school, for giving me a warm and welcoming home from which to research and teach the topics I am passionate about. A very special thanks to F&M colleagues who became faculty at the same time as me, Firouzeh Shokooh-Valle and Secil Yilmaz. Thank you for the ongoing feminist solidarity, intellectual passion, and humor that helped me persevere in the writing!

Although I have now moved on to Dartmouth College, I will always remain deeply grateful to Franklin and Marshall College, which also happens to be my undergraduate alma mater. The Judaic Studies program at F&M set me on my life path, in large part due to the mentorship I received from Annette Aronowicz and the late Matthew Hoffman—may his memory be a blessing.

I am grateful to the Office of College Grants at F&M for providing resources that enabled me to finish my research and this book. I also wish to acknowledge the National Science Foundation and Memorial Foundation for Jewish Culture for funding much of the fieldwork research that went into this book.

Some of the material in this book appeared in earlier publications. Chapter 2 includes excerpts from journal articles that appeared in *The Journal of Middle Eastern Woman's Studies* (2017), *The Journal of Settler Colonial Studies* (2018), and *The Journal of Contemporary Jewry* (2020). Chapter 3 includes an excerpt from my 2023 article in *The Association for Judaic Studies Review*. I am indebted to the feedback provided by journal editors and the anonymous peer reviewers of these previous publications.

Thank you to Rutgers University Press for taking on this manuscript and seeing it through to publication, especially editors Elisabeth Maselli and Christopher Rios-Sueverkruebbe for their valuable insights and assistance along the way. Thank you to the Association for Jewish Studies and the Jordan Schnitzer Family Foundation for awarding me a 2023 Jordan Schnitzer First Book Award which included a subvention to offset the publication costs of this book, making it more accessible to readers around the world.

NOTES

PREFACE

1. I have assigned her a pseudonym here and most individuals quoted in this text have also been given pseudonyms (with the exception of a few high-profile public figures).

2. This is the assertion of John Hall, a sociologist of apocalyptic and messianic movements who claims that messianic yearning and what we call "the apocalypse" is not exclusively religious but rather refers to diverse beliefs and social mobilizations, including forms of state violence and political revolution that are driven by visions of "extreme social and cultural disjuncture" that "undermine normal perceptions of reality" and motivate people to "act in unprecedented ways." John R. Hall, *Apocalypse: From Antiquity to the Empire of Modernity* (Cambridge: Polity, 2009), 2–3.

3. See, for example, the following recent works that approach the study of Israel/Palestine from a global perspective: Israel Drori, *Foreign Workers in Israel: Global Perspectives* (Albany: State University of New York Press, 2009); John Collins, *Global Palestine* (New York: Columbia University Press, 2011); Michael Brenner, "Global Israel: A State Beyond Borders," in *In Search of Israel: The History of an Idea* (Princeton, NJ: Princeton University Press, 2018).

4. There is a growing body of ethnographic work focused on new and emerging Jewish communities that has helped to deconstruct hegemonic notions of "who is a Jew," including recent research on Judaizing Christian churches, groups claiming "lost tribe" status, and crypto-Jews (communities claiming descent from Sephardic Jews who were forcibly converted during the Spanish Inquisition). See, for example, Tudor Parfitt and Netanel Fisher, eds., *Becoming Jewish: New Jews and Emerging Jewish Communities in a Globalized World* (Newcastle upon Tyne, UK: Cambridge Scholars, 2016); Nathan Devir, *New Children of Israel: Emerging Jewish Communities in an Era of Globalization* (Salt Lake City: University of Utah Press, 2017); Noah Tamarkin, *Genetic Afterlives: Black Jewish Indigeneity in South Africa* (Durham, NC: Duke University Press, 2020); Manoela Carpenedo, *Becoming Jewish, Believing in Jesus: Judaizing Evangelicals in Brazil* (New York: Oxford University Press, 2021); Janet Liebman Jacobs, *Hidden Heritage: The Legacy of the Crypto-Jews* (Berkeley: University of California Press, 2002).

5. See, for example, the following histories of Christian Zionism and U.S.-Israel relations: Daniel G. Hummel, *Covenant Brothers: Evangelicals, Jews, and U.S.-Israeli Relations* (Philadelphia: University of Pennsylvania Press, 2019); Shalom Goldman, *Zeal for Zion: Christians, Jews, and the Idea of the Promised Land* (Chapel Hill: University of North Carolina Press, 2009); Yaakov S. Ariel, *An Unusual Relationship: Evangelical Christians and Jews* (New York: New York University Press, 2013).

6. For more background and critical reflection on the notion of the field site as an artificial construction of the ethnographer during anthropological research, see, for example, James Clifford and George E. Marcus, eds., *Writing Culture: The Poetics and Politics of Ethnography* (Berkeley: University of California Press, 1986).

7. I borrow this phrase from Robert Rozehnal in his work on digital Sufism. Rozehnal, *Cyber Sufis: Virtual Expression of the American Muslim Experience* (London: Oneworld, 2019), 4–12.

8. Pierrick Leurent and Irris Makler, "Palestinian 'Knife Intifada' Reflects a Generation's Despair," *France24*, May 6, 2016, https://www.france24.com/en/20160506-reporter-israel-knife -intifada-palestinian-territories-violence.

9. Donna Harraway, "Situated Knowledges: The Science Question in Feminism and the Privilege of Partial Perspective," *Feminist Studies* 14, no. 3 (1988): 575–599.

10. John L. Jackson, *Thin Description: Ethnography and the African Hebrew Israelites of Jerusalem* (Cambridge, MA: Harvard University Press, 2013).

11. See, for example, the scholarship of Ella Shohat, Smadar Lavie, Claris Harbon, Henriette Dahan Kalev, Islad Jad, Rema Hammami, Julie Peteet, and Rhoda Kanaaneh.

CHAPTER 1   INTRODUCTION

1. The biblical prophet Ezekiel described the construction of an immense and eternal future Temple (Ezekiel 40:1–42:20). Ezekiel's visions are generally regarded in rabbinic commentaries as prophesizing the Third and Final Temple of messianic times following the return of Jews to the Land of Israel.

2. For more background on the history of the Third Temple movement in Israel, see the following ethnographic and historical accounts: Sarina Chen, *Soon in Our days: The Temple Mount and National Religious Society* (Beer Sheva: Ben Gurion University Press, 2018; Hebrew); Motti Inbari, *Jewish Fundamentalism and the Temple Mount* (Albany: State University of New York Press, 2009); Gershom Gorenberg, *The End of Days: Fundamentalism and the Struggle for the Temple Mount* (Oxford: Oxford University Press, 2000).

3. By "Children of Israel" I refer to the biblical phrase (Exodus 1:9) and notion within Judaism that the Jewish people are genealogical and spiritual descendants of the biblical Yaacov who is also called Israel (Genesis 35:10). According to the biblical narrative, Israel (Yaacov) and his sons formed the twelve Israelite tribes that were freed from slavery in Egypt and chosen by God to receive the Torah at Mount Sinai. The phrase "Children of Israel" also references the theological notion of Jews as a "chosen nation" (*am nivhar*) selected to inherit the 613 commandments given in the Torah.

4. For an overview of philosemitism in the history of Christianity, see Jonathan Karp and Adam Sutcliffe, *Philosemitism in History* (New York: Cambridge University Press, 2011). There are also a number of important new case studies documenting philosemitic and Judaizing trends that have appeared in Christian-majority countries, including case studies of Christian communities that have adopted Jewish rituals and/or claim Jewish or Israelite descent. See, for example, Carpenedo, *Becoming Jewish*; Devir, *New Children of Israel*.

5. Isaiah 56:7.

6. The phrase "ethnographic object" refers to a particular cultural artifact that an anthropologist studies.

7. Hebrew-Roots Christianity refers to a movement of Christian churches worldwide, coming from offshoots of Protestant Christianity, for example, those identifying as Sacred Name Movement and Messianic Christianity. While the category of Hebrew-Roots Christianity covers a wide spectrum of theological and ritual stances, Hebrew-Roots congregations typically share a few core tenets. These congregations generally emphasize that fact that Jesus was a Jew, and adherents believe that, in order to properly implement Jesus's teachings, Christians must understand the historical Jewish context in which he lived. Thus, they tend to place greater emphasis on the study of the Old Testament as foundational for understanding the New Testament. Some Hebrew-Roots congregations, however, have gone beyond a textual engagement with the Hebrew Bible to adopting forms of Jewish cultural and ritual life including Jewish ritual clothing (e.g., kippot and tallit), Hebrew names, and Jewish holiday observances. In contrast to Jews, Hebrew-Roots Christians maintain that Jesus is the Messiah and salvation can be attained only through belief in him. It is precisely here where Noahides depart from Hebrew-Roots Christianity; once they renounce their belief in Jesus they can longer partici-

pate in Hebrew-Roots congregations and thus reidentify as Noahide according to Jewish legal/rabbinic interpretations. I note for the reader that there are also a number of Sabbath-keeping churches concerned with drawing closer to the Bible (the Sabbath is one of the Ten Commandments) that do not necessarily identify as part of the Hebrew-Roots movement and may not place a great emphasis on adopting specifically Jewish religious customs.

During my research, I also met with ex-Christians who ended up in the Noahide movement after joining Sabbath-keeping churches such as Seventh-day Adventist congregations. In most cases that I documented, Noahides coming from Seventh-day Adventism spent some time in a Hebrew-Roots congregation, such as Messianic Judaism, as an intermediary step before leaving Christianity entirely. For more information on the Hebrew-Roots movement, I recommend Dan Cohn-Sherbok, *Messianic Judaism: A Critical Anthology* (London: Blooms-bury, 2000). For background on Seventh-day Adventism, which first developed in the United States, and its proliferation across Africa, Asia, and Latin America, I recommend the following: Malcolm Bull and Keith Lockhart, *Seeking a Sanctuary: Seventh-Day Adventism and the American Dream*, 2nd ed. (Bloomington: Indiana University Press, 2007); Eva Keller, *The Road to Clarity: Seventh-Day Adventism in Madagascar* (New York: Palgrave Macmillan, 2005); Christie Chui-Shan Chow, *Schism: Seventh-Day Adventism in Post-Denominational China* (Notre Dame, IN: University of Notre Dame Press, 2021).

8. Speculative design, also commonly referred to as "critical design" or "futurescaping," is a design methodology aimed at creating "alternative ways of being" and is typically used to develop design solutions for large-scale economic, political, and social justice issues such as climate change or alternatives to capitalism. Anthony Dunne and Fiona Raby, *Speculative Everything: Design, Fiction, and Social Dreaming* (Cambridge, MA: MIT Press, 2013), 3.

9. See, for example, the following historical and anthropological works that emphasize the reciprocal nature of colonizer-colonized interactions: Peter van der Veer, *Imperial Encounters: Religion and Modernity in India and Britain* (Princeton, NJ: Princeton University Press, 2001); Jean Comaroff, *Body of Power, Spirit of Resistance: The Culture and History of a South African People* (Chicago: University of Chicago Press, 1985); Albert Memmi, *The Colonizer and the Colonized*, trans. Howard Greenfeld (Boston: Beacon, 1991); Ann Laura Stoler, *Along the Archival Grain: Epistemic Anxieties and Colonial Common Sense* (Princeton, NJ: Princeton University Press, 2009).

10. There is of course precedent in the anthropological literature for employing ethnographic methods in the study of political theology. I note for the reader two examples that were particularly useful for me when developing my own research approach. Susan Harding's work on Christian fundamentalism in America provided an intimate ethnographic portrait of how a Christian dispensationalist political theology, which came of age in the second half of the twentieth century, influenced the rhetoric and spiritual identities of born-again Christians, as they learned to read contemporary political events through biblical and messianic lenses. Harding, *The Book of Jerry Falwell: Fundamentalist Language and Politics* (Princeton, NJ: Princeton University Press, 2000). Michael Feige's work on Jewish fundamentalism in the West Bank entered into the daily lives and practices of religious Jewish settlers to reveal the confluence of religious and political ideologies that motivated Jewish settlement expansion over the Green Line after 1967. Feige, *Settling in the Hearts: Jewish Fundamentalism in the Occupied Territories* (Detroit: Wayne State University Press, 2009).

11. See, for example, the 2017 volume of *Israel Studies Review* dedicated to the Temple Mount. While this particular volume takes steps toward complicating the religious extremists versus secular-state binary, the articles still utilize these categories. Moreover, the volume does not examine the ongoing Temple Mount crisis in relation to Israel's broader settler-colonial dynamics.

12. "Changing Perspectives on the Temple Mount," *Israel Studies Review* 32, no. 1 (2017): v–vii.

13. Joyce Dalsheim, *Unsettling Gaza: Secular Liberalism, Radical Religion, and the Israeli Settlement Project* (Oxford: Oxford University Press, 2011).

14. Anidjar provides a succinct explanation of the importance of the theologico-political category in this interview: "The Jew, the Arab: An Interview with Gil Anidjar," Asia Society, n.d., https://asiasociety.org/jew-arab-interview-gil-anidjar. See also Gil Anidjar, *The Jew, the Arab: A History of the Enemy* (Stanford, CA: Stanford University Press, 2003).

15. Talal Asad, *Formations of the Secular: Christianity, Islam, Modernity* (Stanford, CA: Stanford University Press, 2003).

16. Talal Asad, Wendy Brown, Judith Butler, and Saba Mahmood, *Is Critique Secular? Blasphemy, Injury, and Free Speech* (New York: Fordham University Press, 2013).

17. Susan Harding, "Representing Fundamentalism: The Problem of the Repugnant Cultural Other," *Social Research* 58, no. 2 (Summer 1991): 373–393.

18. Harding, "Representing Fundamentalism," 374.

19. Harding, "Representing Fundamentalism," 374.

20. Bruce Lincoln, *Religion, Empire, and Torture: The Case of Achaemenian Persia, with a Postscript on Abu Ghraib* (Chicago: University of Chicago Press, 2007), xi.

21. Richard T. Hughes, *Myths America Lives By: White Supremacy and the Stories That Give Us Meaning* (Urbana: University of Illinois Press, 2018), 2.

22. Michal Kravel-Tovi provides a useful and concise definition of Zionist biopolitical policy: "an institutional channel for population policy through which the Jewish state strives to produce and reproduce the Israeli nation as Jewish." A Jewish demographic majority effectively ensures Jewish dominance in all spheres of cultural, economic, and political Israeli life. Michal Kravel-Tovi, *When the State Winks: The Performance of Jewish Conversion in Israel* (New York: Columbia University Press, 2019), 53. The demographic mission, in the wake of the Holocaust, became a sacred responsibility for the Israeli national collective and is at play in nearly every aspect of state policy making, through the management of Jewish, Palestinian, and other minority lives. Policies and state resources are directed at maximizing Jewish birthrates and enhancing Jewish immigration. Palestinian populations, whose high birthrights are viewed as a threat to Jewish hegemony, are subject to what Jasbir Puar defines as "debilitating" biopolitical strategies. Living under the hazards of military occupation, the loss of lands and natural resources, physical and social fracturing of populations, and limited legal protections debilitates Palestinians.

23. There is now a robust literature that addresses the settler-colonial origins of Zionism and ongoing settler-colonial power dynamics in the State of Israel. See, for example, Nur Masalha, *Imperial Israel and the Palestinians: The Politics of Expansion* (London: Pluto Press, 2000); Lorenzo Veracini, *Israel and Settler Society* (London: Pluto Press, 2006); Ariel Handel, Marco Allegra, and Erez Maggor, eds., *Normalizing Occupation: The Politics of Everyday Life in the West Bank Settlements* (Bloomington: Indiana University Press, 2017); Rashid Khalidi, *The Hundred Years' War on Palestine: A History of Settler Colonialism and Resistance, 1917–2017* (New York: Metropolitan Books, 2020).

24. Jeff Halper, *Decolonizing Israel, Liberating Palestine: Zionism, Settler Colonialism, and the Case for One Democratic State* (London: Pluto Press, 2021), 5–17; Benny Morris, *Righteous Victim: A History of the Zionist-Arab Conflict, 1881–1999* (New York: Knopf, 1999), 21–22.

25. Edward W. Said, *Orientalism* (New York: Vintage, 1979).

26. For an examination of the way Orientalist ideologies influenced Zionist leaders and Israel's treatment of both Palestinians and Mizrahim (Jews from the Middle East and North Africa), I refer the reader to the following works: Edward W. Said, "Zionism from the Standpoint of Its Victims," *Cultural Politics* 11 (1997): 15–38; Yehouda A. Shenhav, *The Arab Jews: A*

Postcolonial Reading of Nationalism, Religion, and Ethnicity (Stanford, CA: Stanford University Press, 2006); Ella Shohat, "The Split Arab/Jew Figure Revisited," *Patterns of Prejudice* 54, no. 1–2 (2020): 46–70.

27. Uri Davis, *Apartheid in Israel: Possibilities for the Struggle Within* (London: Zed, 2003), 199–200.

28. Ilan Pappe, *The Making of the Arab-Israeli Conflict, 1947–51* (New York: I. B. Taurus, 1994), 91–98.

29. Halper, *Decolonizing Israel*, 4.

30. Tom Segev and Arlen Neal Weinstein, *1949: The First Israelis* (New York: Free Press, 1986), 6.

31. For more background on Israel's strategic use of legal frameworks to facilitate the expropriation of Palestinian lands, see, for example, Hadeel S. Abu Hussein, *The Struggle for Land Under Israeli Law: An Architecture of Exclusion* (London: Routledge, 2022).

32. Shira Robinson, *Citizen Strangers: Palestinians and the Birth of Israel's Liberal Settler State* (Stanford, CA: Stanford University Press, 2013).

33. I refer the reader to the following studies of ethnocratic dynamics in Israel and the political/economic position of Palestinians with Israeli citizenship living inside the Green Line: As'ad Ghanem, "The Expanding Ethnocracy: Judaization of the Public Space," *Israel Studies Review* 26, no. 1 (2011): 21–27; Oren Yiftachel, *Ethnocracy: Land and Identity Politics in Israel/Palestine* (Philadelphia: University of Philadelphia Press, 2006); Nadim Rouhana, *Identities in Conflict: Palestinian Citizens in an Ethnic Jewish State* (New Haven, CT: Yale University Press, 1997).

34. Masalha, *Imperial Israel and the Palestinians*; Ilan Pappe, ed., *Israel and South Africa: The Many Faces of Apartheid* (London: Zed Books, 2015).

35. The following accounts document the conditions of Palestinian life under Israeli military occupation in the West Bank: Saree Makdisi, *Palestine Inside Out: An Everyday Occupation* (New York: Norton, 2010); Neve Gordon, *Israel's Occupation* (Berkeley: University of California Press, 2008).

36. See, for example, the following works discussing the spatial and architectural changes that have fragmented Palestinian populations and, in the opinions of the authors, foreclosed a two-state solution. Eyal Weizman, *Hollow Land: Israel's Architecture of Occupation* (London: Verso, 2012); Ian Lustik, *Paradigm Lost: From Two-State Solution to One-State Reality* (Philadelphia: University of Pennsylvania Press, 2019).

37. Arjun Appadurai, *Modernity at Large: Cultural Dimensions of Globalization* (Minneapolis: University of Minnesota Press, 1996).

38. See, for example, Rozehnal, *Cyber Sufis*; Aisha M. Beliso-De Jesús, *Electric Santería: Racial and Sexual Assemblages of Transnational Religion* (New York: Columbia University Press, 2015).

39. See, for example, the following studies of digital religion that engage with questions of authority: Heidi Campbell, "How Religious Communities Negotiate New Media Religiously," in *Digital Religion, Social Media and Culture: Perspectives, Practices, and Futures*, ed. Pauline Hope Cheong, Peter Fisher-Nielsen, Stefan Gelfgren, and Charles Ess (New York: Peter Lang, 2012); Paula Hope Cheong, "Authority," in *Digital Religion: Understanding Religious Practice in New Media Worlds*, ed. Heidi A. Campbell (New York: Routledge, 2013), 72–87.

40. Marla Brettschneider, *The Jewish Phenomenon in Sub-Saharan Africa: The Politics of Contradictory Discourses* (Lewiston, NY: Edwin Mellen Press, 2015), 2–13.

41. Such an "anchored" approach is modeled in the following accounts of globalizing religion: Manuel A. Vásquez and Marie F. Marquardt, *Globalizing the Sacred: Religion Across the Americas* (New Brunswick, NJ: Rutgers University Press, 2003); Beliso-De Jesús, *Electric Santería*.

42. Thomas J. Csordas, *Transnational Transcendence: Essays on Religion and Globalization* (Berkeley: University of California Press, 2009), 3.

43. Csordas, *Transnational Transcendence*, 4.

44. Anna Lowenhaupt Tsing, *Friction: An Ethnography of Global Connection* (Princeton, NJ: Princeton University Press, 2005), 4–5.

45. See, for example, the following works on postcolonial religion: Fedeke N. Castor, *Spiritual Citizenship: Transnational Pathways from Black Power to Ifa in Trinidad* (Durham, NC: Duke University Press, 2017); M. Jacqui Alexander, *Pedagogies of Crossing: Meditations on Feminism, Sexual Politics, Memory, and the Sacred* (Durham, NC: Duke University Press, 2005).

46. For example, Fedeke Castor, in her work on transnational African diasporic communities in Afro-Atlantic religions, brings forth the notion of "spiritual citizenship" to describe "the power of the sacred to inform new ways of belonging to community, the nation, and the transnational." Castor, *Spiritual Citizenship*, 5.

47. A good example of this approach is Devaka Premawardhana's ethnographic study of Pentecostalism in Mozambique: Premawardhana, *Faith in Flux: Pentecostalism and Mobility in Rural Mozambique* (Philadelphia: University of Pennsylvania Press, 2018).

48. "Messianic" is a common shorthand among Hebrew-Roots Christians that stands for "Messianic Judaism," a global movement that syncretizes elements of Judaism and Protestant Christianity.

49. I documented very similar patterns of religious shifting among Noahides in Mexico (from Catholicism to Messianic churches to Noahide). While I could not include the Mexico case study in this book, an analysis of my Mexico data is available in a previous publication: Rachel Feldman, "I Call It 'Rabbi YouTube': Rabbinic Authority in the Digital Age and Global South," *Association for Judaic Studies Review* 46, no. 1 (April 2023).

50. Max Weber's foundational writings on the concept of "charisma" helped initiate the field of religious conversion studies that would be further developed from sociological, psychological, and anthropological perspectives. Weber described the charismatic authority that enables certain individuals to be perceived as having "superhuman" capabilities of "divine origin," that subsequently establishes them as a leader capable of attracting and influencing followers. Weber, *The Theory of Social and Economic Organization*, ed. Talcott Parsons, trans. A. M Henderson (New York: Free Press, 1964).

51. John Lofland and Rodney Stark, "Becoming a World-Saver: A Theory of Conversion to a Deviant Perspective," *American Sociological Review* 30, no. 6 (1965): 862–875.

52. Roger A. Strauss, "Religious Conversion as a Personal and Collective Accomplishment," *Sociological Analysis* 40, no. 2 (1979): 158–165; A. L. Griel, "Previous Dispositions and Conversion to Perspectives of Social and Religious Movements," *Sociological Analysis* 38, no. 2 (1977): 115–125.

53. J. T. Richardson and M. Stewart, "Conversion Process Models and the Jesus Movement," in *Conversion Careers: In and Out of the New Religions,* edited by J. T. Richardson (Beverly Hills, CA: SAGE, 1978), 24–42; T. E. Long and J. K. Hadden, "Religious Conversion and the Concept of Socialization: Integrating the Brainwashing and Drift Models," *Journal for the Scientific Study of Religion* 22, no. 1 (1983): 1–14; Rodney Stark and Roger Finke, *Acts of Faith: Explaining the Human Side of Religion* (Berkeley: University of California Press, 2000).

54. Ronaldo Almeida and Paula Monteiro, "Transito religioso no Brasil," *Sao Paulo Perspectiva* 15, no. 3 (2001): 92–101.

55. Patricia Birman, "Cultos de possess o e pentecostalismo no Brasil: Passagens," *Religio e Sociedade* 17 (1996): 90–109.

56. Alejandro Frigerio, "Analyzing Conversion in Latin America: Theoretical Questions, Methodological Dilemmas, and Comparative Data from Argentina and Brazil," in *Conversion*

of a Continent: Cotemporary Religious Change in Latin America, ed. Timothy J. Steigenga and Edward L. Cleary (New Brunswick, NJ: Rutgers University Press, 2007), 33–51.

57. Benjamin E. Zeller, *Heaven's Gate: America's UFO Religion* (New York: New York University Press, 2014), 1–15.

58. Hanan Mazeh, "Built, Destroyed, and Built Again: Temple and History in Genesis Rabbah in Light of Christian Sources," *Jewish Quarterly Review* 110, no. 4 (2020): 652–678; Dalia Marx, "The Missing Temple: The Status of the Temple in Jewish Culture Following Its Destruction," *European Judaism* 46, no. 2 (2013): 61–78; Moshe Chaim Luzzato, *Secrets of the Future Temple: Mishkney Elyon*, ed. Avraham Greenbaum (Jerusalem: Azamra Institute, 1999).

59. See Maimonides's *Mishneh Torah*, "Laws of Kings and Their Wars," chap. 11.

60. Maimonides, "Laws of Kings and Their Wars," 8:10.

61. Abraham Joshua Heschel, *The Sabbath* (New York: Noonday Press, 1975).

62. Mazeh, "Built, Destroyed, and Built Again," 652.

63. Marx, "Missing Temple."

64. Moshe Chaim Luzzatto, *Secrets of the Future Temple: Mishkney Elyon*, ed. Avraham Greenbaum (Jerusalem: Azamra Institute, 1999).

65. This is based on particular interpretations of Exodus 25:8: "Make for me sanctuary and I will dwell *within you*." For example, Rebbe Nachman of Breslov, an eighteenth-century Jewish mystic, emphasized the importance of personal tikkun (spiritual repair) that precedes the rebuilding of the Temple (*Likutey Halachot, Tzitzit* 3:2, 5:6). In another famous example, according to Meir Leibush ben Yehiel Michel Wisser, a nineteenth-century rabbi from Russia, the structure of the Second Temple parallels the human body, with each of its chambers and vessels symbolizing human organs and bodily functions. For example, the golden altar holding the incense offering represents the nose, and the tablets containing the Ten Commandments symbolize the right and left hemispheres of the brain. See the chapter "R'mazai Hamishkan," in Rabbi L. Reznick, *The Holy Temple Revisited* (Northvale, NJ: Jason Aronson, 1993).

66. Marx, "Missing Temple," 67.

67. Marx, "Missing Temple," 67. In her article Dalia Marx cites the specific Talmudic example of Menakhot 97a: "Rabban Johanan and Rabbi Eleazer both said: While the Temple still stood the altar used to make an atonement for a person, but now that the Temple no longer stands a person's table makes atonement for him."

68. Consider, for example, a sixth-century midrash: "Rabbi Kohen, brother of Rabbi Chiyah bar Abba said: Just as the Shekhinah is found in the Temple in Jerusalem so the Shekhinah will fill the world from one end to the other, and this is what [scripture] means when it says (Ps 72:19): 'And his kavod (glory) will fill the entire world, amen and amen'" (Midrash Esther Rabbah, 1.4).

69. Jill Hammer, *Return to the Place: The Magic, Meditation, and Mystery of Sefer Yetzirah* (Teaneck, NJ: Ben Yehuda Press, 2020), ix.

70. Gershom Scholem, *The Messianic Idea in Judaism: And Other Essays on Jewish Spirituality* (New York: Schocken Books, 1971), 31.

71. Scholem, *Messianic Idea in Judaism*, 8–22.

72. Lawrence Fine, *Physician of the Soul, Healer of the Cosmos: Isaac Luria and His Kabbalistic Fellowship* (Stanford, CA: Stanford University Press, 2003); Martin Buber, *The Legend of the Baal-Shem* (Princeton, NJ: Princeton University Press, 1995).

73. Alexander van der Haven, *From Lowly Metaphor to Divine Flesh: Sarah the Ashkenazi, Sabbatai Tsevi's Messianic Queer and the Sabbatian Movement* (Amsterdam: Menasseh ben Israel Instituut, 2012).

74. Arie Morgenstern and Joel A. Linsider, *Hastening Redemption: Messianism and the Resettlement of the Land of Israel* (Oxford: Oxford University Press, 2006).

75. Yael Zerubavel, *Recovered Roots: Collective Memory and the Making of Israeli National Tradition* (Chicago: University of Chicago Press, 1995).

76. Zerubavel, *Recovered Roots*, 14–19; David Biale, *Blood and Belief: The Circulation of a Symbol between Jews and Christians* (Berkeley: University of California Press, 2007), 162–185.

77. Aviezer Ravitsky, *Messianism, Zionism, and Jewish Religious Radicalism*, trans. Michael Swirsky and Jonathan Chipman (Chicago: University of Chicago Press, 1996), 2–40.

78. For an overview of Kook's life and theology, I recommend Yehudah Mirsky, *Rav Kook: Mystic in a Time of Revolution* (New Haven, CT: Yale University Press, 2014).

79. Kravel-Tovi, *When the State Winks*, 102.

80. Kravel-Tovi, *When the State Winks*, 103.

81. The Merkaz ha-Rav yeshiva is one of Israel's largest and most influential religious-Zionist seminaries, originally founded by Rabbi Avraham Isaac Kook in 1924 and eventually inherited by his son Tzvi Yehuda, who served as "rosh yeshiva" (seminary dean) from 1951 to 1982.

82. For more background on the political and messianic ideological development of Gush Emunim and religious Zionism in Israel, I refer the reader to the following: Gideon Aran, *Kookisk: The Roots of Gush Emunum, the Settlers' Culture, Zionist Theology and Messianism in Our Age* (Jerusalem: Carmel Press, 2013; Hebrew); Shai Held, "What Zvi Yehudah Kook Wrought: The Theopolitical Radicalization of Religious Zionism," in *Rethinking the Messianic Idea in Judaism*, ed. Michael L. Morgan and Steven Weitzman (Bloomington: Indiana University Press, 2015), 229–255; Motti Inbari, *Messianic Religious Zionism Confronts Israeli Territorial Compromises* (New York: Cambridge University Press, 2012).

83. Yoav Peled and Horit Peled, "Religious Zionism: The Quest for Hegemony" (paper, ECPR General Conference, Wroclaw, September 2019), 7–9.

84. Handel, Allegra, and Maggor, *Normalizing Occupation*, 2–3. Today, the image of the stereotypical settler of Gush Emunim (typically depicted as a gun-toting messianic-Zionist Ashkenazi with knitted kippah) does not match the majority of Israelis living in the West Bank, a heterogeneous mix of secular and religious Jews with diverse ethnic and national origins, motivated by the practical benefits of living in the West Bank, drawn to the affordable housing and educational and social services, within the reality of Israel's significantly diminished welfare state and rising cost of living (Handel, Allegra, and Maggor, *Normalizing Occupation*, 6).

85. Handel, Allegra, and Maggor, *Normalizing Occupation*, 9.

86. To this day, as Lavie explains, the Israeli left remains dominated by a secular Ashkenazi upper class who have failed to attract Mizrahim to their parties in significant numbers. Smadar Lavie, *Wrapped in the Flag of Israel: Mizrahi Single Mothers and Bureaucratic Torture* (Lincoln: University of Nebraska Press, 2014), 62–64.

87. Paul Scham, "A Nation That Dwells Alone: Israeli Religious Nationalism in the 21st Century," *Israel Studies* 23, no. 3 (Fall 2018): 211.

88. Tomer Persico provides a summary of this history in "The End Point of Zionism," explaining that, in general, the founders of Gush Emunim and most of Israel's major Orthodox and Ultra-Orthodox rabbinic voices did not openly advocate for Temple rebuilding and forbade Jews from visiting the site. These dynamics have shifted in recent years as rabbinic leaders have increasingly promoted Temple Mount pilgrimage, and the question of the Temple Mount has reemerged as one of the most important issues for the religious Zionist public. Persico, "The End Point of Zionism: Ethnocentrism and the Temple Mount," *Israel Studies Review* 32, no. 1 (2017): 104–122.

89. Persico, "End Point of Zionism," 119.

90. Isaiah 42:6.

91. Su'ad Abdul Khabeer, *Muslim Cool: Race, Religion, and Hip Hop in the United States* (New York: New York University Press, 2016), 227.

92. Nadia Abu El-Haj, *Facts on the Ground: Archeological Practice and Territorial Self-Fashioning in Israeli Society* (Chicago: University of Chicago Press, 2001); Nadia Abu El-Haj, *The Genealogical Science: The Search for Jewish Origins and the Politics of Epistemology* (Chicago: University of Chicago Press, 2012).

93. Abu El-Haj, *Facts on the Ground*.

94. Abu El-Haj, *Facts on the Ground*, 125.

95. David M. Goldenberg, *The Curse of Ham: Race and Slavery in Early Judaism, Christianity, and Islam* (Princeton, NJ: Princeton University Press, 2003), 6–8.

96. Genesis chapter 10 lists the seventy descendants of the sons of Noah. From this verse, rabbinic exegesis develops the idea that the world consists of seventy original nations all speaking their own language. The Noahide / Third Temple movement has reinvigorated this idea and imbues it with messianic meaning in their discourses. In messianic times, following the building of the Third Temple, all "seventy nations" will rediscover their Noahide identity and will come to offer sacrifices in the Temple in Jerusalem as the house of the one true God for all of humanity. The nascent Sanhedrin addresses its public statements to the "seventy nations" and imagines that it will someday replace the United Nations as the supreme court of the Noahide nations of the world.

97. Goldenberg, *Curse of Ham*.

98. Goldenberg, *Curse of Ham*, 3.

99. Stephen R. Haynes, *Noah's Curse: The Biblical Justification of American Slavery* (Oxford: Oxford University Press, 2002), 1–9.

100. Tudor Parfitt, "Joining or Rejoining the Jewish People in Africa," in Parfitt and Fisher, *Becoming Jewish*, 6.

101. Edith Bruder, *The Black Jews of Africa: History, Religion, Identity* (Oxford: Oxford University Press, 2008), 52.

102. Benjamin Braude, "The Sons of Noah and the Construction of Ethnic and Geographical Identities in the Medieval and Early Modern Periods," *William and Mary Quarterly* 54, no. 1 (1997): 103–142.

103. Biale, *Blood and Belief*, 162–163.

104. Abu El-Haj, *Genealogical Science*.

105. Tamarkin, *Genetic Afterlives*.

106. Khaled A. Beydoun, *American Islamophobia: Understanding the Roots and Rise of Fear* (Oakland: University of California Press, 2018).

107. Yulia Egorova, "Redefining the Converted Jewish Self: Race, Religion, and Israel's Bene Menashe," *American Anthropologist* 177, no. 3 (2015): 493–505.

108. Menachem Kellner, *Gam Hem Keruyim Adam: haNokhri beEinei haRambam* [They too are called human: Maimonides's views on non-Jews] (Ramat Gan: Bar Ilan University Press, 2016).

109. The Hebrew word "Mizrahi" (literally "Eastern") has become an umbrella term for Jews with origins in North Africa and the Middle East. As Smadar Lavie explains, in addition to its historical usage by the Israeli government and state demographers to group Jews from the MENA region together, the word "Mizrahi" came into usage as a political and coalition term by activists and intellectuals in Israel in the 1980s and 1990s (Lavie, *Wrapped in the Flag of Israel*, 2).

110. Orna Sasson-Levy, "A Different Kind of Whiteness: Marking and Unmarking of Social Boundaries in the Construction of Hegemonic Ethnicity," *Sociological Forum* 28, no. 1 (2013): 27–50.

111. I direct the reader to the following excellent works that provide analyses of intra-Jewish racial hierarchy in Israel and the history of Mizrahi discrimination in the country: Sami Shalom

Chetrit, *Intra-Jewish Conflict in Israel: White Jews, Black Jews* (London: Routledge, 2010); Shoshana Madmoni-Gerber, *Israeli Media and the Framing of Internal Conflict: The Yemenite Babies Affair* (New York: Palgrave Macmillan, 2009); Lavie, *Wrapped in the Flag of Israel*.

112. Lavie, *Wrapped in the Flag of Israel*, 80.

113. Lavie, *Wrapped in the Flag of Israel*, 119.

CHAPTER 2   BIBLICAL REVIVAL IN CONTEMPORARY ISRAEL

1. This particular quote is reported by David Sheen in his article on Baruch Ben Yosef (born in the United States as Andy Green), who was himself a member of Kahane's KACH party and remains a suspect in the murder of Palestinian human rights activist Alex Odeh. Sheen, "Alleged Assassin of Alex Odeh Finds Safe Harbor in Israel" (Americans for Middle East Understanding, 2020), http://www.ameu.org/Current-Issue/Current-Issue/2020-Volume-53/UPDATED-The-Latest-on-the-Suspected-Murderers-of.aspx.

2. Meir Kahane was an American Israeli and Orthodox Rabbi who first rose to political prominence in the United States when he founded the Jewish Defense League in 1968 an organization that promoted Jewish pride and armed Jewish militancy in response to anti-semitism in America. The organization later dissolved after members were imprisoned for arms smuggling and terrorist activities. In 1971 Kahane moved to Israel, where he founded the ultranationalist KACH party and gained a seat in the Israeli Parliament in 1984. In 1986 KACH was banned in Israel and labeled a terrorist organization in both Israel and the United States, and Kahane was forced to leave Parliament. Kahane was assassinated in 1990 by Egyptian American El Sayyid Nosair, who admitted to murdering Kahane when he was later convicted of aiding in the World Trade Center bombing. For more background on the development of Kahane's political ideology during his time in the United States and in Israel, see Shaul Magid's recent cultural history on the topic, *Meir Kahane: The Public Life and Political Thought of an American Jewish Radical* (Princeton, NJ: Princeton University Press, 2021).

3. Inbari, *Jewish Fundamentalism*.

4. Inbari, *Jewish Fundamentalism*, 33–39.

5. In the 1990s, Rabbi Shlomo Goren, former Chief Ashkenazi Rabbi of Israel who served in the IDF and participated in the capture of East Jerusalem in 1967, fought against the pilgrim-age prohibition, which he saw as a serious obstacle to securing Israeli sovereignty over the Temple Mount. Goren advocated for a change in the public consciousness toward the Temple Mount, persuading public figures and government representatives to ascend the mount in the name of fulfilling the sacred biblical commandment of conquering the Land of Israel.

6. Ariel, *Unusual Relationship*, 202.

7. Ariel, *Unusual Relationship*, 202–208.

8. Craig Larkin and Michael Dumper, "In Defense of Al-Aqsa: The Islamic Movement inside Israel and the Battle for Jerusalem," *Middle East Journal* 66, no. 1 (2012): 31–52.

9. Sophia Brown, "Contested Space: Control and Resistance in Rema Hammami's East Jerusalem," *Journal of Commonwealth Literature* 51, no. 2 (2016): 287–301.

10. Yitzhak Reiter, *Jerusalem and Its Role in Islamic Solidarity* (New York: Palgrave Macmillan, 2008), 109.

11. I was informed of this trend by a spokesperson from the foundation during an interview that I conducted in their offices in East Jerusalem in 2015.

12. Peter Beaumont, "What's Driving the Lone Wolves Who Are Stalking the Streets of Jerusalem?," *Guardian*, October 17, 2015, https://www.theguardian.com/world/2015/oct/18/knife-intifada-palestinian-israel-west-bank.

13. Arnon Segal, "The Vision of a Former Member of the Jewish Underground: A Train to the Temple," *Makor Rishon,* September 6, 2013, https://www.makorrishon.co.il/nrg/online/11/ART2/504/492.html (Hebrew).

14. Dunne and Raby, *Speculative Everything,* 3.

15. Dunne and Raby, *Speculative Everything,* 12.

16. This phrase was commonly used by informants from the Temple Movement and is taken from verses of the prophet Isaiah (56:7): "For My House shall be called a House of Prayer for all Nations."

17. A photograph of the reconstructed menorah can be found online: Temple Institute, "History of the Holy Temple Menorah" (2020), https://templeinstitute.org/history-holy-temple-menorah/.

18. Dunne and Raby, *Speculative Everything,* 31–49.

19. The Temple Institute mission statement can be found here: Temple Institute, "About the Temple Institute" (2020), https://templeinstitute.org/about-us/.

20. According to reports by Israeli NGOs Ir Amim and Keshev (March 1, 2013), "The State of Israel directly funds various Temple movement activities. In the years 2008–2011, the Ministry of Culture, Science and Sports and the Ministry of Education supported the Temple Institute and the Midrasha at an average rate of NIS 412,000 [approximately $150,000] per year. In 2012, the Midrasha, the educational arm of the Temple Institute, received NIS 189,000 [approximately $48,000] from the Ministry of Education." See Ir Amim and Keshev, "Dangerous Liaison: The Dynamics of the Rise of the Temple Movements and Their Implications" (March 1, 2013), http://www.ir-amim.org.il/sites/default/files/Dangerous%20Liaison-Dynamics%20of%20the%20Temple%20Movements.pdf. In 2016, it was also reported that the Ministry of Defense gave the Temple Institute NIS 150,000 ($41,096). See Shachar Ilan, "The Mystery of the Estates committee and the Financing of the Holy Grail: This I How the State Distributes the funds It Inherits," *Calcalist,* October 13, 2016, https://www.calcalist.co.il/local/articles/0,7340,L-3699721,00.html (Hebrew).

21. Rachel Feldman, "Jewish Theocracy at the Biblical Barbeque: The Role of Third Temple Activism and Sacrificial Reenactments in Shaping Self and State," *Journal of Contemporary Jewry* 40 (2020): 431–452.

22. Adam Eliyahu Berkowitz, "Sanhedrin Appoints High Priest in Preparation for the Third Temple," *Israel 365 News,* August 29, 2016, http://www.breakingisraelnews.com/74772/sanhedrin-appoints-high-priest-preparation-third-temple/#GpSzDlOJwZ4tdbFg.97.

23. Indiegogo, "The World's First Institute for Training Kohanim" (n.d.), https://www.indiegogo.com/projects/the-world-s-first-institute-for-training-kohanim.

24. Mario Krämer, "Introduction: Ethnicity as a Political Resource in Different Regions of the World," in *Ethnicity as a Political Resource in different regions of the world,* ed. University of Cologne Forum (Bielefeld, Germany: Transcript-Verlag, 2015), 99–106.

25. Sarina Chen, "The Ethos of Self-Sacrifice in the Rituals of Sacrifices: The Temple Activists Are Shaping a Post-nationalist Orthodox Identity," *Struggle for Modern Jewish Identity* 1 (2014): 273–280 (Hebrew).

26. Rabbi Yisrael Ariel's speech on Jewish theocratic conquest was recorded during a Third Temple conference in Jerusalem on September 9, 2015, by David Sheen and is viewable online: https://www.youtube.com/watch?v=9edV7ta-r-Y.

27. Inbari, *Jewish Fundamentalism,* 51–77.

28. Inbari, *Jewish Fundamentalism,* 13.

29. Shaul Magid provides a thorough analysis of Meir Kahane's particular brand of theocratic post-Zionism and critique of liberalism and antidemocratic ideology in his recent history of Kahane's life and philosophy. Magid, *Meir Kahane,* 159–190.

30. Magid, *Meir Kahane*, 172–177.

31. Michael Schaeffer Omer-Man, "Israel's Chief Rabbi Urges Building Jewish Temple on Temple Mount Haram al-Sharif," +972 *Magazine*, June 11, 2016, https://972mag.com/israels -chief-rabbi-urges-building-jewish-temple-on-temple-mountharam-al-sharif/119972/.

32. Nir Hasson, "One Third of Israeli Jews Want the Temple Rebuilt in Jerusalem, Poll Finds," *Haaretz*, July 12, 2013. www.haaretz.com/israel-news.premium-1.535336.

33. Yossi Verter, "Temple Mount Extremists Making Inroads in Both Knesset and Israeli Government," *Haaretz*, October 30, 2015, http://www.haaretz.com/israel-news/.premium-1.683179.

34. Marissa Newman, "Temple Mount Activists Convene in Knesset, Urge PM to 'Open Gates' to Jewish Prayer," *Times of Israel*, November 7, 2016, http://www.timeofisrael.com/temple -mount-activists-convene-in-knesset-urge-pm-to-open-gates-to-jewish-prayer/.

35. Persico, "End Point of Zionism."

36. For additional information and news coverage of the debate, see, for example, the following report that was published on the Channel 7 website: Shimon Cohen, "They Looked for the Temple Mount in the Curriculum and Didn't Find It," *Arutz Sheva*, November 17, 2021, https://www.inn.co.il/news/531959 (Hebrew).

37. Yehouda A. Shenhav, "How Did the Mizrahim Become Religious and Zionist? Zionism, Colonialism, and the Religionization of the Arab Jew," *Israel Studies Forum* 19, no. 1 (2003): 73.

38. Sasson-Levy, "Different Kind of Whiteness," 29–34.

39. Nissim Leon, "The Secular Origins of Mizrahi Traditionalism," *Israel Studies* 13, no. 3 (2008): 23.

40. Sasson-Levy, "Different Kind of Whiteness," 36.

41. Nir Hasson, "Ten People Were Arrested on the Eve of Passover for Attempting to Offer a Passover Sacrifice on the Temple Mount," *Haaretz*, April 23, 2016, www.haaretz.co.il/news /education/1.2924506 (Hebrew).

42. Ido Ben Porat, "Fifteen Right Wing Activists Were Arrested on the Way to the Temple Mount," *Arutz Sheva*, May 12, 2016, www.inn.co.il/News/News.aspx/321895 (Hebrew).

43. According to police reports, 5,658 Jews visited the Mount in 2009 and nearly 11,000 in 2014. See, for example, the following reports citing these police estimates: http://the—temple .blogspot.fr/2015/01/blog-post_11.html (Hebrew); http://www.jpost.com/Israel-News/Jewish -visitors-to-Temple-Mount-increase-by-92-percent-since-2009-389154 (English). Temple activists volunteer to document visitor numbers weekly and post the data online. Weekly numbers can be accessed on the Facebook page of the "Yaraeh" (It Will Be Seen), https://www .facebook.com/yaraeh.temple.mount, as well as on the Facebook page of "Beyadenu" (The Temple Mount Is in Our Hands), a 2021 merger of the former Temple Mount Faithful with Students for the Temple Mount, https://www.facebook.com/Beyadenu. Numbers tend to spike during Jewish holidays and on days of repentance and fasting. On Tisha B'Av 2021, a fasting day commemorating the destruction of the Second Temple, a record 1,679 Jews, including Knesset members Amichai Chikli and Yomtov Kalfon, ascended to the Temple Mount through guided pilgrimage tours under the protection and coordination of the police. On the same day, Prime Minister Naftali Bennett issued a public statement affirming Jewish "freedom of worship" on the Temple Mount, a controversial move that seemed to signal a change in policy by breaking with a long-term "status quo" agreement between Israel and the Waqf that enables Jews to visit but not to engage in prayer or ritual on the site. Amos Harel, "Bennet's Announcement about Jewish Pilgrimage to the Temple Mount Is Portrayed as a Change in the Israeli Position," *Haaretz*, July 18, 2021, https://www.haaretz.co.il/news/politics/.premium .HIGHLIGHT-1.10010627 (Hebrew).

44. A report written by Temple Movement activists on Haredi participation was posted on *Temple Blogspot*, an important blog active at the time of my research, but no longer active

now. Accessed December 2017. http://the-temple.blogspot.co.il/2016/11/blog-post_18.html (Hebrew).

45. Temple Mount guides refer to the act of going to the Temple Mount as an *aliyah*, meaning to go up or ascend. In Hebrew, aliyah refers to both spiritual and physical ascent in a number of contexts. The phrase *aliyah laregel* literally means to ascend by foot and is the closest equivalent to the English word "pilgrimage." In the biblical sense, aliyah refers to those who would travel to Jerusalem to bring offerings to the Temple during the three yearly pilgrimage festivals. In the twentieth century, it has most famously been used to refer to the waves of Jewish immigrants moving to the Land of Israel.

46. On February 29, 2016, members of Women for the Temple argued against rabbinic mikveh restrictions before the Knesset's Committee on Gender Equality.

47. As is the case in many of Israel's hotspot military checkpoints in the West Bank, the Haram ash-Sharif is predominantly policed by Mizrahi Jews, Ethiopian Jews, Druze, and Christian Palestinian soldiers. Mizrahi soldiers are often sent to do the "dirty work" of protecting an Ashkenazi elite in Israel, a dynamic that reflects broader racial inequalities and power dynamics in Israel. Tom Mehager examines these dynamics in "Terrorist Shooting in Hebron: The Syndrome of the Mizrahi Guard," *Haokets*, March 28, 2016, www.haokets.org (Hebrew).

48. First attributed to Ori Tzvi Greenberg (1896–1981), a revisionist Zionist and political leader who advocated for Jewish sovereignty over all of the historic Land of Israel.

49. Rina made these comments during an interview with Channel 7 News. The link to her interview is no longer available online.

50. Rabbi Yitzhak Ginsburgh is an American Israeli rabbi whose teachings blend messianic religious Zionism with Chabad mysticism to advocate for the rebuilding of the Third Temple and the revival of a Jewish monarchy in the Land of Israel. He has also participated in the production of materials and resources for Noahides, notably through the publication of his popular book *Kabbalah and Meditation for the Nations*.

51. According to Youssef Mukhemer, the former president of the Murabitoun in an online interview available through Jordan News Agency, accessed September 2018, http://petra.gov .jo/Public_News/Nws_NewsDetails.aspx?lang=1&site_id=2&NewsID=169397&Type=P) (Arabic).

52. Devorah Margolin, "Women's Liberation: Violence and Palestinian Women in the Third Intifada," *Haaretz*, October 27, 2015, http://www.haaretz.com/opinion/.premium-1.682558.

53. Tamar El Or and Haim Watzman, *Next Year I Will Know More: Literacy and Identity among Young Orthodox Women in Israel* (Detroit: Wayne State University Press, 2002); Yael Israel-Cohen, *Between Feminism and Orthodox Judaism: Resistance, Identity, and Religious Change in Israel* (Leiden: Brill, 2012).

54. Jewish Orthodoxy typically does not ordain women with the title of "rabbi." However, programs like the one offered at Midreshet Lindenbaum, while still controversial in the Orthodox world, allow women to undertake the same course of study as male rabbis and become arbiters of Jewish Law. The ordination program requires five years of intensive study and passing exams equivalent to those required for male rabbis.

55. Idit Bartov, Interview with Idit Bartov. "In the Halakha of the Temple Mount, The Women are Leading the Men," *Mishelach* July 30, 2014, http://www.mishelach.co.il/2014/07 (Hebrew).

56. See Babylonian Talmud, Chullin Daf, 60b. This is a midrash on Genesis 1:16 explaining why the moon, originally equal in size and light to the sun, was diminished. According to the parable, the moon (representing feminine energy) complained about sharing power with the sun and was diminished by God, who eventually brings an atonement offering for decreasing the light of the moon. This parable is often read in religious circles as an explanation for male

dominance, the sacred but concealed power of women, and the eventual rectification of the moon's light (feminine energy) in messianic times as alluded to in the blessing for the new lunar month: "May the light of the moon be like the light of sun and like the light of the seven days of Creation, as it was before it was diminished."

57. Nira Yuval-Davis, *Gender and Nation* (London: SAGE, 1997), 39.

58. Paola Bacchetta and Margaret Power, *Right Wing Women: From Conservatives to Extremists around the World* (New York: Routledge, 2002); Amrita Basu, "The Gendered Imagery and Women's Leadership of Hindu Nationalism," *Reproductive Health Matters* 4, no. 8 (1996): 70–76.

59. bell hooks, "Feminism and Militarism: A Comment," *Women's Studies Quarterly* 23, nos. 3–4 (1995): 58–64; Laura Duhan Kaplan, "Woman as Caretaker: An Archetype That Supports Patriarchal Militarism." *Hypatia* 9, no. 2 (1994): 123–133; Michaela Di Leonardo, "Morals, Mothers, and Militarism: Antimilitarism and Feminist Theory," *Feminist Studies* 11, no. 3 (1985): 611–615.

60. Yifat Ehrlich, "The Temple Mount in Their Hands," *Yediot Ahronot* (Latest News), November 6, 2016 (Hebrew).

61. See also the video coverage of Women for the Temple by Israel's Channel 1 news: https://www.youtube.com/watch?v=HEjfoVRZOgI#t=142 (Hebrew). Ido Ben Porat, "Defense Minister Outlaws Temple Mount Screamers," *Arutz Sheva*, September 9, 2015, www.israelnational news.com/News/News.aspx/200493; Ben Porat, "Fifteen Right Wing Activists Were Arrested"; Ari Soffer, "Temple Mount: Jews Harassed Ordered to 'Respect Ramadan,'" *Arutz Sheva*, June 30, 2014, www.israelnationalnews.com/News/News.aspx/182344.

62. Tamara Neuman, "Maternal 'Anti-Politics' in the Formation of Hebron's Jewish Enclave," *Journal of Palestine Studies* 33, no. 2 (2004): 51–70.

63. Lihi Ben Shitrit, *Righteous Transgressions: Women's Activism on the Israeli and Palestinian Religious Right Wing* (Princeton, NJ: Princeton University Press, 2015), 81–82; Feige, *Settling in the Hearts*, 212; Gideon Aran and Tamar El-Or, "Giving Birth to a Settlement: Maternal Thinking and Political Action of Jewish Women in the West Bank," *Gender and Society* 9, no. 1 (1995): 60–78.

64. Aran and El-Or , 52–56.

65. Feige, *Settling in the Hearts*, 212–228.

66. Kobi Cohen-Hattab, "Zionism, Tourism, and the Battle for Palestine: Tourism as a Political-Propaganda Tool," *Israel Studies* 9, no. 1 (2004): 61–85.

67. Tamar Katriel, *Performing the Past: A Study of Israeli Settlement Museums* (New York: Routledge, 2009).

68. Cohen-Hattab, "Zionism, Tourism, and the Battle for Palestine," 71.

69. In Hebrew, the word *madrikh* (guide) is used to refer to a guide in a number of contexts, such as secular tourism guides. The word can also refer to a leader or teacher in a spiritual context. For example, religious seminaries often appoint more advanced students to be *madrikhim* (guides), spiritual mentors for younger students.

70. Cohen-Hattab, "Zionism, Tourism, and the Battle for Palestine," 72.

71. Cohen-Hattab, "Zionism, Tourism, and the Battle for Palestine," 71.

72. Gideon Bar, "Reconstructing the Past: The Creation of Jewish Sacred Space in the State of Israel 1948–1967," *Israel Studies* 13, no. 3 (2008): 1–21.

73. Jackie Feldman, "Constructing a Shared Bible Land: Jewish Israeli Guiding Performances for Protestant Pilgrims," *American Ethnologist* 34, no. 2 (2007): 351–374.

74. Hava Schwartz, "The Return to the Monument: The Looming Absence of the Temple," *Israel Studies Review* 32, no. 1 (2017): 48–66.

75. Schwartz, "Return to the Monument," 61.

76. Joel Beinin, "Mixing, Separation, and Violence in Urban Spaces and the Rural Frontier in Palestine," *Arab Studies Journal* 21, no. 1 (2013): 14–47.

77. Akhil Gupta, "Blurred Boundaries: The Discourse of Corruption, the Culture of Politics, and the Imagined State," *American Ethnologist* 22, no. 2 (1995): 375–402.

78. James Ferguson and Akhil Gupta, "Spatializing States: Toward an Ethnography of Neoliberal Community," *American Ethnologist* 29, no. 4 (2002): 981–1002.

79. Christopher Krupa, "State by Proxy: Privatized Government in the Andes," *Comparative Studies in Society and History* 52, no. 2 (2010): 319–350.

80. Krupa, "State by Proxy," 319.

81. Robinson, *Citizen Strangers*, 10.

82. The 2015 survey conducted by the Palestinian Center for Policy and Survey Research, "Palestinian Public Opinion Poll No-58," can be accessed online: http://www.pcpsr.org/en/node/625.

83. See the following online report: "Dichter: Waqf Sovereignty on Temple Mount Ended Friday," *Israel National News*, July 18, 2017, http://www.israelnationalnews.com/News/Flash.aspx/393019.

84. Sheked Orbak, "And So Right Wing Organizations Annex the Human Rights Discourse," *Haaretz*, February 23, 2017, http://www.haaretz.co.il/magazine/.premium-1.3882719 (Hebrew).

85. Schlomo Fischer, "From Yehuda Etzion to Yehuda Glick: From Redemptive Revolution to Human Rights on the Temple Mount," *Israel Studies Review* 32, no. 1 (2017): 88–103; Nicola Perugini and Neve Gordon, *The Human Right to Dominate* (Oxford: Oxford University Press, 2015).

86. Perugini and Gordon, *Human Right to Dominate*, 15.

87. Perugini and Gordon, *Human Right to Dominate*, 17.

88. Perugini and Gordon, *Human Right to Dominate*, 23.

89. The term "apartheid" has been used by scholars of Israel/Palestine and human rights activists to argue that Israel's system of control over Palestinians and self-definition as a Jewish state (whereby rights and privileges are distributed according to one's particular racial status) meets the international definition of an apartheid state. The term "apartheid" is also commonly used to draw a comparison between the conditions of apartheid South Africa and those under Israeli control over the occupied Palestinian territories, most notably in the West Bank, where Palestinians cannot travel freely, can reside only in specific Palestinian cantons, have limited access to land and natural resources, and are subject to Israeli military law (meanwhile Jews in the West Bank enjoy unrestricted mobility along with and the protection and rights afforded them by Israeli citizenship). Some extend the apartheid analogy to Palestinians holding citizenship inside of Israel's internationally recognized borders established after the 1948 War of Independence, arguing that Palestinians living inside Israel proper are still subject to a form of second-class citizenship and have limited access to land and resources.

90. Asad et al., *Is Critique Secular?*

91. Yehouda Shlezinger, "Temple Mount Activist Eyes the Presidency," *Israel Hayom*, October 14, 2020, https://www.israelhayom.com/2020/10/14/temple-mount-activist-eyes-the-presidency/.

CHAPTER 3   "BORN AGAIN, AGAIN"

1. I take this phrase from Noahide preacher Rod Bryant, a former Christian pastor and army chaplain who founded Netiv, the Texas-based Noahide education center described in chapter 3.

2. Goldman, *Zeal for Zion*, 270–308.

3. Goldman, *Zeal for Zion*, 308.

4. Here I refer to those congregations and denominations belonging to a syncretic religious movement often referred to as "Messianic Judaism" that combines belief in Jesus as the messiah with observance of Jewish ritual traditions and holidays.

5. Ariel, *Unusual Relationship*, 1–14.

6. Harding, *Book of Jerry Falwell*, 3–20.

7. Harding, *Book of Jerry Falwell*.

8. Harding, *Book of Jerry Falwell*, 228–241.

9. Hummel, *Covenant Brothers*, 168.

10. Hummel, *Covenant Brothers*, 13.

11. Hummel, *Covenant Brothers*, 227.

12. Hummel, *Covenant Brothers*, 7.

13. The earliest known listing of the Seven Laws can be found in the Tosefta, a second-century compilation of Jewish Law that was not included in the Mishnah.

14. See Tractate Sanhedrin, 56a–60a.

15. David Novak, *The Image of the Non-Jew in Judaism* (Portland, OR: Littman Library of Jewish Civilization, 1983).

16. Novak, *Image of the Non-Jew in Judaism*, 20.

17. Novak, *Image of the Non-Jew in Judaism*, 153.

18. Maxwell Luria, introduction to Elijah Benamozegh, *Israel and Humanity* (Mahwah, NJ: Paulist Press, 1995), 20.

19. Novak, *Image of the Non-Jew in Judaism*, 25.

20. Novak, *Image of the Non-Jew in Judaism*, 26.

21. Novak, *Image of the Non-Jew in Judaism*, 28.

22. Novak, *Image of the Non-Jew in Judaism*, 28–29.

23. Novak, *Image of the Non-Jew in Judaism*, 31.

24. See, for example, Babylonian Talmud, Tractate Sanhedrin, 58b: "And Reish Lakish says: A gentile who observed Shabbat is liable to receive the death penalty, as it is stated: 'And day and night shall not cease' (Genesis 8:23), which literally means: And day and night they shall not rest. This is interpreted homiletically to mean that the descendants of Noah may not take a day of rest. And the Master said that their prohibition is their death penalty, i.e., the punishment for any prohibition with regard to descendants of Noah is execution. Ravina says: If a descendant of Noah observes a day of rest on any day of the week, even one not set aside for religious worship, e.g., on a Monday, he is liable."

25. See, for example, Tractate Sanhedrin, 59a: "And Rabbi Yoḥanan says: A gentile who engages in Torah study is liable to receive the death penalty; as it is stated: 'Moses commanded us a law [torah], an inheritance of the congregation of Jacob' (Deuteronomy 33:4), indicating that it is an inheritance for us, and not for them. The Gemara answers: There, in the baraita, the reference is to a gentile who engages in the study of their seven mitzvot. It is a mitzva for a gentile to study the halakhot that pertain to the seven Noahide mitzvot, and when he does so he is highly regarded."

26. Maimonides, "Laws of Kings and Their Wars."

27. Maimonides, "Laws of Kings and Their Wars," 8:10.

28. Eugene Korn, "Gentiles, the World to Come, and Judaism: The Odyssey of a Rabbinic Text," *Modern Judaism* 14, no. 3 (1994): 281.

29. Maimonides, "Laws of Kings and Their Wars," 8:11.

30. Maimonides, "Laws of Kings and Their Wars."

31. Korn, "Gentiles, the World to Come, and Judaism," 266.

32. Novak, *Image of the Non-Jew in Judaism*, 153–175.

33. Maimonides, "Laws of Kings and Their Wars," 12:1–2.

34. Maimonides, "Laws of Kings and Their Wars," 12:4–5.

35. Maimonides, "Laws of Kings and Their Wars," 9:9: "A non-Jew who busied himself with Torah is liable with his life. From Heaven, because others will see him perform Mitzvohs and being engaged in Torah and will be deceived. They will think him a practicing Jew and err after him. . . . He must involve himself in their Seven Commandments only. . . . There is no reason to mention (that he is culpable) if he invented his own holiday. The principle here is that we do not permit them to make a new religion and create new commandments for themselves based on their own reasoning. They may only become Righteous Converts and accept upon themselves all the Commandments, or they must observe their own (Seven) Laws only, and not add or detract from them."

36. Maimonides, "Laws of Kings and Their Wars," 9:9.

37. Novak, *Image of the Non-Jew in Judaism*, 15.

38. Aimé Pallière, *The Unknown Sanctuary: A Pilgrimage from Rome to Israel*, New ed. (New York: Bloch, 1971), 134.

39. Pallière, *Unknown Sanctuary*.

40. Benamozegh, *Israel and Humanity*, 45.

41. Benamozegh, *Israel and Humanity*, 262.

42. Pallière, *Unknown Sanctuary*, 23.

43. Pallière, *Unknown Sanctuary*, 23–26.

44. Pallière, *Unknown Sanctuary*, 47.

45. Pallière, *Unknown Sanctuary*, 136.

46. Pallière, *Unknown Sanctuary*, 139.

47. Pallière, *Unknown Sanctuary*, 139.

48. Pallière, *Unknown Sanctuary*, 150.

49. Pallière, *Unknown Sanctuary*, 167.

50. Jeffrey Kaplan, *Radical Religion in America: Millenarian Movements from the Far Right to the Children of Noah* (Syracuse, NY: Syracuse University Press, 1997), 115.

51. Jeffrey Kaplan, *Radical Religion in America*.

52. Kaplan, *Radical Religion in America*, xv.

53. Kaplan, *Radical Religion in America*.

54. Kaplan gives the example of the Christian Identity movement, an offshoot of British Israelism founded on antisemitic and white supremacist ideologies. Christian Identity promoted the belief that Caucasians were the lost tribes of Israel and Jews were the offspring of Satan who had stolen their identity and "robbed them of knowledge of their covenantal birthright." Kaplan, *Radical Religion in America* 3–4.

55. In his autobiography, Jones claims that one of the script writers of the film participated in his excavations as a volunteer and based the character of Indiana Jones on him.

56. Detailed in Jones's autobiography *A Door of Hope*.

57. Jones, *Door of Hope*, 60.

58. Jones, *Door of Hope*, 146.

59. In 2006 the nascent Sanhedrin invited American Noahide leaders to form a Noahide council called the High Council of Bnei Noah.

60. Kahane's speech is available online: NETIV, "Rabbi Meir Kahane 1990 Speech to the Bnei Noach," YouTube, August 24, 2016, https://www.youtube.com/watch?v=7CiZtwg-S04&t=551s.

61. Magid, *Meir Kahane*, 75–106.

62. Magid, *Meir Kahane*, 75–106.

63. Shaul Magid describes Kahane's vision of Zionism as stemming fundamentally from his belief in Jewish separatism. Magid, *Meir Kahane*, 176.

64. Magid, *Meir Kahane*. Magid documents Kahane's militant and ultranationalist vision of Zionism, a vision that he argues stemmed from Kahane's ideological obsession with remedying diasporic Jewish weakness.

65. J. David Davis, *Finding the God of Noah: The Spiritual Journey of a Baptist Minister from Christianity to the Laws of Noah* (Brooklyn: KTAV, 1997), 79.

66. Davis, *Finding the God of Noah*, 85.

67. Davis, *Finding the God of Noah*, 86.

68. Davis, *Finding the God of Noah*, 131.

69. Davis, *Finding the God of Noah*, 134.

70. Davis, *Finding the God of Noah*, 193.

71. Davis, *Finding the God of Noah*, 172.

72. Davis, *Finding the God of Noah*, 173.

73. Davis, *Finding the God of Noah*, 176–177.

74. Donny Fuchs, "The Sons of Noach: Genuine Righteous Gentiles Revisited," *Jewish Press*, October 19, 2017, http://www.jewishpress.com/indepth/columns/fuchs-focus/the-sons-of -noach-genuine-righteous-gentiles-revisited/2017/10/19/.

75. Oren Golan, "Charting Frontiers of Online Religious Communities: The Case of Chabad Jews," in Campbell, *Digital Religion*, 155–163.

76. From the text of a letter written by the Rebbe in English to Army Chaplain Brig. Gen. Israel Drazin in 1986, first printed in *Wellsprings* no. 7 (vol. 3, no. 5, 1987). Republished more recently in Yehoishophot Oliver, *To Perfect the World: The Lubavitcher Rebbe's Call to Teach the Noahide Code to All Mankind* (Brooklyn: SIE, 2015), a compilation of translated talks given by the Rebbe. Published in 2015 by Sichos in English, copyrighted by Rabbi Yehoishophot Oliver and Ask Noah International.

77. In order to make this claim, the Rebbe grounds his argument in Maimonides's discussion of the Noahide laws in the *Mishneh Torah*, where Maimonides writes, "Moses was commanded by the Almighty to compel all the inhabitants of the world to accept the commandments given to Noah's descendants" (8:10). According to Maimonides, Moses was commanded not only to bestow 613 commandments of Mosaic Law upon the Children of Israel but also to transmit the Seven Noahide Laws to the Gentile nations. From this line the Rebbe concludes that all Jews remain beholden to the mission of Moses. Just as they are commanded to uphold Mosaic Law, Jews are also required by Torah Law to continue transmission of Noahide Laws. According to the Rebbe, Jews are required by God to deliver knowledge of the Noahide code to the nations through peaceful verbal persuasion.

78. Oliver, *To Perfect the World*, 5. The Torah refers to the "souls that they [Abraham and Sarah] made in Charan" (Bereshit 12:5). Rashi interprets this verse to mean that Abraham and Sarah converted Gentiles, convincing them to abandon idolatry and believe in the one true God, which is according to the Rebbe, a biblical precedent for Noahide outreach.

79. Oliver, *To Perfect the World*, 8–20.

80. Oliver, *To Perfect the World*, 39. The Rebbe is quoted as having stated, "One should approach a Gentile and explain to him—in a pleasant manner—that since God cares about his personal welfare, He sent the Jew, who possesses a spark of Moshe, to convey his command that was issued to Moshe at Mount Sinai (as part of the giving of the Torah to the Jewish people) for the Gentile nations to abide by the Noahide Code. One should also explain to him that this is beneficial for civilizing the world. These words will surely succeed in having their intended effect."

81. The resolution text from 1991 is available online on the Congress website at https://www .congress.gov/bill/102ndcongress/house-joint-resolution/104/text.

82. Oliver, *To Perfect the World*, 42.

83. Judy Maltz, "'Thou Shalt Not Kill' Applies to You Too, Jewish Campaign Tells Palestinians and Israeli Arabs," *Haaretz*, December 10, 2015, https://www.haaretz.com/israel-news/2015-12-10/ty-article/.premium/thou-shalt-not-kill-applies-to-you-too-chabad-tells-arabs/0000017f-f086-dc28-a17f-fcb7f43e0000.

84. Elliot Wolfson, *Open Secret: Postmessianic Messianism and the Mystical Revision of Menaḥęm Mendel Schneerson* (New York: Columbia University Press, 2009), 132.

85. Updated information on Netiv and Bryant's biography comes from Shloime Zionce, "Nothing but the Truth: Rod (Reuven) Bryant Explains How He Became a Leader in the International Movement to Keep the Sheva Mitzvos Bnei Noach," *Ami Magazine*, September 18, 2019, https://www.amimagazine.org/2019/09/18/nothing-but-the-truth/.

86. Zionce, "Nothing but the Truth."

87. Zionce, "Nothing but the Truth."

88. Zionce, "Nothing but the Truth."

89. Zionce, "Nothing but the Truth."

90. The lecture is titled "Clarifying Common Misconceptions about the Noahide." It can be viewed online: NETIV, "Clarifying Common Misconceptions about the Noahide" (July 28, 2019), https://www.youtube.com/watch?v=stScFNb-37Q.

91. NETIV, "Clarifying Common Misconceptions."

92. NETIV, "Clarifying Common Misconceptions."

93. NETIV, "Clarifying Common Misconceptions."

94. NETIV, "Clarifying Common Misconceptions."

95. Campbell, "How Religious Communities Negotiate New Media Religiously," 5.

96. Christopher Helland, "Online-Religion/Religion-Online and Virtual Communities," in *Religion on the Internet: Research Prospects and Promises*, ed. J. K. Hadden and D. E Cowan (New York: JAI Press, 2000), 205–223; Morten T. Hojsgaard and Margit Warburg, eds., *Religion and Cyberspace* (New York: Routledge, 2005); Eileen Barker, "Crossing the Boundary: New Challenges to Religious Authority and Control as a Consequence of Access to the Internet," in Hojsgaard and Warburg, *Religion and Cyberspace*, 67–85; Bryan S. Turner, "Religious Authority and the New Media," *Media, Theory, Culture & Society* 24, no. 2 (2007): 117–134.

97. Stewart M. Hoover, "Religious Authority in the Media Age," in *The Media and Religious Authority*, ed. Stewart M. Hoover (University Park: Pennsylvania State University Press, 2016), 15–36.

98. Ayala Fader, *Hidden Heretics: Jewish Doubt in the Digital Age* (Princeton, NJ: Princeton University Press, 2019); Rozehnal, *Cyber Sufis*; Gary Bunt, *Hastag Islam: How Cyber-Islamic Environments Are Transforming Religious Authority* (Chapel Hill: University of North Carolina Press, 2018); Campbell, "How Religious Communities Negotiate New Media Religiously."

99. Cheong, "Authority," 75.

100. Michal Raucher, "Yoatzot Halacha: Ruling the Internet, One Question at a Time," in *Digital Judaism: Jewish Negotiations with Digital Media and Culture*, ed. Heidi Campbell (New York: Routledge, 2015), 57–73.

101. Heidi Campbell and Oren Golan, "Creating Digital Enclaves: Negotiation of the Internet among Bounded Religious Communities," *Media, Culture, and Society* 33, no. 5 (2011): 709–724.

102. Heidi Campbell, *Digital Creatives and the Rethinking of Religious Authority* (Abingdon: Routledge, 2021), 73–100.

103. Cheong, "Authority," 72–87; Nabil Echchaibi, "From Audio Tapes to Video Blogs: The Delocalisation of Authority in Islam," *Nations and Nationalism* 17, no. 1 (2011): 25–44.

104. Brettschneider, *Jewish Phenomenon*.

105. Brettschneider, *Jewish Phenomenon*, 2–13.

106. Brettschneider, *Jewish Phenomenon*, 21.

107. The Noahide Academy homepage can be viewed here: https://www.noahide-academy .com.

108. These quotes were taken from the "About Us" page of the Noahide Academy website: https://www.noahide-academy.com/about-us/.

109. The Philippines page of the Noahide Academy website can be viewed online: https:// www.noahide-academy.com/philippines-noahide-community/.

110. Kenton J. Clymer, *Protestant Missionaries in the Philippines, 1898–1916: An Inquiry into the American Colonial Mentality* (Urbana: University of Illinois Press, 1986), 154.

111. Wolfson, *Open Secret*, 229.

112. Wolfson, *Open Secret*, 231.

113. Wolfson, *Open Secret*, 236.

114. Alfred A. Cave, "Canaanites in a Promised Land: The American Indian and the Providential Theory of Empire," *American Indian Quarterly* 12, no. 4 (1988): 277–297.

115. Lincoln, *Religion, Empire, and Torture*, 16.

116. The full text of the declaration is available online at https://www.noahideworldcenter .com/full-declaration-in-languages/.

117. A map of Brit Olam's global affiliated Noahide communities is available on their website: https://noahideworldcenter.org/pages/communities.

118. "Rabbi David Lau Blesses Noahides and Brit Olam. Noahide World Center, June 13, 2014, video, 5:00, https://www.youtube.com/watch?v=PHlHSy_2udE.

CHAPTER 4　"RIGHTEOUS AMONG THE NATIONS"

1. For more background on religious diversification in the Philippines, see, for example, the following scholarship: Jayeel S. Cornelio, "Institutional Religion and Modernity-in-Transition: Christianity's Innovations in Philippines and Latin America," *Philippine Studies* 56, no. 3 (2008): 345–358; Christl Kessler and Jurgand Ruland, "Responses to Rapid Social Change: Populist Religion in the Philippines," *Pacific Affairs* 79, no. 1 (2006): 73–96; Gerry M. Lanuza, "The New Cult Phenomenon in Philippine Society," *Philippines Studies* 47, no. 4 (1999): 492–514; Raymundo Go, The Philippine Council of Evangelical Churches: Its Background, Context, and Formation among Post–World War II Churches (Carlisle: Langham Monographs, 2019); Vicente L. Rafael, White Love: And Other Events in Filipino History (Durham, NC: Duke University Press, 2000); James A. Beckford and Araceli Suzara, "A New Religious and Healing Movement in the Philippines," *Religion* 24, no. 2 (1994): 117–141.

2. Manuel Victor J. Sapitula and Jayeel S. Cornelio, "A Religious Society? Advancing the Sociology of Religion in the Philippines," *Philippine Sociological Review* 62 (2014): 1–9.

3. The term *conversos* refers to Sephardic Jews who were forcibly converted to Catholicism during the Inquisition and later resettled in the Spanish colonies, where some continued to live in hiding as crypto-Jews passing down Jewish customs in secrecy inside the home.

4. See, for example, recent case studies of emerging Jewish communities, lost tribe claims, and contestations over recognition documented in the following scholarship: Devir, *New Children of Israel*; Parfitt, "Joining or Rejoining the Jewish People in Africa"; Stuart Charme, "Newly Found Jews and the Politics of Recognition," *Journal of the American Academy of Religion* 80, no. 2 (2012): 387–410; Courtney Handman, "Israelite Genealogies and Christian Commitment: The Limits of Language Ideologies in Guhu-Samane Christianity," *Anthropological Quarterly* 84, no. 3 (2011): 655–677.

5. Go, *Philippine Council of Evangelical Churches*, 55–111.

6. Cornelio, "Institutional Religion and Modernity-in-Transition."

7. Go, *Philippine Council of Evangelical Churches*, 67.

8. Luis Q. Lacar, "Balik-Islam: Christian Converts to Islam in the Philippines, c. 1970–98," *Islam and Christian-Muslim Relations* 12, no. 1 (2001): 41.

9. Teresita Cruz-Del Rosario, "Return to Mecca: Balik-Islam among Filipino Migrants in Singapore," *Transitions: Journal of Transient Migration* 2, no. 2 (2018): 95–97.

10. Cruz-Del Rosario, "Return to Mecca," 95–97.

11. Cruz-Del Rosario, "Return to Mecca," 52.

12. Philippine Survey Authority, "Survey on Overseas Filipinos" (December 2, 2022), https://psa.gov.ph/statistics/survey/labor-and-employment/survey-overseas-filipinos.

13. See, for example, the following scholarship on conversion to Islam among Filipino/a foreign workers: Teresita Cruz-Del Rosario, "Return to Mecca," 97; Attiya Ahmed, *Everyday Conversions: Islam, Domestic Work, and South Asian Migrant Women in Kuwait* (Durham, NC: Duke University Press, 2017).

14. Liat Ayalon and Sharon Shiovitz-Ezra, "The Experience of Loneliness among Live-In Filipino Homecare Workers in Israel: Implications for Social Workers," *British Journal of Social Work* 40, no. 8 (2010): 2538–2559.

15. In the Jewish tradition, it is customary to dispose of texts that contain the name of God through burial.

16. Wolfson, *Open Secret*, 231.

17. Wolfson, *Open Secret*, 238.

18. Wolfson, *Open Secret*, 233.

19. Kellner, *Gam Hem Keruyim Adam*, 215.

20. The song is available online: Salve Gamora, "Bro. Jerome Pagalan Suson—Singing 'Baruch Ad-nai,'" YouTube, April 23, 2015, https://www.youtube.com/watch?v=43Ej9zhf98I.

21. Bonnie M. Harris, *Philippine Sanctuary: A Holocaust Odyssey* (Madison: University of Wisconsin Press, 2020), 69.

22. Brettschneider, *Jewish Phenomenon*, 9.

23. Zvi Ben-Dor Benite, *The Ten Lost Tribes* (Oxford: Oxford University Press, 2009), 58.

24. Benite, *Ten Lost Tribes*.

25. Benite, *Ten Lost Tribes*, 3.

26. Benite, *Ten Lost Tribes*, 24.

27. Bruder, *Black Jews of Africa*, 13.

28. Yulia Egorova and Shahid Perwez, "The Children of Ephraim: Being Jewish in Andhra Pradesh," *Anthropology Today* 26, no. 6 (2010): 14–18.

29. Egorova and Perwez, "Children of Ephraim," 15.

30. Egorova and Perwez, "Children of Ephraim."

31. Noah Tamarkin, "Religion as Race, Recognition as Democracy: Lemba 'Black Jews' in South Africa," *Annals of the American Academy of Political and Social Science* 637 (2011): 161.

32. Tamarkin, *Genetic Afterlives*.

33. As Yulia Egorova explains in her article on the Bnei Menashe resettlement, according to most historians and anthropologists, the Bnei Menashe practiced an indigenous animist religion until their conversion to Christianity in the nineteenth century and began identifying with the tribe of Menashe only in the 1950s. Egorova, "Redefining the Converted Jewish Self," 496.

34. In the case of the Bene Menashe, Orthopraxis provides a path toward social inclusion into Israeli society. In her work on the topic, Yulia Egorova explains, "Because of the racialized way in which the Bene Menashe immigrants are perceived in Israel, they are forced to emphasize their religious 'superiority' vis-à-vis other migrants to be able to develop a positive sense of self" ("Redefining the Converted Jewish Self," 495). Through religion, the Bene Menashe can override their racial otherness and become proper citizens who reinforce the political agenda of the state (494).

35. Kravel-Tovi addresses these dynamics (Orthopraxis as a conduit for national inclusion) in her recent ethnography of state-sponsored conversion in Israel among immigrants from the former Soviet Union. Her work also addresses the ways in which conversions are vetted and legitimated in Israel and how conversion facilitates state biopolitical goals. Kravel-Tovi, *When the State Winks*.

36. Bruder, *Black Jews of Africa*, 192.

37. Jonathan Freedman, "Conversos, Marranos, and Crypto-Jews," in *Boundaries of Jewish Identity*, ed. Susan A. Glenn and Naomi B. Sokoloff (Seattle: University of Washington Press, 2010), 190.

38. Freedman, "Conversos, Marranos, and Crypto-Jews," 192.

39. Freedman, "Conversos, Marranos, and Crypto-Jews," 193–194.

40. Kravel-Tovi, *When the State Winks*, 80.

41. Examples of previous research from the early twentieth century that investigated the arrival of Sephardic Jewish conversos to the Philippines include George Alexander Kohut, "Jewish Heretics in the Philippines in the Sixteenth and Seventeenth Century," *Publications of the American Jewish Historical Society* 12, no. 12 (1904): 149–156; Charles H. Cunningham, "The Inquisition in the Philippines: The Salcedo Affair," *Catholic Historical Review* 3, no. 4 (1918): 417–445.

CONCLUSION

1. Rabbi Oury Cherki's writings on Zionism can be found online on the Brit Olam: World Noahide Center website: https://noahideworldcenter.org.

2. I refer here again to Motti Inbari's use of the phrase "post-Zionism" to describe the "theocratic post-Zionism" of Third Temple activists and religious-nationalists post-1967. Inbari, *Jewish Fundamentalism*, 51–77.

3. For a historical and ethnographic treatment of Jewish indigeneity-making practices in Israel/Palestine, see Rachel Feldman and Ian McGonigle, eds., *Settler-Indigeneity in the West Bank* (Montreal: McGill-Queens University Press, 2023).

4. Veracini, *Israel and Settler Society*, 14–22.

5. Adam Eliyahu Berkowitz, "Trump's Jerusalem Declaration: 'Enormous Steps Towards Bringing the Temple,'" *Israel 365 News*, December 7, 2017, https://www.breakingisraelnews.com/99002/trumps-jerusalem-declaration-next-step-third-temple/#/.

6. See, for example, Ezra 1:1–2 and Isaiah 45:1.

7. Adam Eliyahu Berkowitz, "Trump's Peace Deal Is Akin to Decree of King Cyrus Paving the Path for the Third Temple Says Israeli Politician," *Israel 365 News*, January 20, 2020, https://www.israel365news.com/144207/trumps-peace-deal-is-akin-to-decree-of-king-cyrus-paving-the-path-for-the-third-temple-says-israeli-politician/.

8. Tuly Weisz, "Unto the Nations—Trump Isn't Cyrus Yet," *Jerusalem Post*, March 27, 2019, https://www.jpost.com/opinion/unto-the-nations-trump-isnt-cyrus-yet-584939.

9. Tara Isabella Burton, "The Biblical Story the Christian Right Uses to Defend Trump," *Vox*, March 5, 2018, https://www.vox.com/identities/2018/3/5/16796892/trump-cyrus-christian-right-bible-cbn-evangelical-propaganda.

10. Hummel, *Covenant Brothers*, 168.

11. Daniel Seidemann, "The UAE-Israel Accord Is a Victory for Temple Mount Extremists," *+972 Magazine*, September 1, 2020, https://www.972mag.com/temple-mount-jerusalem-uae-israel/.

12. For more information on the Syrian edict against conversion, see the following article: Zevulun Lieberman, "A Sefardic Ban on Converts," *Tradition: A Journal of Orthodox Jewish Thought* 23, no. 2 (Winter 1988): 22–25.

13. Goldenberg, *Curse of Ham.*

14. For background on Ashkenazi Ultra-Orthodox anti-Zionism, see, for example, Aviezer Ravitzky, *Messianism, Zionism, and Jewish Religious Radicalism,* trans. Michael Swirsky and Jonathan Chipman (Chicago: University of Chicago Press, 1996); Motti Inbari, *Jewish Radical Ultra-Orthodoxy Confronts Modernity, Zionism and Women's Equality* (Cambridge: Cambridge University Press, 2016). For background on secular and religious Mizrahi challenges to Zionism, see, for example, Moshe Behar and Zvi Ben-Dor Benite, *Modern Middle Eastern Jewish Thought: Writings on Identity, Politics, and Culture, 1893–1958* (Waltham, MA: Brandeis University Press, 2013).

15. Sue Surkes, "Israel Chief Rabbi Urges Rebuilding Jerusalem Temple," *Times of Israel,* June 9, 2016, https://www.timesofisrael.com/israel-chief-rabbi-urges-rebuilding-jerusalem -temple/.

16. Jeremy Sharon, "Non-Jews in Israel Must Keep Noahide Laws, Chief Rabbi Says," *Jerusalem Post,* March 28, 2016, https://www.jpost.com/Israel-News/Non-Jews-are-forbidden-by -Jewish-law-to-live-in-Israel-chief-rabbi-says-449395.

17. Scholem, *Messianic Idea in Judaism,* 36.

18. Marx, Dalia. "The Missing Temple: The Status of the Temple in Jewish Culture Following Its Destruction." *European Judaism* 46, no. 2 (2013): 64.

19. Rebbe Nachman of Breslov, *Likutey Halachot, Tzitzit* 3:2, 5:6.

20. Marx, Dalia. "The Missing Temple: The Status of the Temple in Jewish Culture Following Its Destruction." *European Judaism* 46, no. 2 (2013): 66.

21. As Mahmood Mamdani explains, liberal ideologies developed in tandem with modern colonial projects as abstract concepts of "autonomy, sovereignty, and self-preservation" were articulated to rationalize conquest. Mamdani, *Neither Settler nor Native: The Making and Unmaking of Permanent Minorities* (Cambridge, MA: Belknap, 2020), 9.

22. This is a famous and often quoted phrase taken from the daily Jewish liturgy that is recited at the conclusion of the "Amidah" prayer: "May it be your will, O my God and God of my fathers, that the Temple be rebuilt speedily in our days, and give us our portion in your Torah, and there we will worship you with reverence as in ancient days and former years."

BIBLIOGRAPHY

Abu El-Haj, Nadia. *Facts on the Ground: Archeological Practice and Territorial Self-Fashioning in Israeli Society*. Chicago: University of Chicago Press, 2001.

———. *The Genealogical Science: The Search for Jewish Origins and the Politics of Epistemology*. Chicago: University of Chicago Press, 2012.

Abu Hussein, Hadeel S. *The Struggle for Land under Israeli Law: An Architecture of Exclusion*. London: Routledge, 2022.

Ahmed, Attiya. *Everyday Conversions: Islam, Domestic Work, and South Asian Migrant Women in Kuwait*. Durham, NC: Duke University Press, 2017.

Alexander, M. Jacqui. *Pedagogies of Crossing: Meditations on Feminism, Sexual Politics, Memory, and the Sacred*. Durham, NC: Duke University Press, 2005.

Almeida, Ronaldo, and Paula Monteiro. "Transito religioso no Brasil." *Sao Paulo Perspectiva* 15, no. 3 (2001): 92–101.

Anidjar, Gil. *The Jew, the Arab: A History of the Enemy*. Stanford, CA: Stanford University Press, 2003.

Appadurai, Arjun. *Modernity at Large: Cultural Dimensions of Globalization*. Minneapolis: University of Minnesota Press, 1996.

Aran, Gideon. *Kookisk: The Roots of Gush Emunum, the Settlers' Culture, Zionist Theology and Messianism in Our Age*. Jerusalem: Carmel Press, 2013 (Hebrew).

Aran, Gideon, and Tamar El-Or. "Giving Birth to a Settlement: Maternal Thinking and Political Action of Jewish Women in the West Bank." *Gender and Society* 9, no. 1 (1995): 60–78.

Ariel, Yaakov S. *An Unusual Relationship: Evangelical Christians and Jews*. New York: New York University Press, 2013.

Asad, Talal. *Formations of the Secular: Christianity, Islam, Modernity*. Stanford, CA: Stanford University Press, 2003.

Asad, Talal, Wendy Brown, Judith Butler, and Saba Mahmood. *Is Critique Secular? Blasphemy, Injury, and Free Speech*. New York: Fordham University Press, 2013.

Ayalon, Liat, and Sharon Shiovitz-Ezra. "The Experience of Loneliness among Live-In Filipino Homecare Workers in Israel: Implications for Social Workers." *British Journal of Social Work* 40, no. 8 (2010): 2538–2559.

Azoulay, Ariella, and Adi Ophir. *The One-State Condition: Occupation and Democracy in Israel/ Palestine*. Stanford, CA: Stanford University Press, 2013.

Bacchetta, Paola, and Margaret Power. *Right Wing Women: From Conservatives to Extremists around the World*. New York: Routledge, 2002.

Bar, Gideon. "Reconstructing the Past: The Creation of Jewish Sacred Space in the State of Israel 1948–1967." *Israel Studies* 13, no. 3 (2008): 1–21.

Bartov, Idit. "In the Halakha of the Temple Mount, the Women Are Leading the Men." *Mishelach*. July 30, 2014. http://www.mishelach.co.il/2014/07 (Hebrew).

Basu, Amrita. "The Gendered Imagery and Women's Leadership of Hindu Nationalism." *Reproductive Health Matters* 4, no. 8 (1996): 70–76.

Beaumont, Peter. "What's Driving the Lone Wolves Who Are Stalking the Streets of Jerusalem?" *Guardian*, October 17, 2015. https://www.theguardian.com/world/2015/oct/18 /knife-intifada-palestinian-israel-west-bank.

Beckford, James A., and Araceli Suzara. "A New Religious and Healing Movement in the Philippines." *Religion* 24, no. 2 (1994): 117–141.

Behar, Moshe, and Zvi Ben-Dor Benite. *Modern Middle Eastern Jewish Thought: Writings on Identity, Politics, and Culture, 1893–1958.* Waltham, MA: Brandeis University Press, 2013.

Beinin, Joel. "Mixing, Separation, and Violence in Urban Spaces and the Rural Frontier in Palestine." *Arab Studies Journal* 21, no. 1 (2013): 14–47.

Beliso-De Jesús, Aisha M. *Electric Santería: Racial and Sexual Assemblages of Transnational Religion.* New York: Columbia University Press, 2015.

Benamozegh, Elijah. *Israel and Humanity.* Translated by Maxwell Luria. Mahwah, NJ: Paulist Press, 1995.

Benite, Zvi Ben-Dor. *The Ten Lost Tribes.* Oxford: Oxford University Press, 2009.

Ben Porat, Ido. "Defense Minister Outlaws Temple Mount Screamers." *Arutz Sheva,* September 9, 2015. www.israelnationalnews.com/News/News.aspx/200493.

———. "Fifteen Right Wing Activists Were Arrested on the Way to the Temple Mount." *Arutz Sheva,* May 12, 2016. www.inn.co.il/News/News.aspx/321895 (Hebrew).

Ben Shitrit, Lihi. *Righteous Transgressions: Women's Activism on the Israeli and Palestinian Religious Right Wing.* Princeton, NJ: Princeton University Press, 2015.

Berkowitz, Adam Eliyahu. "Sanhedrin Appoints High Priest in Preparation for the Third Temple." *Israel 365 News,* August 29, 2016. http://www.breakingisraelnews.com/74772/sanhedrin-appoints-high-priest-preparation-third-temple/#GpSzDlOJwZ4tdbFg.97.

———. "Trump's Jerusalem Declaration: 'Enormous Steps towards Bringing the Temple.'" *Israel 365 News,* December 7, 2017. https://www.breakingisraelnews.com/99002/trumps-jerusalem-declaration-next-step-third-temple/#/.

———. "Trump's Peace Deal Is Akin to Decree of King Cyrus Paving the Path for the Third Temple Says Israeli Politician." *Israel 365 News,* January 20, 2020. https://www.israel365news.com/144207/trumps-peace-deal-is-akin-to-decree-of-king-cyrus-paving-the-path-for-the-third-temple-says-israeli-politician/.

Beydoun, Khaled A. *American Islamophobia: Understanding the Roots and Rise of Fear.* Oakland: University of California Press, 2018.

Biale, David. *Blood and Belief: The Circulation of a Symbol between Jews and Christians.* Berkeley: University of California Press, 2007.

Birman, Patricia. "Cultos de possess o e pentecostalismo no Brasil: Passagens." *Religio e Sociedade* 17 (1996): 90–109.

Braude, Benjamin. "The Sons of Noah and the Construction of Ethnic and Geographical Identities in the Medieval and Early Modern Periods." *William and Mary Quarterly* 54, no. 1 (1997): 103–142.

Brenner, Michael. "Global Israel: A State Beyond Borders." In *In Search of Israel: The History of an Idea,* 230–265. Princeton, NJ: Princeton University Press, 2018.

Brettschneider, Marla. *The Jewish Phenomenon in Sub-Saharan Africa: The Politics of Contradictory Discourses.* Lewiston, NY: Edwin Mellen Press, 2015.

Brown, Sophia. "Contested Space: Control and Resistance in Rema Hammami's East Jerusalem." *Journal of Commonwealth Literature* 51, no. 2 (2016): 287–301.

Bruder, Edith. *The Black Jews of Africa: History, Religion, Identity.* Oxford: Oxford University Press, 2008.

Buber, Martin. *The Legend of the Baal-Shem.* Princeton, NJ: Princeton University Press, 1995.

Bucaille, Laetitia. *Growing Up Palestinian: Israeli Occupation and the Intifada Generation.* Princeton, NJ: Princeton University Press, 2004.

Bull, Malcolm, and Keith Lockhart. *Seeking a Sanctuary: Seventh-Day Adventism and the American Dream.* 2nd ed. Bloomington: Indiana University Press, 2007.

Bunt, Gary. *Hastag Islam: How Cyber-Islamic Environments Are Transforming Religious Authority*. Chapel Hill: University of North Carolina Press, 2018.

Burton, Tara Isabella. "The Biblical Story the Christian Right Uses to Defend Trump." *Vox*, March 5, 2018. https://www.vox.com/identities/2018/3/5/16796892/trump-cyrus-christian -right-bible-cbn-evangelical-propaganda.

Campbell, Heidi. *Digital Creatives and the Rethinking of Religious Authority*. Abingdon: Routledge, 2021.

———, ed. *Digital Judaism: Jewish Negotiations with Digital Media and Culture*. London: Routledge, 2015.

———. "How Religious Communities Negotiate New Media Religiously." In *Digital Religion, Social Media and Culture: Perspectives, Practices, and Futures*, edited by Pauline Hope Cheong, Peter Fisher-Nielsen, Stefan Gelfgren, and Charles Ess, 81–96. New York: Peter Lang, 2012.

Campbell, Heidi, and Oren Golan. "Creating Digital Enclaves: Negotiation of the Internet among Bounded Religious Communities." *Media, Culture, and Society* 33, no. 5 (2011): 709–724.

Campbell, Heidi, and Ruth Tsuria, eds. *Digital Religion: Understanding Religious Practice in Digital Media*. New York: Routledge, 2021.

Carpenedo, Manoela. *Becoming Jewish, Believing in Jesus: Judaizing Evangelicals in Brazil*. New York: Oxford University Press, 2021.

Castor, Fedeke N. *Spiritual Citizenship: Transnational Pathways from Black Power to Ifa in Trinidad*. Durham, NC: Duke University Press, 2017.

Cave, Alfred A. "Canaanites in a Promised Land: The American Indian and the Providential Theory of Empire." *American Indian Quarterly* 12, no. 4 (1988): 277–297.

Charme, Stuart. "Newly Found Jews and the Politics of Recognition." *Journal of the American Academy of Religion* 80, no. 2 (2012): 387–410.

Chen, Sarina. "The Ethos of Self-Sacrifice in the Rituals of Sacrifices: The Temple Activists Are Shaping a Post-nationalist Orthodox Identity." *Struggle for Modern Jewish Identity* 1 (2014): 273–280 (Hebrew).

———. *Soon in Our Days: The Temple Mount and National Religious Society*. Beer Sheva: Ben Gurion University Press, 2018 (Hebrew).

Cheong, Pauline Hope. "Authority." In *Digital Religion: Understanding Religious Practice in New Media Worlds*, edited by Heidi A. Campbell, 72–87. New York: Routledge, 2013.

Cheong, Pauline Hope, Peter Fisher-Nielsen, Stefan Gelfgren, and Charles Ess, eds. *Digital Religion, Social Media, and Culture: Perspectives, Practices, and Futures*. New York: Peter. Lang, 2012.

Cheong, Pauline Hope, Shirlena Huang, and Jessie P. H. Poon. "Religious Communication and Epistemic Authority of Leaders in Wired Faith Organizations." *Information, Communication, and Society* 11, no. 1 (2011): 89–100.

Chetrit, Sami Shalom. *Intra-Jewish Conflict in Israel: White Jews, Black Jews*. London: Routledge, 2010.

Chow, Christie Chui-Shan. *Schism: Seventh-Day Adventism in Post-denominational China*. Notre Dame, IN: University of Notre Dame Press, 2021.

Clifford, James, and George E. Marcus, eds. *Writing Culture: The Poetics and Politics of Ethnography*. Berkeley: University of California Press, 1986.

Clymer, Kenton J. *Protestant Missionaries in the Philippines, 1898–1916: An Inquiry into the American Colonial Mentality*. Urbana: University of Illinois Press, 1986.

Cohen, Shimon. "They Looked for the Temple Mount in the Curriculum and Didn't Find It." *Arutz Sheva*. November 17, 2021. https://www.inn.co.il/news/531959 (Hebrew).

Cohen-Hattab, Kobi. "Zionism, Tourism, and the Battle for Palestine: Tourism as a Political-Propaganda Tool," *Israel Studies* 9, no. 1 (2004): 61–85.

Cohn-Sherbok, Dan. *Messianic Judaism: A Critical Anthology*. London: Bloomsbury, 2000.

Collins, John. *Global Palestine*. New York: Columbia University Press, 2011.

Comaroff, Jean. *Body of Power, Spirit of Resistance: The Culture and History of a South African People*. Chicago: University of Chicago Press, 1985.

Cornelio, Jayeel S. "Institutional Religion and Modernity-in-Transition: Christianity's Innovations in Philippines and Latin America." *Philippine Studies* 56, no. 3 (2008): 345–358.

Cruz-Del Rosario, Teresita. "Return to Mecca: Balik-Islam among Filipino Migrants in Singapore." *Transitions: Journal of Transient Migration* 2, no. 2 (2018): 95–97.

Csordas, Thomas J. *Transnational Transcendence: Essays on Religion and Globalization*. Berkeley: University of California Press, 2009.

Cunningham, Charles H. "The Inquisition in the Philippines: The Salcedo Affair." *Catholic Historical Review* 3, no. 4 (1918): 417–445.

Dalsheim, Joyce. *Unsettling Gaza: Secular Liberalism, Radical Religion, and the Israeli Settlement Project*. Oxford: Oxford University Press, 2011.

Davis, Uri. *Apartheid in Israel: Possibilities for the Struggle Within*. London: Zed, 2003.

Davis, J. David. *Finding the God of Noah: The Spiritual Journey of a Baptist Minister from Christianity to the Laws of Noah*. Brooklyn: KTAV, 1997.

Devir, Nathan. *New Children of Israel: Emerging Jewish Communities in an Era of Globalization*. Salt Lake City: University of Utah Press, 2017.

Di Leonardo, Michaela. "Morals, Mothers, and Militarism: Antimilitarism and Feminist Theory." *Feminist Studies* 11, no. 3 (1985): 611–615.

Drori, Israel. *Foreign Workers in Israel: Global Perspectives*. Albany: State University of New York Press, 2009.

Dulin, John. "Messianic Judaism as a Mode of Christian Authenticity: Exploring the Grammar of Authenticity through Ethnography of a Contested Identity." *Anthropos* 108, no. 1 (2013): 35–51.

Dunne, Anthony, and Fiona Raby. *Speculative Everything: Design, Fiction, and Social Dreaming*. Cambridge, MA: MIT Press, 2013.

Echchaibi, Nabil. "From Audio Tapes to Video Blogs: The Delocalisation of Authority in Islam." *Nations and Nationalism* 17, no. 1 (2011): 25–44.

Egorova, Yulia. "Redefining the Converted Jewish Self: Race, Religion, and Israel's Bene Menashe." *American Anthropologist* 177, no. 3 (2015): 493–505.

Egorova, Yulia, and Shahid Perwez. "The Children of Ephraim: Being Jewish in Andhra Pradesh." *Anthropology Today* 26, no. 6 (2010): 14–18.

Ehrlich, Yifat. "The Temple Mount in Their Hands." *Yediot Ahronot* [Latest news], November 6, 2016 (Hebrew).

El Or, Tamar, and Haim Watzman. *Next Year I Will Know More: Literacy and Identity among Young Orthodox Women in Israel*. Detroit: Wayne State University Press, 2002.

Fader, Ayala. *Hidden Heretics: Jewish Doubt in the Digital Age*. Princeton, NJ: Princeton University Press, 2019.

Feige, Michael. *Settling in the Hearts: Jewish Fundamentalism in the Occupied Territories*. Detroit: Wayne State University Press, 2009.

Feldman, Jackie. "Constructing a Shared Bible Land: Jewish Israeli Guiding Performances for Protestant Pilgrims." *American Ethnologist* 34, no. 2 (2007): 351–374.

Feldman, Rachel. "I Call It 'Rabbi YouTube': Rabbinic Authority in the Digital Age and Global South." *Association for Judaic Studies Review* 46, no. 1 (April 2023): 1–24.

————. "Jewish Theocracy at the Biblical Barbeque: The Role of Third Temple Activism and Sacrificial Reenactments in Shaping Self and State." *Journal of Contemporary Jewry* 40 (2020): 431–452.

Feldman, Rachel, and Ian McGonigle, eds. *Settler-Indigeneity in the West Bank.* Montreal: McGill-Queens University Press, 2023.

Ferguson, James, and Akhil Gupta. "Spatializing States: Toward an Ethnography of Neoliberal Community." *American Ethnologist* 29, no. 4 (2002): 981–1002.

Fine, Lawrence. *Physician of the Soul, Healer of the Cosmos: Isaac Luria and His Kabbalistic Fellowship.* Stanford, CA: Stanford University Press, 2003.

Fischer, Schlomo. "From Yehuda Etzion to Yehuda Glick: From Redemptive Revolution to Human Rights on the Temple Mount." *Israel Studies Review* 32, no. 1 (2017): 88–103.

Freedman, Jonathan. "Conversos, Marranos, and Crypto-Jews." In *Boundaries of Jewish Identity,* edited by Susan A. Glenn and Naomi B. Sokoloff, 188–202. Seattle: University of Washington Press, 2010.

Frigerio, Alejandro. "Analyzing Conversion in Latin America: Theoretical Questions, Methodological Dilemmas, and Comparative Data from Argentina and Brazil." In *Conversion of a Continent: Cotemporary Religious Change in Latin America,* edited by Timothy J. Steigenga and Edward L. Cleary, 33–51. New Brunswick, NJ: Rutgers University Press, 2007.

Fuchs, Donny. "The Sons of Noach: Genuine Righteous Gentiles Revisited." *Jewish Press,* October 19, 2017. http://www.jewishpress.com/indepth/columns/fuchs-focus/the-sons -of-noach-genuine-righteous-gentiles-revisited/2017/10/19/

Ghanem, As'ad. "The Expanding Ethnocracy: Judaization of the Public Space." *Israel Studies Review* 26, no. 1 (2011): 21–27.

Go, Raymundo. *The Philippine Council of Evangelical Churches: Its Background, Context, and Formation among Post–World War II Churches.* Carlisle: Langham Monographs, 2019.

Golan, Oren. "Charting Frontiers of Online Religious Communities: The Case of Chabad Jews." In *Digital Religion,* edited by Heidi Campbell, 155–163. London: Routledge, 2013.

Goldenberg, David M. *The Curse of Ham: Race and Slavery in Early Judaism, Christianity, and Islam.* Princeton, NJ: Princeton University Press, 2003.

Goldman, Shalom. *Zeal for Zion: Christians, Jews, and the Idea of the Promised Land.* Chapel Hill: University of North Carolina Press, 2009.

Gordon, Neve. *Israel's Occupation.* Berkeley: University of California Press, 2008.

Gorenberg, Gershom. *The End of Days: Fundamentalism and the Struggle for the Temple Mount.* Oxford: Oxford University Press, 2000.

Griel, A. L. "Previous Dispositions and Conversion to Perspectives of Social and Religious Movements." *Sociological Analysis* 38, no. 2 (1977): 115–125.

Gupta, Akhil. "Blurred Boundaries: The Discourse of Corruption, the Culture of Politics, and the Imagined State." *American Ethnologist* 22, no. 2 (1995): 375–402.

Hall, John R. *Apocalypse: From Antiquity to the Empire of Modernity.* Cambridge: Polity, 2009.

Halper, Jeff. *Decolonizing Israel, Liberating Palestine: Zionism, Settler Colonialism, and the Case for One Democratic State.* London: Pluto Press, 2021.

Hammer, Jill. *Return to the Place: The Magic, Meditation, and Mystery of Sefer Yetzirah.* Teaneck, NJ: Ben Yehuda Press, 2020.

Handel, Ariel, Marco Allegra, and Erez Maggor, eds. *Normalizing Occupation: The Politics of Everyday Life in the West Bank Settlements.* Bloomington: Indiana University Press, 2017.

Handman, Courtney. "Israelite Genealogies and Christian Commitment: The Limits of Language Ideologies in Guhu-Samane Christianity." *Anthropological Quarterly* 84, no. 3 (2011): 655–677.

Harding, Susan Friend. *The Book of Jerry Falwell: Fundamentalist Language and Politics*. Princeton, NJ: Princeton University Press, 2000.

———. "Representing Fundamentalism: The Problem of the Repugnant Cultural Other." *Social Research* 58, no. 2 (Summer 1991): 373–393.

Harel, Amos. "Bennet's Announcement about Jewish Pilgrimage to the Temple Mount Is Portrayed as a Change in the Israeli Position." *Haaretz*, July 18, 2021. https://www.haaretz.co.il/news/politics/.premium.HIGHLIGHT-1.10010627 (Hebrew).

Harraway, Donna. "Situated Knowledges: The Science Question in Feminism and the Privilege of Partial Perspective." *Feminist Studies* 14, no. 3 (1988): 575–599.

Harris, Bonnie M. *Philippine Sanctuary: A Holocaust Odyssey*. Madison: University of Wisconsin Press, 2020.

Harris-Shapiro, Carol. *Messianic Judaism: A Rabbi's Journey through Religious Change in America*. Boston: Beacon, 1999.

Hasson, Nir. "One Third of Israeli Jews Want the Temple Rebuilt in Jerusalem, Poll Finds." *Haaretz*, July 12, 2013. www.haaretz.com/israel-news.premium-1.535336.

———. "Ten People Were Arrested on the Eve of Passover for Attempting to Offer a Passover Sacrifice on the Temple Mount." *Haaretz*, April 23, 2016. www.haaretz.co.il/news/education/1.2924506 (Hebrew).

Haynes, Stephen R. *Noah's Curse: The Biblical Justification of American Slavery*. Oxford: Oxford University Press, 2002.

Held, Shai. "What Zvi Yehudah Kook Wrought: The Theopolitical Radicalization of Religious Zionism." In *Rethinking the Messianic Idea in Judaism*, edited by Michael L. Morgan and Steven Weitzman, 229–255. Bloomington: Indiana University Press, 2015.

Helland, Christopher. "Online-Religion/Religion-Online and Virtual Communities." In *Religion on the Internet: Research Prospects and Promises*, edited by J. K. Hadden and D. E Cowan, 205–223. New York: JAI Press, 2000.

Heschel, Abraham Joshua. *The Sabbath*. New York: Noonday Press, 1975.

Hojsgaard, Morten T., and Margit Warburg, eds. *Religion and Cyberspace*. New York: Routledge, 2005.

hooks, bell. "Feminism and Militarism: A Comment." *Women's Studies Quarterly* 23, nos. 3–4 (1995): 58–64.

Hoover, Stewart M., ed. *The Media and Religious Authority*. University Park: Pennsylvania State University Press, 2016.

Höschele, Stefan. *Christian Remnant–African Folk Church: Seventh-Day Adventism in Tanzania, 1903–1980*. Leiden: Brill, 2007.

Hughes, Richard T. *Myths America Lives By: White Supremacy and the Stories That Give Us Meaning*. Urbana: University of Illinois Press, 2018.

Hummel, Daniel G. *Covenant Brothers: Evangelicals, Jews, and U.S.-Israeli Relations*. Philadelphia: University of Pennsylvania Press, 2019.

Inbari, Motti. *Jewish Fundamentalism and the Temple Mount*. Albany: State University of New York Press, 2009.

———. *Jewish Radical Ultra-Orthodoxy Confronts Modernity, Zionism and Women's Equality*. Cambridge: Cambridge University Press, 2016.

———. *Messianic Religious Zionism Confronts Israeli Territorial Compromises*. New York: Cambridge University Press, 2012.

Israel-Cohen, Yael. *Between Feminism and Orthodox Judaism: Resistance, Identity, and Religious Change in Israel*. Leiden: Brill, 2012.

Jackson, John L. *Thin Description: Ethnography and the African Hebrew Israelites of Jerusalem*. Cambridge, MA: Harvard University Press, 2013.

Jacobs, Janet Liebman. *Hidden Heritage: The Legacy of the Crypto-Jews*. Berkeley: University of California Press, 2002.

Jones, Vendyl. *A Door of Hope*. Springdale, AR: Lightcatcher Books, 2005.

Joseph, Suad. *Gender and Citizenship in the Middle East*. Syracuse, NY: Syracuse University Press, 2000.

Kaplan, Jeffrey. *Radical Religion in America: Millenarian Movements from the Far Right to the Children of Noah*. Syracuse, NY: Syracuse University Press, 1997.

Kaplan, Laura Duhan. "Woman as Caretaker: An Archetype That Supports Patriarchal Militarism." *Hypatia* 9, no. 2 (1994): 123–133.Karp, Jonathan, and Adam Sutcliffe. *Philosemitism in History*. New York: Cambridge University Press, 2011.

Katriel, Tamar. *Performing the Past: A Study of Israeli Settlement Museums*. New York: Routledge, 2009.

Keller, Eva. *The Road to Clarity: Seventh-Day Adventism in Madagascar*. New York: Palgrave Macmillan, 2005.

Kellner, Menachem. *Gam Hem Keruyim Adam: haNokhri beEinei haRambam* [They too are called human: Maimonides's views on non-Jews]. Ramat Gan: Bar Ilan University Press, 2016.

Kessler, Christl, and Jurgand Ruland. "Responses to Rapid Social Change: Populist Religion in the Philippines." *Pacific Affairs* 79, no. 1 (2006): 73–96.

Khabeer, Su'ad Abdul. *Muslim Cool: Race, Religion, and Hip Hop in the United States*. New York: New York University Press, 2016.

Khalidi, Rashid. *The Hundred Years' War on Palestine: A History of Settler Colonialism and Resistance, 1917–2017*. New York: Metropolitan Books, 2020.

Kimmerling, Baruch. *Zionism and Territory: The Socio-territorial Dimensions of Zionist Politics*. Berkeley: University of California Institute of International Relations, 1983.

Kohut, George Alexander. "Jewish Heretics in the Philippines in the Sixteenth and Seventeenth Century." *Publications of the American Jewish Historical Society* 12, no. 12 (1904): 149–156.

Korn, Eugene. "Gentiles, the World to Come, and Judaism: The Odyssey of a Rabbinic Text." *Modern Judaism* 14, no. 3 (1994): 265–287.

Krämer, Mario. "Introduction: Ethnicity as a Political Resource in Different Regions of the World." In *Ethnicity as a Political Resource*, edited by the University of Cologne Forum, 99–106. Bielefeld, Germany: Transcript Verlag, 2015.

Kravel-Tovi, Michal. *When the State Winks: The Performance of Jewish Conversion in Israel*. New York: Columbia University Press, 2019.

Krupa, Christopher. "State by Proxy: Privatized Government in the Andes." *Comparative Studies in Society and History* 52, no. 2 (2010): 319–350.

Lacar, Luis Q. "Balik-Islam: Christian Converts to Islam in the Philippines, c. 1970–98." *Islam and Christian-Muslim Relations* 12, no. 1 (2001): 39–60.

Lanuza, Gerry M. "The New Cult Phenomenon in Philippine Society." *Philippines Studies* 47, no. 4 (1999): 492–514.

Larkin, Craig, and Michael Dumper. "In Defense of Al-Aqsa: The Islamic Movement Inside Israel and the Battle for Jerusalem." *Middle East Journal* 66, no. 1 (2012): 31–52.

Lavie, Smadar. *Wrapped in the Flag of Israel: Mizrahi Single Mothers and Bureaucratic Torture*. Lincoln: University of Nebraska Press, 2014.

Leon, Nissim. "The Secular Origins of Mizrahi Traditionalism." *Israel Studies* 13, no. 3 (2008): 22–42.

Lieberman, Zevulun. "A Sefardic Ban on Converts." *Tradition: A Journal of Orthodox Jewish Thought* 23, no. 2 (Winter 1988): 22–25.

Lincoln, Bruce. *Religion, Empire, and Torture: The Case of Achaemenian Persia, with a Postscript on Abu Ghraib*. Chicago: University of Chicago Press, 2007.

Lofland, John, and Rodney Stark. "Becoming a World-Saver: A Theory of Conversion to a Deviant Perspective." *American Sociological Review* 30, no. 6 (1965): 862–875.

Long, T. E., and J. K. Hadden. "Religious Conversion and the Concept of Socialization: Integrating the Brainwashing and Drift Models." *Journal for the Scientific Study of Religion* 22, no. 1 (1983): 1–14.

Lustik, Ian. *Paradigm Lost: From Two-State Solution to One-State Reality*. Philadelphia: University of Pennsylvania Press, 2019.

Luzzato, Moshe Chaim. *Secrets of the Future Temple: Mishkney Elyon*. Edited by Avraham Greenbaum. Jerusalem: Azamra Institute, 1999.

Madmoni-Gerber, Shoshana. *Israeli Media and the Framing of Internal Conflict: The Yemenite Babies Affair*. New York: Palgrave Macmillan, 2009.

Magid, Shaul. *Meir Kahane: The Public Life and Political Thought of an American Jewish Radical*. Princeton, NJ: Princeton University Press, 2021.

Makdisi, Saree. *Palestine Inside Out: An Everyday Occupation*. New York: Norton, 2010.

Maltz, Judy. "'Thou Shalt Not Kill' Applies to You Too, Jewish Campaign Tells Palestinians and Israeli Arabs." *Haaretz*, December 10, 2015. https://www.haaretz.com/israel-news/2015-12-10/ty-article/.premium/thou-shalt-not-kill-applies-to-you-too-chabad-tells-arabs/0000017f-f086-dc28-a17f-fcb7f43e0000.

Mamdani, Mahmood. *Neither Settler nor Native: The Making and Unmaking of Permanent Minorities*. Cambridge, MA: Belknap, 2020.

Margolin, Devorah. "Women's Liberation: Violence and Palestinian Women in the Third Intifada." *Haaretz*, October 27, 2015. http://www.haaretz.com/opinion/.premium-1.682558.

Marx, Dalia. "The Missing Temple: The Status of the Temple in Jewish Culture Following Its Destruction." *European Judaism* 46, no. 2 (2013): 61–78.

Masalha, Nur. *Imperial Israel and the Palestinians: The Politics of Expansion*. London: Pluto Press, 2000.

Mazeh, Hanan. "Built, Destroyed, and Built Again: Temple and History in Genesis Rabbah in Light of Christian Sources." *Jewish Quarterly Review* 110, no. 4 (2020): 652–678.

McGonigle, Ian. *Genomic Citizenship: The Molecularization of Identity in the Contemporary Middle East*. Cambridge, MA: MIT Press, 2021.

Mehager, Tom. "Terrorist Shooting in Hebron: The Syndrome of the Mizrahi Guard." *Haokets*, March 28, 2016. www.haokets.org (Hebrew).

Memmi, Albert. *The Colonizer and the Colonized*. Translated by Howard Greenfeld. Boston: Beacon, 1991.

Mirsky, Yehudah. *Rav Kook: Mystic in a Time of Revolution*. New Haven, CT: Yale University Press, 2014.

Morgenstern, Arie, and Joel A. Linsider. *Hastening Redemption: Messianism and the Resettlement of the Land of Israel*. Oxford: Oxford University Press, 2006.

Morris, Benny. *Righteous Victim: A History of the Zionist-Arab Conflict, 1881–1999*. New York: Knopf, 1999.

Neuman, Tamara. "Maternal 'Anti-Politics' in the Formation of Hebron's Jewish Enclave." *Journal of Palestine Studies* 33, no. 2 (2004): 51–70.

Newman, Marissa. "Temple Mount Activists Convene in Knesset, Urge PM to 'Open Gates' to Jewish Prayer." *Times of Israel*, November 7, 2016. http://www.timeofisrael.com/temple-mount-activists-convene-in-knesset-urge-pm-to-open-gates-to-jewish-prayer/.

Novak, David. *The Image of the Non-Jew in Judaism*. Portland, OR: Littman Library of Jewish Civilization, 1983.

Oliver, Yehoishophot. *To Perfect the World: The Lubavitcher Rebbe's Call to Teach the Noahide Code to All Mankind.* Brooklyn: SIE, 2015.

Omer-Man, Michael Schaeffer. "Israel's Chief Rabbi Urges Building Jewish Temple on Temple Mount Haram al-Sharif." *+972 Magazine,* June 11, 2016. https://972mag.com /israels-chief-rabbi-urges-building-jewish-temple-on-temple-mountharam-al-sharif /119972/.

Orbak, Sheked. "And So Right Wing Organizations Annex the Human Rights Discourse." *Haaretz,* February 23, 2017. http://www.haaretz.co.il/magazine/.premium-1.3882719 (Hebrew).

Pallière, Aimé. *The Unknown Sanctuary: A Pilgrimage from Rome to Israel.* New ed. New York: Bloch, 1971.

Pappe, Ilan, ed. *Israel and South Africa: The Many Faces of Apartheid.* London: Zed Books, 2015.

———. *The Making of the Arab-Israeli Conflict, 1947–51.* New York: I. B. Taurus, 1994.

Parfitt, Tudor, and Netanel Fisher, eds. *Becoming Jewish: New Jews and Emerging Jewish Communities in a Globalized World.* Newcastle upon Tyne, UK: Cambridge Scholars, 2016.

Peled, Yoav, and Horit Peled. "Religious Zionism: The Quest for Hegemony." Paper presented at the ECPR General Conference, Wroclaw, September 2019.

Persico, Tomer. "The End Point of Zionism: Ethnocentrism and the Temple Mount." *Israel Studies Review* 32, no. 1 (2017): 104–122.

Perugini, Nicola, and Neve Gordon. *The Human Right to Dominate.* Oxford: Oxford University Press, 2015.

Premawardhana, Devaka. *Faith in Flux: Pentecostalism and Mobility in Rural Mozambique.* Philadelphia: University of Pennsylvania Press, 2018.

Puar, Jasbir K. *The Right to Maim: Debility, Capacity, Disability.* Durham, NC: Duke University Press, 2017.

Rafael, Vicente L. *White Love: And Other Events in Filipino History.* Durham, NC: Duke University Press, 2000.

Raucher, Michal. "Yoatzot Halacha: Ruling the Internet, One Question at a Time." In *Digital Judaism: Jewish Negotiations with Digital Media and Culture,* edited by Heidi Campbell, 57–73. New York: Routledge, 2015.

Ravitzky, Aviezer. *Messianism, Zionism, and Jewish Religious Radicalism.* Translated by Michael Swirsky and Jonathan Chipman. Chicago: University of Chicago Press, 1996.

Reiter, Yitzhak. *Jerusalem and Its Role in Islamic Solidarity.* New York: Palgrave Macmillan, 2008.

Reznick, Rabbi L. *The Holy Temple Revisited.* Northvale, NJ: Jason Aronson, 1993.

Richardson, J. T., and M. Stewart. "Conversion Process Models and the Jesus Movement." In *Conversion Careers: In and Out of the New Religions,* edited by J. T. Richardson, 24–42. Beverly Hills, CA: SAGE, 1978.

Robinson, Shira. *Citizen Strangers: Palestinians and the Birth of Israel's Liberal Settler State.* Stanford, CA: Stanford University Press, 2013.

Rouhana, Nadim. *Identities in Conflict: Palestinian Citizens in an Ethnic Jewish State.* New Haven, CT: Yale University Press, 1997.

Rozehnal, Robert. *Cyber Sufis: Virtual Expression of the American Muslim Experience.* London: Oneworld, 2019.

Said, Edward W. *Orientalism.* New York: Vintage, 1979.

———. *The Politics of Dispossession: The Struggle for Palestinian Self-Determination, 1969–1994.* New York: Pantheon Books, 1994.

———. "Zionism from the Standpoint of Its Victims." *Cultural Politics* 11 (1997): 15–38.

Sapitula, Manuel Victor J., and Jayeel S. Cornelio. "A Religious Society? Advancing the Sociology of Religion in the Philippines." *Philippine Sociological Review* 62 (2014): 1–9.

Sasson-Levy, Orna. "A Different Kind of Whiteness: Marking and Unmarking of Social Boundaries in the Construction of Hegemonic Ethnicity." *Sociological Forum* 28, no. 1 (2013): 27–50.

Scham, Paul. "A Nation That Dwells Alone: Israeli Religious Nationalism in the 21st Century." *Israel Studies* 23, no. 3 (Fall 2018): 207–215.

Scholem, Gershom. *The Messianic Idea in Judaism: And Other Essays on Jewish Spirituality.* New York: Schocken Books, 1971.

Schwartz, Hava. "The Return to the Monument: The Looming Absence of the Temple." *Israel Studies Review* 32, no. 1 (2017): 48–66.

Segal, Arnon. "The Vision of a Former Member of the Jewish Underground: A Train to the Temple." *Makor Rishon.* September 6, 2013. https://www.makorrishon.co.il/nrg/online/11/ART2/504/492.html (Hebrew).

Segev, Tom, and Arlen Neal Weinstein. *1949: The First Israelis.* New York: Free Press, 1986.

Seidemann, Daniel. "The UAE-Israel Accord Is a Victory for Temple Mount Extremists." +972 *Magazine*, September 1, 2020. https://www.972mag.com/temple-mount-jerusalem-uae-israel/.

Sharon, Jeremy. "Non-Jews in Israel Must Keep Noahide Laws, Chief Rabbi Says." *Jerusalem Post*, March 28, 2016. https://www.jpost.com/Israel-News/Non-Jews-are-forbidden-by-Jewish-law-to-live-in-Israel-chief-rabbi-says-449395.

Sheen, David. "Alleged Assassin of Alex Odeh Finds Safe Harbor in Israel." Americans for Middle East Understanding, 2020. http://www.ameu.org/Current-Issue/Current-Issue/2020-Volume-53/UPDATED-The-Latest-on-the-Suspected-Murderers-of.aspx.

Shenhav, Yehouda A. *The Arab Jews: A Postcolonial Reading of Nationalism, Religion, and Ethnicity.* Stanford, CA: Stanford University Press, 2006.

———. "How Did the Mizrahim Become Religious and Zionist? Zionism, Colonialism, and the Religionization of the Arab Jew." *Israel Studies Forum* 19, no. 1 (2003): 73.

Shenhav, Yehouda, and Yossi Yonah, eds. *Racism in Israel.* Jerusalem: Van Leer Institute and Hakibbutz Hameuchad, 2008 (Hebrew).

Shlezinger, Yehuda. "Temple Mount Activist Eyes the Presidency." *Israel Hayom*, October 14, 2020. https://www.israelhayom.com/2020/10/14/temple-mount-activist-eyes-the-presidency/.

Shohat, Ella. *On the Arab-Jew, Palestine, and Other Displacements: Selected Writings.* London: Pluto Press, 2017.

———. "The Split Arab/Jew Figure Revisited." *Patterns of Prejudice* 54, no. 1–2 (2020): 46–70.

Smooha, Sammy. "Minority Status in an Ethnic Democracy: The Status of the Arab Minority in Israel." *Ethnic and Racial Studies* 13, no. 3 (1990): 389–413.

Soffer, Ari. "Temple Mount: Jews Harassed Ordered to 'Respect Ramadan.'" *Arutz Sheva*, June 30, 2014. www.israelnationalnews.com/News/News.aspx/182344.

Stark, Rodney, and Roger Finke. *Acts of Faith: Explaining the Human Side of Religion.* Berkeley: University of California Press, 2000.

Stoler, Ann Laura. *Along the Archival Grain: Epistemic Anxieties and Colonial Common Sense.* Princeton, NJ: Princeton University Press, 2009.

Strauss, Roger A. "Religious Conversion as a Personal and Collective Accomplishment." *Sociological Analysis* 40, no. 2 (1979): 158–165.

Surkes, Sue. "Israel Chief Rabbi Urges Rebuilding Jerusalem Temple." *Times of Israel*, June 9, 2016. https://www.timesofisrael.com/israel-chief-rabbi-urges-rebuilding-jerusalem-temple/.

Tamarkin, Noah. *Genetic Afterlives: Black Jewish Indigeneity in South Africa.* Durham, NC: Duke University Press, 2020.

———. "Religion as Race, Recognition as Democracy: Lemba 'Black Jews' in South Africa." *Annals of the American Academy of Political and Social Science* 637 (2011): 148–164.

Taragin-Zeller, Lea. *The State of Desire: Religion and Reproductive Politics in the Promised Land.* New York: New York University Press, 2023.

Tsing, Anna Lowenhaupt. *Friction: An Ethnography of Global Connection.* Princeton, NJ: Princeton University Press, 2005.

Turner, Bryan S. "Religious Authority and the New Media," *Media, Theory, Culture & Society* 24, no. 2 (2007): 117–134.

van der Haven, Alexander. *From Lowly Metaphor to Divine Flesh: Sarah the Ashkenazi, Sabbatai Tsevi's Messianic Queer and the Sabbatian Movement.* Amsterdam: Menasseh ben Israel Instituut, 2012.

van der Veer, Peter. *Imperial Encounters: Religion and Modernity in India and Britain.* Princeton, NJ: Princeton University Press, 2001.

Vásquez, Manuel A., and Marie F. Marquardt. *Globalizing the Sacred: Religion Across the Americas.* New Brunswick, NJ: Rutgers University Press, 2003.

Veracini, Lorenzo. *Israel and Settler Society.* London: Pluto Press, 2006.

Verter, Yossi. "Temple Mount Extremists Making Inroads in Both Knesset and Israeli Government." *Haaretz,* October 30, 2015. http://www.haaretz.com/israel-news/.premium-1.683179.

Weber, Max. *The Theory of Social and Economic Organization.* Edited by Talcott Parsons. Translated by A. M. Henderson. New York: Free Press, 1964.

Weiner, Moshe. *The Divine Code.* Pittsburgh: Ask Noah International, 2011.

Weisz, Tuly. "Unto the Nations—Trump Isn't Cyrus Yet." *Jerusalem Post,* March 27, 2019. https://www.jpost.com/opinion/unto-the-nations-trump-isnt-cyrus-yet-584939.

Weizman, Eyal. *Hollow Land: Israel's Architecture of Occupation.* London: Verso, 2012.

Wolfson, Elliot. *Open Secret: Postmessianic Messianism and the Mystical Revision of Menaḥem Mendel Schneerson.* New York: Columbia University Press, 2009.

Yiftachel, Oren. *Ethnocracy: Land and Identity Politics in Israel/Palestine.* Philadelphia: University of Philadelphia Press, 2006.

Yitzhaki, Aharon. *The Mask: Introduction to the Ethnic Strategy in the State of Israel-Comparative Research.* Israel: Kotarot (Hebrew).

Yuval-Davis, Nira. *Gender and Nation.* London: SAGE, 1997.

Zeller, Benjamin E. *Heaven's Gate: America's UFO Religion.* New York: New York University Press, 2014.

Zerubavel, Yael. *Recovered Roots: Collective Memory and the Making of Israeli National Tradition.* Chicago: University of Chicago Press, 1995.

INDEX

ABOUT THE AUTHOR

RACHEL Z. FELDMAN is an assistant professor of religious studies at Dartmouth College and recipient of the 2023 Jordan Schnitzer First-Book Prize awarded by the Association for Jewish Studies. She is the coeditor of *Settler Indigeneity in the West Bank* with Ian McGonigle.